FAITH WORKS

FAITH WORKS

The Gospel According to the Apostles

JOHN F. MacARTHUR, JR.

WORD PUBLISHING

Dallas · London · Vancouver · Melbourne

Faith Works: The Gospel According to the Apostles

Library of Congress Cataloging-in-Publication Data

MacArthur, John, 1939–
    Faith works : the gospel according to the Apostles / John F. MacArthur.
        p. cm.
    ISBN 0-8499-0841-8
    1. Faith. 2. Faith—Biblical teaching. I. Title.
BV4637.M227   1992
234'.2—dc20   92–46041
                                                                CIP

Printed in the United States of America.

To Lance Quinn

a Timothy to me in every sense—who fulfills my
goal by going beyond his teacher.

The grace of God has appeared, bringing salvation to all men, instructing us to deny ungodliness and worldly desires and to live sensibly, righteously and godly in the present age, looking for the blessed hope and the appearing of the glory of our great God and Savior, Christ Jesus.

Titus 2:11–13

The Lord knows how much I owe (and every reader owes) to Phil Johnson for this book. He is my dear friend and the perfect complement to me in every aspect related to writing. He carefully, skillfully pulls my voice out of the air and transforms it into ink. I could not do it without him.

Contents

Introduction

This is not a typical sequel. It is more of a *pre*quel, a start-from-the-beginning approach to the subject it deals with. It fleshes out the framework of doctrine that was only hinted at in its predecessor, *The Gospel According to Jesus.* That book was an analysis of Jesus' evangelistic ministry. It contrasted our Lord's preaching, teaching, and private ministry with the methods of twentieth-century evangelicalism. This book deals with the apostles' doctrine of salvation, showing that the gospel according to Jesus is also the gospel according to the apostles. Thus the entire New Testament message stands in stark contrast to the hollow "gospel" many are proclaiming today.

Perhaps you are thinking, *No, thanks. I'll leave the doctrinal studies to professional theologians. Give me a good devotional book instead.*

But please read on. This is not a technical study or an academic treatise. It is not a textbook for theologians. It is a message that has burned in my heart through all the years of my ministry. Far from being a dry dissertation, it is a passionate look at the most essential of all Christian truths. If salvation is important to you (what could possibly be *more* important?) you cannot afford to ignore the issues this book addresses. If you are inclined to think that a "doctrinal" book is the antithesis of a "devotional" book, I hope to change your mind.

I believe Christians today are starved for doctrinal content. Five years ago, when I was writing *The Gospel According to Jesus,* this issue came to the forefront of my thinking. Several publishers warned me that the book was "too doctrinal" to sell. The whole point of the book was to answer a doctrinal controversy that had festered beneath the surface of evangelicalism for years. I could not write the book without plunging into doctrine. When I finally completed the book, I had to admit it seemed rather like a textbook. It employed theological terminology you might encounter in a Bible college or seminary classroom, but is unfamiliar to many laymen. It was set in small type, heavily footnoted, and began with a critical appraisal of some dispensationalists' soteriology—not the kind of reading the average lay person wants for daily devotions.

In the end the book was published as an academic study, edited and marketed by the publisher's textbook division.

Naturally I hoped the book would gain a broader audience, but I admit I was astonished when it became one of the most widely read Christian books of the 1980s. It was the first "doctrinal" book to become a bestseller in years. It was obvious that *The Gospel According to Jesus* struck a chord—or hit a nerve, depending on which side of the debate you stand.

Almost immediately after the book was published, I began to get letters from lay readers asking for more on the subject. They wanted practical advice: *How should we explain the gospel to children? What tracts are available that present the way of salvation fully and biblically?* They wanted help understanding their own spiritual experiences: *I came to Christ as a child and didn't surrender to Him as Lord until several years later. Does that invalidate my salvation?* They wanted spiritual counsel: *I've been struggling with sin and lack of assurance for years. Can you help me understand genuine faith and how I can have it?* They wanted clarification: *What about Lot and the Corinthians who lived in disobedience? They were still redeemed people, weren't they?* They wanted simplified explanations: *I don't easily understand theological terminology like "dispensationalism" and "soteriology." Can you explain the lordship controversy to me in plain English?*

This book is for those people. It's a simpler treatment, which is appropriate, because the gospel itself is simple. Moreover, I contend that the biblical issues at the heart of the lordship controversy are all very simple as well. It doesn't take an accomplished theologian to discern the sense of difficult passages like 1 John 2:3–4: "By this we know that we have come to know Him, if we keep His commandments. The one who says, 'I have come to know Him,' and does not keep His commandments, is a liar, and the truth is not in him."

I am once again using footnotes, mostly to document the quotations a book like this requires. I have again included a section on dispensationalism, because I wanted to explain in more detail what it is and what bearing it has on the lordship controversy. Nevertheless, this is a book for every Christian. It is not meant to be an advanced study. Each key term is defined the first time I use it, and I have included a glossary. My goal has been to explain the issues so that even a newcomer to the faith can understand what I'm talking about.

Unfortunately, the lordship controversy has become needlessly muddled by complex arguments couched in theological jargon. All of this tends to intimidate people who sincerely want to understand the issues. Many lay Christians—and some Christian leaders—have concluded that the issues are too deep to fathom. Others have allowed themselves to be misled by oversimplified arguments or distracted by emotionally charged rhetoric, rather than thinking through the issues carefully for themselves. I hope this book will help provide an antidote to the confusion and garbled logic that have commandeered the lordship debate over the past half decade.

My purpose is not to answer critics. I have a file drawer full of reviews of *The Gospel According to Jesus.* Most have been positive, and I appreciate the encouragement and affirmation. But I have also read very carefully all the negative reviews (and there have been many). I have studied them with an open heart, asked my staff and the faculty of The Master's Seminary to evaluate every criticism, and returned to Scripture to study prayerfully the biblical issues. The process has helped sharpen my thinking, and for that I am grateful. Some readers have noticed that later editions of the book have included some wording changes that clarify or refine what I was saying.

Overall, however, I must confess that I have been deeply disappointed with the *quality* of the critics' response. The overwhelming majority of criticisms have nothing whatever to do with biblical matters. Some reviewers have complained that the lordship issue is too divisive, the message too hard, or my position too dogmatic. Others have argued semantics or taken exception to my terminology. Some have feigned indignation, claiming *The Gospel According to Jesus* is an unfair personal attack on them, their friends, or this or that organization. A few vocal critics have declared the book unbalanced, accused me of paving the road back to Rome, said I am abandoning dispensationalism, labeled me a hyper-Calvinist, faulted me for being too Arminian, or (most grievously) denounced me as a teacher of works-salvation.

To all who have asked me to reply to those charges, I have simply said read the book for yourself and judge whether they are fair complaints. I believe they are all answered by *The Gospel According to Jesus.*

The problem with all such criticisms is that none of them deals with the *biblical* particulars. As I said in that first book, I'm not really troubled if what I teach messes up someone's dispensational chart. I'm not ultimately concerned with whether something is compatible with a particular system of theology. Nor is my agenda to promote some novel theological scheme. My only aim is to discern and teach what the Scriptures say. I make no apology for that. If we're going to discuss doctrinal matters, let's allow the Bible to settle the question.

Many critics were willing to condemn "lordship salvation" for calling sinners to full surrender, but not one bothered to explain why Jesus Himself said to the unsaved multitudes, "If anyone wishes to come after Me, let him deny himself, and take up his cross, and follow Me" (Mark 8:34). Several called me a legalist for teaching that a transformed life is the inevitable consequence of genuine faith. But no one offered any other possible explanation of 2 Corinthians 5:17: "If any man is in Christ, he is a new creature; the old things passed away; behold, new things have come." Many were eager to argue theological fine points, hypothetical cases, logical ramifications, rational premises, semantic differences, and so on. Almost no one has been willing to grapple with the pertinent biblical texts.

Modern evangelicalism seems poorly equipped to handle controversies like the lordship issue. We have been conditioned to hear only brief, insipid "sound bites." In considering issues of this magnitude, we need to listen, reason, and ponder matters carefully, then come to resolution and agreement. Many seem to think the lordship controversy ought to be settled through a public showdown similar to the televised presidential debates. I have been repeatedly challenged to match wits with leading no-lordship advocates in a public forum. I have consistently declined, and I want to explain why.

My experience with such debates has convinced me that they are not particularly edifying. Listeners come away thinking they fully understand the issues, but the typical debate format allows time only to scratch the surface. The real issues are not going to be settled in one- and two-hour sessions. In practice, the real issues rarely are dealt with. Instead, public debates tend to major on the minors. Debates, in the end, merely offer the most clever participants a forum in which to score points. Worst of all, debates contribute to the perception of personal hostility.

A speech contest cannot resolve the differences in this controversy. Moreover, such an approach has no biblical warrant. I know of no occasion in Scripture when debate was used to come to a proper understanding and consensus on a doctrinal question.

In *The Gospel According to Jesus,* I expressed a desire that the book would be a catalyst for discussion and ultimate resolution of the issues. Since the book's release I have met privately with a number of key Christian leaders from the other side—and my door remains open. I don't view any of these men as enemies, nor do I regard our disagreement as a personal feud. In the scope of all that we believe, we agree far more than we disagree. But there's no denying that these matters pertaining to the gospel are fundamental and therefore our disagreement on them is a serious matter. Surely everyone involved will agree that we cannot simply act as if nothing of importance is at stake.

Ultimately, the best forum in which to air this kind of doctrinal dispute is through careful, biblically reasoned dialogue, preferably in written form. It is easier in writing to measure one's words carefully, to be comprehensive, and to avoid the kind of divisiveness we all are rightly concerned about. We need to clarify the issues, not escalate the emotional pitch of our disagreement.

My desire is to present the case biblically, clearly, graciously, fairly, and in terms that every Christian can understand. My approach will be to examine some of the key passages from the epistles and Acts that reveal how the apostles proclaimed the gospel and how they unfolded the truths of salvation to the early church. There is so much clear revelation on this theme that you may feel you are being given the same thing over and over—and you are—because it is so crucial to the Holy Spirit's purpose in communicating the matter of salvation that these truths are woven into the fabric of many epistles.

I think you'll agree that the gospel according to the apostles is the same gospel Jesus preached. I believe you'll also be convinced that their gospel differs dramatically from the diluted message popular with so many today. And I pray you'll find this book an encouragement as you seek to put your own faith to work.

1

Prologue

In the gospel, I find satisfaction to my mind that I find nowhere else. . . . There is no problem of my life but that the gospel deals with it and answers it. I find intellectual rest and an answer to all my questions.

And, thank God, my heart and my desires are also satisfied. I find complete satisfaction in Christ. There is no desire, there is nothing that my heart can crave for but He can more than satisfy. All the restlessness of desire is quelled by Him as He breathes His peace into my troubles and problems and restlessness. . . .

So I am given rest in spite of my circumstances. The gospel enables me to say with the Apostle Paul, "I am persuaded"—which means, I am certain—"that neither death nor life nor angels, nor principalities, nor powers, nor things present nor things to come, Nor height, nor depth, nor any other creature shall be able to separate us from the love of God, which is in Christ Jesus our Lord" (Rom. 8:38–39). That is perfect rest which is independent of circumstances; that is to be calm in the midst of storm.

D. Martyn Lloyd-Jones[1]

*W*hile I was writing this book my whole life suddenly changed.

One afternoon while waiting for my son to join me at the golf course, I received a telephone call informing me that my wife, Patricia,

---

[1] D. Martyn Lloyd-Jones, *The Heart of the Gospel* (Wheaton, Ill.: Crossway, 1991), 165–66.

and our youngest daughter, Melinda, had been involved in a very serious automobile accident. Patricia had been gravely injured and was being airlifted to a hospital about an hour away from where I was. No other details were available. Inadvertently leaving my golf clubs on the practice tee, I immediately got in my car and headed for the hospital.

That hour-long drive to the hospital will be forever etched in my memory. A thousand thoughts flooded my mind. I realized, of course, that I might never see Patricia alive again. I thought of the gaping hole that would exist in my life without her. I reflected on the essential part she has had in my life and ministry over the years. I wondered how I could ever manage without her. I remembered when we first met, how we grew to love each other, and hundreds of other little things about our life together. I would give anything to keep her, but I realized now that choice was not mine to make.

A supernatural peace flooded my soul. My grief, sorrow, uncertainty, and fears were all enveloped in that restful peace. I knew that Patricia and I were both in our Lord's hands, and under the circumstances that was the only place I could imagine any sense of safety. I did not know His design. I could not see His purposes. I could not understand what had happened or why. But I could rest in the knowledge that His plan for us was ultimately for our good and for His glory.

When I arrived at the emergency room, I learned that Melinda had been badly bruised and cut but was not seriously injured. She was severely shaken but not in any danger.

A doctor came out to explain Patricia's injuries to me. Her neck was broken. Two vertebrae were severely crushed. The damage had occurred above the crucial nerves in the spinal cord that control breathing. In most cases like hers, the victim dies immediately. But our Lord had providentially spared her.

She had also sustained a severe blow to the head. The impact of the roof crushing down on her head as the car flipped was powerful enough to have killed her. They were giving her massive doses of a new drug designed to stop swelling in the brain. The surgeon was concerned that the head injury could yet prove fatal. He had used more than forty sutures to close the wound in her scalp. Her jaw and several bones in her face were broken. She would not be out of danger for several days.

Emergency room personnel were about to move Patricia to surgery, where doctors would attach a steel halo to her head by means of four bolts drilled directly into the skull. The device would suspend her head and stabilize her neck while the vertebrae healed. She would wear the halo for several months and after that undergo a grueling program of physical rehabilitation.

In the next few days doctors discovered additional injuries. The right collarbone was broken. Worse, Patricia's right arm was paralyzed. She could move her fingers and grip things, but her arm hung limply and she had no sensation in it. Her left hand was broken and needed a cast. That meant Patricia could not use either hand.

This all has brought a wonderful opportunity for me to serve my wife. All our lives together she has cared for my needs, served the family, and ministered to us in a myriad of ways. Now it is my turn, and I have relished the opportunity. My love for her and my appreciation of all that she does has grown by magnitudes.

As of this writing, Patricia is still in the halo. It is a remarkable contraption, a huge steel yoke that suspends her head by resting the weight of it on four steel rods rising from a plastic upper-body vest. It holds her head and neck immobile in traction.

I am glad to report that she is out of danger now. If God graciously permits, by the time this book is published she will be out of the halo. She has regained some use of her right arm, and doctors tell us she could be on the way to a full recovery.

This whole experience has been the most difficult trauma of our lives together. Yet through it all both Patricia and I have learned again—in a very practical way—that faith works. Our faith in Christ—the same faith with which we first trusted Him as Lord—has remained strong and enabled us to trust Him through this trial.

We have understood as never before the sweetness of our Lord's invitation in Matthew 11:28–30: "Come to Me, all who are weary and heavy-laden, and I will give you rest. Take My yoke upon you, and learn from Me, for I am gentle and humble in heart; and you shall find rest for your souls. For My yoke is easy, and My load is light." We have found again and again that though the yoke does not always *seem* easy and the burden does not always *feel* light, living under the precious reality of Christ's lordship offers the only truly restful life, no matter what.

That is, after all, the heart of the gospel according to Jesus. The apostles knew this truth both from the Lord's teaching and from their own experience. It was the heart of their message to an unsaved world. They preached that faith *works;* it cannot fail or remain passive, but immediately goes to work in the life of the believer. It works *for* us and *in* us and *through* us. Faith is sustained and it sustains us in the midst of life's trials. It motivates us in the face of life's difficulties. It carries us through life's tragedies. Because faith works, it enables us to enjoy a supernatural spiritual rest.

Our experience throughout Patricia's ordeal has given me a new vigor for this book. I am constantly reminded that my confidence in the lordship of Jesus Christ is the foundation and the support of my life. The immense provision of His saving grace enables us to endure.

The lordship of Christ is not some dry and musty abstract doctrinal subject. The gospel is not an academic matter. Faith is not a theoretical pursuit. The grace of God is not a conjectural reality. How we understand the truths of the gospel will ultimately determine how we live our lives. All these issues are dynamic, intensely practical, and supremely relevant in our day-to-day lives. Please bear that in mind as you study these pages.

2

A Primer on the "Lordship Salvation" Controversy

> Beloved, while I was making every effort to write you about our common salvation, I felt the necessity to write to you appealing that you contend earnestly for the faith which was once for all delivered to the saints.
>
> Jude 3

Why do you want to do another book on 'lordship salvation'?" a friend recently asked. "Hasn't that issue been beaten to death?"

I admit that a part of me echoes that sentiment. Originally I had no intention of writing a sequel to *The Gospel According to Jesus*. That book was in preparation for several years, and when I finally completed it I was eager to move on to something different. Although I felt there was much more that *could* be said, I was satisfied that the book adequately covered the subject. I was not trying to place myself at the nucleus of an ongoing debate. Most of all, I did not want the "lordship salvation" controversy to become the single focus of my ministry.

That was five years ago. Today I sense something of what Jude must have felt when he penned the verse quoted above. An urgent prompting in the deepest part of my soul constrains me to say more.

Is This Really a Crucial Issue?

A major reason for my concern has to do with some popular misconceptions that cloud the whole controversy. "Lordship salvation" has become the most talked about and least understood theological topic in evangelical Christendom. Nearly everyone seems to know *about* the debate; few truly understand the issues. It is easy to find strong opinions on both sides. But ferreting out people with genuine understanding is another matter. Many suppose the whole thing is a superficial conflict and the church would be better off if everyone forgot about it. One very well known Christian leader told me he had purposely avoided reading any books on the matter; he didn't want to be forced to take sides. Another told me the issue is unnecessarily divisive.

Yet this is not theological trivia. How we proclaim the gospel has eternal ramifications for non-Christians and defines who we are as Christians. Nor is the lordship question a theoretical or hypothetical problem. It raises several fundamental questions that have repercussions at the most practical level of Christian living.

How should we proclaim the gospel? Do we present Jesus to unbelievers as Lord, or as Savior only? What are the essential truths of the gospel message? What does it mean to be *saved*? How can a person know his or her faith is real? Can we have absolute assurance of salvation? What kind of transformation is accomplished in the new birth? How do we explain sin in the Christian's life? How far in sinning can a Christian go? What relationship is there between faith and obedience? Every area of Christian living is affected by one or more of those questions.

Of course, that's not to say the lordship discussion is purely pragmatic. A number of crucial doctrines have surfaced in the debate: dispensationalism, election, the *ordo salutis* ("order of salvation"), the relationship of sanctification and justification, eternal security, perseverance of the saints, and so on.

Don't be put off. You may not immediately recognize some of those terms or be able to define them all, but if you're a Christian, every one of them is important to you. You ought to have a basic understanding of what they mean and how they relate to Scripture and the gospel message. Doctrine is not the exclusive domain of seminary professors. All true Christians must be concerned with understanding sound doctrine. Doctrine properly understood can never be a merely academic pursuit. It is the discipline of discerning and digesting what God is saying to us in His Word so we can live lives that glorify Him. Doctrine forms the belief system that controls and compels behavior. What could be more practical—or more important?

Let's keep that perspective in mind as we approach this controversial topic. Do we disagree on doctrinal matters? Let's look together at what *God's Word* says. Theological systems, polemics, elegant rhetoric, or bombast and bravado may persuade some people, but not those who seek to know the mind of God. God's truth is revealed in His Word, and it is there we must ultimately go to settle this or any other doctrinal issue.

What Is "Lordship Salvation" All About?

The gospel call to faith presupposes that sinners must repent of their sin and yield to Christ's authority. That, in a sentence, is what "lordship salvation" teaches.

I don't like the term *lordship salvation.* I reject the connotation intended by those who coined the phrase. It insinuates that a submissive heart is extraneous or supplementary to saving faith. Although I have reluctantly used the term to describe my views, it is a concession to popular usage. Surrender to Jesus' lordship is not an addendum to the biblical terms of salvation; the summons to submission is at the heart of the gospel invitation throughout Scripture.

Those who criticize lordship salvation like to level the charge that we teach a system of works-based righteousness. Nothing could be further from the truth. Although I labored to make this as plain as possible in *The Gospel According to Jesus,* some critics continue to hurl that allegation. Others have imagined that I am advocating a new or modified doctrine of salvation that challenges the Reformers' teaching or radically redefines faith in Christ. Of course, my purpose is just the opposite.

Therefore, let me attempt to state the crucial points of my position as plainly as possible. These articles of faith are fundamental to all evangelical teaching:

- Christ's death on the cross paid the full penalty for our sins and purchased eternal salvation. His atoning sacrifice enables God to justify sinners freely without compromising the perfection of divine righteousness (Rom. 3:24–26). His resurrection from the dead declares His victory over sin and death (1 Cor. 15:54–57).

- Salvation is by grace through faith in the Lord Jesus Christ alone—plus and minus nothing (Eph. 2:8–9).

- Sinners cannot earn salvation or favor with God (Rom. 8:8).

- God requires of those who are saved no preparatory works or prerequisite self-improvement (Rom. 10:13; 1 Tim. 1:15).
- Eternal life is a gift of God (Rom. 6:23).
- Believers are saved and fully justified before their faith ever produces a single righteous work (Eph. 2:10).
- Christians can and do sin (1 John 1:8, 10). Even the strongest Christians wage a constant and intense struggle against sin in the flesh (Rom. 7:15–24). Genuine believers sometimes commit heinous sins, as David did in 2 Samuel 11.

Alongside those truths, I believe Scripture teaches these:

- The gospel calls sinners to faith joined in oneness with repentance (Acts 2:38; 17:30; 20:21; 2 Pet. 3:9). Repentance is turning from sin (Acts 3:19; Luke 24:47). It is not a work but a divinely bestowed grace (Acts 11:18; 2 Tim. 2:25). Repentance is a change of heart, but genuine repentance will effect a change of behavior as well (Luke 3:8; Acts 26:18–20).
- Salvation is all God's work. Those who believe are saved utterly apart from any effort on their own (Titus 3:5). Even faith is a gift of God, not a work of man (Eph. 2:1–5, 8). Real faith therefore cannot be defective or short-lived but endures forever (Phil. 1:6, cf. Heb. 11).
- The object of faith is Christ Himself, not only a creed or a promise (John 3:16). Faith therefore involves personal commitment to Christ (2 Cor. 5:15). In other words, all true believers follow Jesus (John 10:27–28).
- Real faith inevitably produces a changed life (2 Cor. 5:17). Salvation includes a transformation of the inner person (Gal. 2:20). The nature of the Christian is different, new (Rom. 6:6). The unbroken pattern of sin and enmity with God will not continue when a person is born again (1 John 3:9–10).
- The "gift of God," eternal life (Rom. 6:23), includes all that pertains to life and godliness (2 Pet. 1:3; Rom. 8:32), not just a ticket to heaven.

- Jesus is Lord of all, and the faith He demands involves unconditional surrender (Rom. 6:17–18; 10:9–10). He does not bestow eternal life on those whose hearts remain set against Him (James 4:6).

- Those who truly believe will love Christ (1 Pet. 1:8–9; Rom. 8:28–30; 1 Cor. 16:22). They will therefore long to obey Him (John 14:15, 23).

- Behavior is an important test of faith. Obedience is evidence that one's faith is real (1 John 2:3). On the other hand, the person who remains utterly unwilling to obey Christ does not evidence true faith (1 John 2:4).

- Genuine believers may stumble and fall, but they *will* persevere in the faith (1 Cor. 1:8). Those who later turn completely away from the Lord show that they were never truly born again (1 John 2:19).

That is my position on "lordship salvation." Anyone who supposes I have some deeper agenda has misunderstood what I am saying.

Radical or Orthodox?

Most Christians will recognize that the points I've listed are not new or radical ideas. The preponderance of Bible-believing Christians over the centuries have held these to be basic tenets of orthodoxy. They are standard precepts of doctrine affirmed, for example, by all the great Reformed and Calvinist creeds. Though our Wesleyan brethren might disagree on a few of the particulars, most of them would quickly affirm that the lordship of Christ is at the heart of the gospel message.[1] No major orthodox movement in the history of Christianity has ever taught that sinners can spurn the lordship of Christ yet lay claim to Him as Savior.

The truth is, the no-lordship gospel is a fairly recent development. Although most advocates of the no-lordship view write and speak as if their teaching represented historic mainstream evangelical Christianity, it does not. Except for a circle of North American pastors, authors, and conference speakers, practically no church leader in the world defends no-lordship doctrine as orthodox. Until recently in

---

[1]Wesleyans believe, for example, that genuine believers can fall away from the faith, but they generally teach that those who do fall away lose their salvation. Their system makes no room for "Christians" who live in continuous rebellion against Christ.

Eastern Europe and the Soviet Union, for example, being a Christian could literally cost a person everything. There the notion of faith without commitment is unthinkable. In England and the rest of Europe, Christian leaders I have met condemn no-lordship teaching as an American aberration. The same is true in other parts of the world I'm familiar with.

This is not to say that no-lordship teaching poses no threat outside the United States. Over the past three or four decades gospel tracts, how-to books on witnessing, radio and television broadcasts, and other media have carried the no-lordship message to the uttermost parts of the earth. The so-called simple-faith gospel—no repentance, no surrender, no commitment, no changed life—has had a horrific influence on the vocabulary of evangelism. Because no-lordship terminology ("accept Jesus as Savior" now, "make Him Lord" later) has become familiar and comfortable, many Christians' thinking about the gospel is fuzzy. When so many of the purveyors of no-lordship salvation brashly level charges of heresy against those who oppose their teaching, is it any wonder sincere Christians are genuinely confused? Which system represents true orthodoxy?

What Does the No-lordship Gospel Teach?

I have listed sixteen beliefs of lordship salvation. The first seven are tenets every major no-lordship advocate would also affirm:

- Christ's death purchased eternal salvation.
- The saved are justified through faith in Christ alone.
- Sinners cannot earn divine favor.
- God requires no preparatory works or pre-salvation reformation.
- Eternal life is a gift.
- Believers are saved before their faith produces any righteous works.
- Christians sin, sometimes horribly.

On that much we all agree. Those who espouse the no-lordship position, however, differ dramatically from lordship salvation on the remaining nine points. Instead they teach:

- Repentance is a change of mind about Christ (*SGS* 96, 99).[2] In the context of the gospel invitation, *repentance* is just a synonym for *faith* (*SGS* 97–99). No turning from sin is required for salvation (*SGS* 99).

- The whole of salvation, including faith, is a gift of God (*SGS* 96). But faith might not last. A true Christian can completely cease believing (*SGS* 141).

- Saving faith is simply being convinced or giving credence to the truth of the gospel (*SGS* 156). It is confidence that Christ can remove guilt and give eternal life, not a personal commitment to *Him* (*SGS* 119).

- *Some* spiritual fruit is inevitable in every Christian's experience. The fruit, however, might not be visible to others (*SGS* 45). Christians can even lapse into a state of permanent spiritual barrenness (*SGS* 53–54).

- Only the *judicial* aspects of salvation—such as justification, adoption, imputed righteousness, and positional sanctification—are guaranteed for believers in this life (*SGS* 150–52). *Practical* sanctification and growth in grace require a postconversion act of dedication.[3]

- Submission to Christ's supreme authority as Lord is not germane to the saving transaction (*SGS* 71–76). Neither dedication nor *willingness* to be dedicated to Christ are issues in salvation (*SGS* 74). The news that Christ died for our sins and rose from the dead is the *complete* gospel. Nothing else must be believed for salvation (*SGS* 40–41).

- Christians may fall into a state of lifelong carnality. A whole category of "carnal Christians"—born-again people who continuously live like the unsaved—exists in the church (*SGS* 31, 59–66).

- Disobedience and prolonged sin are no reason to doubt the reality of one's faith (*SGS* 48).

---

[2]Throughout this book, I will use the abbreviation *SGS* in reference to Charles Ryrie, *So Great Salvation* (Wheaton, Ill.: Victor, 1989).

[3]Charles C. Ryrie, *Balancing the Christian Life* (Chicago: Moody, 1969), 186.

- A believer may utterly forsake Christ and come to the point of not believing. God has guaranteed that He will not disown those who thus abandon the faith (*SGS* 141). Those who have once believed are secure forever, even if they turn away (*SGS* 143).

Some of the more radical advocates of no-lordship doctrine do not stop there. They further stipulate:

- Repentance is not essential to the gospel message. In no sense is repentance related to saving faith (*AF* 144–46).[4]
- Faith is a human act, not a gift from God (*AF* 219). It occurs in a decisive moment but does not necessarily continue (*AF* xiv, 107). True faith can be subverted, be overthrown, collapse, or even turn to unbelief (*AF* 111).
- To "believe" unto salvation is to believe the *facts* of the gospel (*AF* 37–39). "Trusting Jesus" means believing the "saving facts" about Him (*AF* 39), and to believe those facts is to appropriate the gift of eternal life (*AF* 40). Those who add any suggestion of commitment have departed from the New Testament idea of salvation (*AF* 27).
- Spiritual fruit is not guaranteed in the Christian life (*AF* 73–75, 119). Some Christians spend their lives in a barren wasteland of defeat, confusion, and every kind of evil (*AF* 119–25).
- Heaven is guaranteed to believers (*AF* 112) but Christian victory is not (*AF* 118–19). One could even say "the saved" still need salvation (*AF* 195–99). Christ offers a whole range of postconversion deliverance experiences to supply what Christians lack (*AF* 196). But these other "salvations" all require the addition of human works, such as obedience, submission, and confession of Jesus as Lord (*AF* 74, 119, 124–25, 196). Thus God is dependent to some degree on human effort in achieving deliverance from sin in this life (*AF* 220).

---

[4] *AF* refers to Zane Hodges, *Absolutely Free!* (Grand Rapids, Mich.: Zondervan, 1989).

- Submission is not in any sense a condition for eternal life (*AF* 172). "Calling on the Lord" means *appealing* to Him, not *submitting* to Him (*AF* 193–95).

- Nothing guarantees that a true Christian will love God (*AF* 130–31). Salvation does not necessarily even place the sinner in a right relationship of harmonious fellowship with God (*AF* 145–60).

- If people are sure they believe, their faith *must* be genuine (*AF* 31). *All* who claim Christ by faith as Savior—even those involved in serious or prolonged sin—should be assured that they belong to God come what may (*AF* 32, 93–95). It is dangerous and destructive to question the salvation of professing Christians (*AF* 18–19, 91–99). The New Testament writers *never* questioned the reality of their readers' faith (*AF* 98).

- It is possible to experience a moment of faith that guarantees heaven for eternity (*AF* 107), then to turn away permanently and live a life that is utterly barren of any spiritual fruit (*AF* 118–19). Genuine believers might even cease to name the name of Christ or confess Christianity (*AF* 111).

Appendix 1 (pages 213–17) is a chart in which the major differences and similarities of the various views are shown side by side.

What Is Really at the Heart of the Lordship Debate?

It should be obvious that these are real doctrinal differences; the lordship controversy is not a semantic disagreement. The participants in this debate hold widely differing perspectives.

Nevertheless, the issues have often been obscured by semantic distractions, distorted interpretations of lordship teaching, mangled logic, and emotion-laden rhetoric. Often it is easier to misconstrue a point than answer it, and sadly that is the tack many have taken. All it has done is confuse the real issues.

Please allow me to address some of the most troublesome fallacies that have hampered understanding and resolution of the lordship question.

The lordship controversy is *not* a dispute about whether salvation is by faith only or by faith plus works. No true Christian would ever suggest that works need to be added to faith in order to secure salvation. No one who properly interprets Scripture would ever propose that human effort or fleshly works can be *meritorious*—worthy of honor or reward from God.[5]

The lordship controversy *is* a disagreement over the nature of true faith. Those who want to eliminate Christ's lordship from the gospel see faith as simple trust in a set of truths about Christ. Faith, as they describe it, is merely a personal appropriation of the promise of eternal life. Scripture describes faith as more than that—it is a wholehearted trust in Christ personally (e.g., Gal. 2:16; Phil. 3:9). Not merely faith *about* Him; faith *in* Him. Note the difference: If I say I believe some promise you have made, I am saying far less than if I say I trust *you*. Believing in a person necessarily involves some degree of commitment. Trusting Christ means placing oneself in His custody for both life and death. It means we rely on His counsel, trust in His goodness, and entrust ourselves for time and eternity to His guardianship. Real faith, saving faith, is all of me (mind, emotions, and will) embracing all of Him (Savior, Advocate, Provider, Sustainer, Counselor, and Lord God).

Those who have such faith will love Christ (Rom. 8:28; 1 Cor. 16:22; 1 John 4:19). They will therefore want to do His bidding. How could someone who truly believes in Christ continue to defy His authority and pursue what He hates? In this sense, then, the crucial issue for lordship salvation is not merely authority and submission, but the affections of the heart. Jesus as Lord is far more than just an authority figure; He's also our highest treasure and most precious companion. We obey Him out of sheer delight.

So the gospel demands surrender, not only for authority's sake, but also because surrender is the believer's highest joy. Such surrender is not an extraneous adjunct to faith; it is the very essence of believing.

Lordship salvation does *not* teach true Christians are perfect or sinless. Wholehearted commitment to Christ does not mean that we never disobey or that we live perfect lives. The vestiges of our sinful flesh make it inevitable that we will often do what we do not want to do (Rom. 7:15). But commitment to Christ *does* mean that obedience rather than disobedience will be our distinguishing trait. God will deal with the sin in our lives and we will respond to His loving chastisement

---

[5]Though, curiously, no-lordship doctrine is often married to a view that sees postsalvation works as meritorious. Zane Hodges, for one, holds this view. He teaches that eternal life may be obtained freely by faith, but the abundant life of John 10:10 is a reward that may be acquired only by works (*AF* 230).

by becoming more holy (Heb. 12:5–11). I labored to make this clear in *The Gospel According to Jesus*. For example, I wrote, "Those with true faith will fail—and in some cases, frequently—but a genuine believer will, as a pattern of life, confess his sin and come to the Father for forgiveness (1 John 1:9)" (p. 192).

Nevertheless, a few critics have tried to portray lordship salvation as a thinly disguised form of perfectionism. One dear brother—a Christian radio personality—wrote me to suggest that qualifying comments in the book like the one I just quoted are actually inconsistent with my overall position. He assumed that these were "disclaimers" added by an editor trying to "tone down" my book. He evidently surmised that my real intent was to teach sinless perfection as the test of true salvation. He had missed the point entirely.

Of course Christians sin. They disobey. They fail. We *all* fall far short of perfection in this life (Phil. 3:12–5). "We all stumble in many ways" (James 3:2). Even the most mature and godly Christians "see in a mirror dimly" (1 Cor. 13:12). Our minds need constant renewing (Rom. 12:2). But that doesn't invalidate the truth that salvation in some real sense makes us practically righteous. The same epistle that describes the Christian's hatred of and battle with sin (Rom. 7:8–24) first says that believers are free from sin and slaves of righteousness (6:18). The same apostle who wrote, "If we say that we have no sin, we are deceiving ourselves" (1 John 1:8) later wrote, "No one who abides in Him sins" (3:6). In one place he says, "If we say that we have not sinned, we make Him a liar, and His word is not in us" (1:10), and in another, "No one who is born of God practices sin, because His seed abides in Him" (3:9).

There's a true paradox—not an inconsistency—in those truths. All Christians sin (1 John 1:8), but all Christians also obey: "By this we know that we have come to know Him, if we keep His commandments" (1 John 2:3). Sin and carnality are still present with all believers (Rom. 7:21), but they cannot be the hallmark of one's character (Rom. 6:22).

Scripture clearly and repeatedly confirms the lordship viewpoint on this matter: "Beloved, do not imitate what is evil, but what is good. The one who does good is of God; the one who does evil has not seen God" (3 John 11). That speaks of *direction*, not *perfection*. But it clearly makes behavior a test of faith's reality.

The sinner's role in salvation is *not* the main issue in the lordship controversy. The heart of the debate deals with how much *God* does in redeeming the elect.

What happens at regeneration? Is the believing sinner really born again (John 3:3, 7; 1 Peter 1:3, 23)? Is our old self really dead, "crucified . . . that we should no longer be slaves to sin" (Rom. 6:6)? Are believers really "partakers of the divine nature" (2 Pet. 1:4)? Is it true that "if any man is in Christ, he is a new creature; the old things passed away; behold, new things have come" (2 Cor. 5:17)? Can we really say, "Having been freed from sin, [we are] slaves of righteousness" (Rom. 6:18)?

Lordship salvation says yes.

This, after all, is the whole point of redemption: "Whom He foreknew, He also predestined to become conformed to the image of His Son" (Rom. 8:29). Does that conforming work of God—sanctification—begin in this lifetime? Again, lordship salvation says yes.

Scripture agrees. "We all, with unveiled face beholding as in a mirror the glory of the Lord, are being transformed into the same image from glory to glory" (2 Cor. 3:18). Though "it has not appeared as yet what we shall be," it is nevertheless certain that "when He appears, we shall be like Him. . . . And everyone who has this hope fixed on Him purifies himself, just as He is pure" (1 John 3:2–3).

There's more: "Whom He predestined, these He also called; and whom He called, these He also justified; and whom He justified, these He also glorified" (Rom. 8:30). Notice God's part in salvation begins with election and ends in glory. In between, every aspect of the redemptive process is God's work, not the sinner's. God will neither terminate the process nor omit any aspect of it.

Titus 3:5 is clear: Salvation—all of it—is "not on the basis of deeds which we have done." It is God's work, done "according to His mercy." It is not merely a declaratory transaction, legally securing a place in heaven but leaving the sinner captive to his sin. It involves a transformation of the disposition, the very nature, through "the washing of regeneration and renewing by the Holy Spirit" as well.

The question is *not* whether we're saved by grace, but *how* grace operates in salvation. No-lordship advocates love to portray themselves as champions of grace. But they characterize grace in an anemic way that misses the whole point. God's grace is a spiritual dynamic that works in the lives of the redeemed, "instructing us to deny ungodliness and worldly desires and to live sensibly, righteously and godly in the present age" (Titus 2:12). True grace is more than just a giant freebie, opening the door to heaven in the sweet by and by, but leaving us to wallow in sin in the bitter here and now. Grace is God presently at work in our lives. By grace "we are His workmanship, created in Christ

Jesus for good works, which God prepared beforehand, that we should walk in them" (Eph. 2:10). By grace He "gave Himself for us, that He might redeem us from every lawless deed and purify for Himself a people for His own possession, zealous for good deeds" (Titus 2:14).

That ongoing work of grace in the Christian's life is as much a certainty as justification, glorification, or any other aspect of God's redeeming work. "I am confident of this very thing, that He who began a good work in you will perfect it until the day of Christ Jesus" (Phil. 1:6). Salvation is wholly God's work, and He finishes what He starts. His grace *is* sufficient. And potent. It cannot be defective in any regard. "Grace" that does not affect one's behavior is not the grace of God.

Repentance is *not* incidental to the gospel. What is the gospel, after all, but a call to repentance (Acts 2:38; 3:19; 17:30)? In other words, it demands that sinners make a change—stop going one way and turn around to go the other (1 Thess. 1:9). Paul's evangelistic invitations always demanded repentance: "God is now declaring to men that all everywhere should repent" (Acts 17:30). Here's how Paul described His own ministry and message: "I did not prove disobedient to the heavenly vision, but kept declaring both to those of Damascus first, and also at Jerusalem and then throughout all the region of Judea, and even to the Gentiles, *that they should repent and turn to God, performing deeds appropriate to repentance*" (Acts 26:19–20, emphasis added). Repentance is what leads to life (Acts 11:18) and to the knowledge of the truth (2 Tim. 2:25). Thus salvation is impossible apart from repentance.

Advocates of the no-lordship position frequently suggest that preaching repentance adds something to the biblical doctrine of salvation by grace through faith alone.

But faith presupposes repentance. How can those who are mortal enemies of God (Rom. 5:10) sincerely believe in His Son *without* repenting? How can anyone truly comprehend the truth of salvation from sin and its consequences, unless that person also genuinely understands and hates what sin is? The whole sense of faith is that we trust Christ to liberate us from the power and penalty of sin. Therefore sinners cannot come to sincere faith apart from a complete change of heart, a turnaround of the mind and affections and will. That is repentance. It is not a supplement to the gospel invitation; it is precisely what the gospel demands. Our Lord Himself described His primary mission as that of calling sinners to repentance (Matt. 9:13).

We often speak of the salvation experience as "conversion." That is biblical terminology (Matt. 18:3; John 12:40; Acts 15:3). *Conversion* and *repentance* are closely related terms. Conversion occurs when a sinner turns to God in repentant faith. It is a complete turnaround, an absolute change of moral and volitional direction. Such a radical reversal is the response the gospel calls for, whether the plea to sinners is phrased as "believe," "repent," or "be converted." Each entails the others.

If someone is walking away from you and you say, "Come here," it is not necessary to say "*turn around* and come." The U-turn is implied in the direction "come." In like manner, when our Lord says, "Come to Me" (Matt. 11:28), the about-face of repentance is understood. Nowhere does Scripture issue an evangelistic appeal that does not at least imply the necessity of repentance. Our Lord offers nothing to impenitent sinners (Matt. 9:13; Mark 2:17; Luke 5:32).

Again, repentance is not a human work. Jesus said, "No one can come to Me, unless the Father who sent Me draws him" (John 6:44). It is God who grants repentance (Acts 11:18; 2 Tim. 2:5). Repentance is *not* pre-salvation self-improvement. It is *not* a question of atoning for sin or making restitution *before* turning to Christ in faith. It is an inward turning from sin to Christ. Though it is not itself a "work" the sinner performs, genuine repentance will certainly produce good works as its inevitable fruit (Matt. 3:8).

The lordship salvation controversy is *not* churchwide. Because of the publicity given to the lordship debate over the past five years, one might get the impression that the entire worldwide evangelical movement is split over these issues. But as I noted earlier, modern no-lordship theology is primarily a North American phenomenon. Certainly it has been exported to some parts of the world by missionaries and others trained in American schools, but I know of no prominent Christian leaders from outside North America who have undertaken to defend the no-lordship view on doctrinal grounds.

To be even more specific, the modern lordship controversy is primarily a dispute among dispensationalists. Appendix 2 explains dispensationalism and why it is at the heart of the lordship debate. Without getting into a technical discussion about theology at this point, let me simply note that one arm of the dispensationalist movement has developed and defended no-lordship doctrine. Their influence on the evangelical culture has been widespread. As the lordship controversy has been debated on radio talk shows and in other popular formats, it has begun to seem like a monumental conflict threatening to divide Protestant Christianity in a major way. The truth is, only one branch of dispensationalism has risen to defend the no-lordship view.

Who are the defenders of no-lordship dispensationalism? Nearly all of them stand in a tradition that has its roots in the teaching of Lewis Sperry Chafer. I will show in Appendix 2 that Dr. Chafer is the father of modern no-lordship teaching. Every prominent figure on the no-lordship side descends from Dr. Chafer's spiritual lineage. Though Dr. Chafer did not invent or originate any of the key elements of no-lordship teaching, he codified the system of dispensationalism on which all contemporary no-lordship doctrine is founded. That system is the common link between those who attempt to defend no-lordship doctrine on theological grounds.

The New Testament epistles do *not* present a different gospel than Jesus Himself preached. One of the hallmarks of Dr. Chafer's brand of dispensationalism was the way he segmented the New Testament, and particularly the teachings of Christ. As we'll note in Appendix 2, Chafer believed many of our Lord's sermons and evangelistic invitations were intended for people in another dispensation. He contrasted Jesus' "kingdom teachings" and His "grace teachings." Only the "grace teachings," according to Chafer, can be legitimately applied to this present age.

Many dispensationalists have abandoned that kind of thinking, but some still do not believe the gospel according to Jesus is even relevant to the discussion of lordship salvation. "Of course Jesus taught a lordship message," one old-line dispensationalist brother wrote me. "He was preaching to people under law. Under grace we must be careful to preach a grace message. We must preach the gospel according to the apostles."

So for the remainder of this book we will focus on the apostles' preaching and teaching. We will take an especially close look at the apostle Paul's teaching. We will examine what the apostles taught about the key doctrinal issues in the lordship debate: faith, grace, repentance, justification, sanctification, sin, works, assurance, perseverance, and the gospel message. A clear fact will emerge: The gospel according to Jesus *is* the same as the gospel according to the apostles. The faith it calls for is not dormant, but dynamic; it is a repentant, submissive, trusting, enduring faith that works.

3

Without Faith, It Is Impossible to Please Him

> Faith is the acceptance of a gift at the hands of Christ. . . . It is a very wonderful thing; it involves a change of the whole nature of man; it involves a new hatred of sin and a new hunger and thirst after righteousness. Such a wonderful change is not the work of man; faith itself is given us by the Spirit of God. Christians never make themselves Christians; but they are made Christians by God.
>
> . . . It is quite inconceivable that a man should be given this faith in Christ, that he should accept this gift which Christ offers, and still go on contentedly in sin. For the very thing which Christ offers us is salvation from sin—not only salvation from the guilt of sin, but also salvation from the power of sin. The very first thing that the Christian does, therefore, is to keep the law of God: he keeps it no longer as a way of earning his salvation—for salvation has been given him freely by God—but he keeps it joyously as a central part of salvation itself. The faith of which Paul speaks is, as Paul himself says, a faith that works through love; and love is the fulfilling of the whole law. . . . The faith that Paul means when he speaks of justification by faith alone is a faith that works.
>
> J. Gresham Machen[1]

At the heart of the no-lordship error is a disastrous misunderstanding about the nature of faith. No-lordship teaching depicts faith as

---

[1] J. Gresham Machen, *What Is Faith?* (New York: Macmillan, 1925), 203–4.

inherently inert—even antithetical to works, obedience, and surrender to the will of God. The disciples of no-lordship doctrine have much to say *about* faith. After all, "simple faith" is the foundation of their whole system. Unfortunately, most rely on sketchy definitions of *faith* ("being convinced or giving credence to something or someone," *SGS* 156) and *believe* ("to hold something as true," *SGS* 155). Many are loath to define the words at all. One has written,

> In every other sphere of life, except religion, we do not puzzle ourselves with introspective questions about the "nature" of our faith.
> . . . Let it be clearly stated here that English words like to "believe" or "faith" function as fully adequate equivalents to their Greek counterparts. There is not some hidden residue of meaning in the Greek words that is not conveyed by their normal English renderings. . . .
>
> It follows that a Greek reader who met the words "he who believes in Me has everlasting life," would understand the word "believe" exactly as we do. The reader *most certainly* would not understand this word to imply submission, surrender, repentance, or anything else of this sort. For those readers, as for us, "to believe" meant "to believe."
>
> Surely it is one of the conceits of modern theology to suppose that we can define away simple terms like "belief" and "unbelief" and replace their meanings with complicated elaborations. The confusion produced by this sort of process has a pervasive influence in the church today (*AF* 27–29).

Those statements summarize the thesis of a chapter titled "Faith Means Just That—Faith!"

All right. Let's suppose that *faith* and *believe* are satisfactory equivalents of the Greek words *pistis* ("faith, faithfulness") and *pisteuō* ("to believe, entrust"). What do English dictionaries say about *faith*?

The *Oxford American Dictionary* says faith is "1. reliance or trust in a person or thing. 2. belief in religious doctrine. 3. a system of religious belief, *the Christian faith*. 4. loyalty, sincerity."

Wait a minute. "Loyalty, sincerity"? Would no-lordship teaching grant that those are elements of true faith? Aren't such concepts specifically excluded from the no-lordship definition of faith?

We turn to the authoritative *Oxford English Dictionary* (OED), which lists more than a full page of meanings for *faith*. It defines faith as "confidence, reliance, trust"; "belief proceeding from reliance on testimony or authority"; "the duty of fulfilling one's trust; allegiance owed to a superior, fealty; the obligation of a promise or engagement"; and "the quality of fulfilling one's trust; faithfulness, fidelity, loyalty." The OED even includes a theological definition:

> That kind of faith (distinctively called *saving* or *justifying* faith) by which, in the teaching of the N. T. a sinner is justified in the sight of God. This is variously defined by theologians (see quots.), but there is general agreement in regarding it as a conviction practically operative on the character and will, and thus opposed to the mere intellectual assent to religious truth (sometimes called *speculative faith*).

Would no-lordship doctrine be in agreement with those definitions? Certainly not. The patrons of no-lordship salvation redefine *faith* precisely to strip the word of any idea of loyalty, faithfulness, allegiance, submission, duty, fidelity, obligation, and "things of this sort."

So the no-lordship partisan finds no support in an appeal to the standard English meaning of the word *faith*. What about *believe*?

According to the OED, *believe* is a verb meaning "to have confidence or faith *in* (a person); and consequently to rely upon, trust to." The dictionary notes that *believe* is derived from root words that mean "to hold estimable, valuable, pleasing, or satisfactory, to be satisfied with."

To be satisfied with Christ. Coming straight from the English dictionary, that frankly is a better definition of *believing* than those who plead for no-lordship salvation have yet proposed. It explicitly sets believing apart from mere abstract acquiescence to academic facts. It describes a faith that *cannot* be placed in opposition to commitment, surrender, repentance, delighting in the Lord, and "things of this sort."

Ultimately, however, it is not the dictionary, but Scripture, to which we must turn for a definition of faith. One chapter in the New Testament, Hebrews 11, is given to us for the express purpose of defining and describing *faith*. The writer to the Hebrews tells us precisely *what faith is* and *what faith does*. Here we find that the faith represented by no-lordship teaching bears little resemblance to the faith Scripture speaks about.

What Faith Is

Hebrews 11 begins, "Now faith is the assurance of things hoped for, the conviction of things not seen. For by it the men of old gained approval. By faith we understand that the worlds were prepared by the word of God, so that what is seen was not made out of things which are visible" (vv. 1–3).

The entire chapter deals with the supremacy and superiority of faith. It confronts the Pharisaism of first-century Judaism, which taught that righteousness, forgiveness from sins, and ultimate salvation could be achieved only through a rigorous system of meritorious works. Jewish tradition had so twisted God's law that most Jews saw it as the way to earn favor with God. Even after being shown the basic truths of Christ, some of the Hebrews were unwilling to abandon their religion based on works-righteousness.

Works-based salvation is and always has been despised by God (cf. Rom. 8:3; Gal. 2:16; Phil. 3:9; 1 Tim. 1:9). God has never redeemed man by works, but always by faith (cf. Gen. 15:6). "The righteous will live by his faith" (Hab. 2:4), is not a truth about the New Covenant alone. As Hebrews 11 makes clear, from Adam on, the instrument of God's salvation has been faith, not works. Works are a byproduct of faith, never a means of salvation.

Habakkuk 2:4 is quoted three times in the New Testament: Romans 1:17, Galatians 3:11, and Hebrews 10:38. Romans explains what is meant by "the righteous." Galatians is something of a commentary on the words "will live." Hebrews 11 plumbs the depths of the phrase "by faith."

Habakkuk 2:4 forms a bridge from Hebrews 10 and its great theme of justification by faith. The saints named in chapter 11 are examples of people who were justified by faith and who lived by faith. Faith is both the way to life and the way to live. Faith is the *only* way; without it no one can please God (v. 6).

What is faith? "Faith is the assurance of things hoped for, the conviction of things not seen" (11:1). That verse is a couplet of Hebrew-style poetry. It defines *faith* in two parallel and almost identical phrases. It is not meant to be a full theological definition. Nevertheless, all the crucial elements that summarize the biblical doctrine of faith are suggested by this verse and the examples of faith that follow.

Faith is the assurance of things hoped for. Faith transports God's promises into the present tense. In other words, real faith implicitly takes God at His word. Faith is a supernatural confidence in—and therefore reliance on—the One who has made the promises. It is not an uncertain hope for something that may come to pass in a vague, indefinite hereafter. It is a trust that brings absolute here-and-now certainty to "things hoped for."

The word translated "assurance" (Gk., *hupostasis*) appears two other times in Hebrews. In 1:3 it is rendered "nature" in the phrase "exact representation of His nature," speaking of Christ's likeness to the Father. In 3:14 the word is "assurance," as in 11:1. It refers to essence, substance, real content—reality as opposed to mere appearance. *Hupostasis* is made up of *stasis* "to stand" and *hupo* "under." It refers to a foundation, the ground on which something is built. A Greek dictionary notes that *hupostasis* was used in ancient Greek literature as a legal term referring to "documents bearing on the ownership of a person's property, deposited in archives, and forming the evidence of ownership." That is the sense conveyed in Hebrews 11:1. The Greek dictionary offers this translation: "Faith is the title-deed of things hoped for."[2]

In a similar vein, the King James Version's rendering of Hebrews 11:1 is a good one: "Faith is the substance of things hoped for, the evidence of things not seen." Faith, far from being ambiguous or unsure, is concrete conviction. It is the present confidence of a future reality, "the *assurance* of things hoped for."

The assurance this verse describes is not personal assurance of salvation but rather absolute certainty with regard to the gospel message. It is saying that faith is a God-wrought conviction about the truth of the Bible's promises and the trustworthiness of Christ. The verse is not saying that faith automatically guarantees full assurance of one's personal salvation.

One question that has been raised by the lordship debate is whether the essence of saving faith is personal assurance. Radical no-lordship doctrine teaches that faith is assurance and assurance is faith. "A person who has *never been sure* of eternal life has *never believed* the saving message of God" (*AF* 51). Also, "It is utterly impossible for us to give credence to the gospel message without knowing that we are saved" (*AF* 50). On the other hand, if you are sure you are saved, you must be: "People know whether they believe something or not, and that is the real issue where God is concerned" (*AF* 31). That teaching makes no place at all for the possibility of *false* assurance.

In chapter 10 we will deal with this matter more thoroughly. As we shall see, there is much more to full assurance of one's salvation than simply believing the objective promises of Scripture. There is much more to faith than a feeling of assurance. Hebrews 11:1 simply means

---

[2]James Hope Moulton and George Milligan, *The Vocabulary of the Greek Testament* (Grand Rapids, Mich.: Eerdmans, 1930), 660.

that faith is a supernatural certainty about the truth of the gospel and the reliability of Christ.[3]

This sure faith must be God's work in us. Although the truth of the gospel is confirmed by many evidences, human nature is predisposed to reject the truth about Christ. So apart from the work of the Spirit in us, we can never believe in the sense this verse describes.

Hebrews 11:1 faith is not like the everyday faith that we speak of. We drink water out of a faucet, believing it is safe. We drive our automobiles in freeway traffic, trusting that the brakes will work. We submit to the surgeon's knife and the dentist's drill by faith. When we drop film off at the drugstore, we trust that the prints will be ready at the promised time (cf. *SGS* 118). We believe in the basic integrity of our governmental leaders (*AF* 27–28). The capacity for that kind of faith is intrinsic to human nature. But it is not the faith Hebrews 11:1 describes.

To begin with, natural faith rests on an object that is not necessarily reliable. The water *might* actually be tainted. The brakes *could* fail. Surgeons *do* make mistakes. The drugstore *may not* deliver your prints on time. The president *probably will* default on some of his campaign promises. But when we believe unto eternal life, we trust something more real and Someone more trustworthy than anything or anyone we could ever comprehend with the natural senses. Our senses may lie; God cannot (Titus 1:2). People fail; God does not (Num. 23:19). Circumstances change; God never does (Mal. 3:6). So the faith described in Hebrews 11 is focused on an infinitely more dependable *object* than any of the day-to-day varieties of faith.

Also, the *nature* of faith is different in the spiritual realm. Natural faith relies on the physical senses. We tend to believe only what we or others can see, hear, taste, and feel. When we trust the water, our brakes, the surgeon, the drugstore, or the president, we do so because our senses and human experience tell us these things are generally worthy of our confidence. Hebrews 11:1 faith, on the other hand, is a *supernatural* conviction—a solid, unshakable assurance that is contrary to human nature. It includes a capacity to lay hold of spiritual reality imperceptible to the natural man: "A natural man does not accept the things of the Spirit of God; for they are foolishness to him, and he cannot understand them, because they are spiritually appraised" (1 Cor. 2:14). Hebrews

---

[3]Hebrews 11:1 certainly affirms that *an element* of assurance is at the heart of faith itself. As we shall see in chapter 10, saving faith in Christ is the foundation of all assurance. One's sense of personal security grows deeper and stronger with spiritual maturity, but the seed of that assurance is present even at the beginning of saving faith.

11:27 characterizes Moses' faith the same way ("he endured, as seeing Him who is unseen").

The clear implication of all this is that faith is a gift of God. If faith were a mere human decision, it would be no assurance at all. It might be a bad decision. If believing were merely a function of the human mind, faith would be no grounds for confidence. The mind can easily be deceived, mistaken, deluded, or misinformed. Real faith, however, is a divinely implanted assurance that rises above the natural functioning of the human mind. After all, the natural man *cannot* see Him who is unseen (v. 27).

But seeing the unseen is the nature of faith.

Faith is . . . the conviction of things not seen. This parallel phrase carries the same truth even further. *Conviction* implies a deeper manifestation of the inward assurance. People of faith are prepared to live out their belief. Their lives reflect a commitment to what their minds and hearts are assured is true. They are so sure of promises and blessings yet future that they behave as if those promises were already realized (Heb. 11:7–13; cf. Rom. 4:17–21).

"Conviction of things not seen" echoes the apostle Peter's description of saving faith (1 Pet. 1:8–9): Although we have not yet seen Christ, we love Him. Though we do not see Him now, we believe in Him—we are committed to Him—with inexpressible and glorious joy, obtaining faith's outcome, the salvation of our souls. Such faith is unassailable. No matter what tests it, no matter the cost, this faith endures. In fact, all the examples in Hebrews 11 show people whose faith was severely tested. In every case, their faith remained strong. To those examples we could add Job, whose faith Satan tried to destroy with the severest kinds of personal tragedy, and Peter, whom Satan sifted like wheat—but his faith didn't fail (Luke 22:32). To this end, Jesus prayed for Peter. He prays just as successfully for *all* the saved (Rom. 8:34; Heb. 7:25; 1 John 2:2). No matter what attacks this faith, it cannot be destroyed.

How can such faith fail to be life-changing? It can't. This faith is a firm and supernatural conviction that governs the true believer's behavior, as the examples in Hebrews 11 also demonstrate. People of faith obey, worship, endure, sacrifice, and work *by faith*. Our works are not fleshly efforts, but the inevitable byproduct of a rock-solid conviction that the "things not seen" are nevertheless real. We obey because we are committed to the object of our faith.

Commitment is the disputed element of faith around which the lordship controversy swirls. No-lordship theology denies that believing in Christ involves any element of personal commitment to Him. It is impossible to harmonize the no-lordship view of faith with Hebrews 11. The whole point of this chapter is to highlight examples of people who were *committed* to what they *believed*. More precisely, they were *committed* to the God they *believed* in—even to death.

Systematic theology usually recognizes three elements of faith: knowledge (*notitia*), assent (*assensus*), and trust (*fiducia*). Augustus H. Strong and Louis Berkhof both refer to *notitia* as the "intellectual element" of faith. *Assensus* is the "emotional element." *Fiducia* is the "voluntary [volitional] element."[4] Real faith therefore involves the whole person—mind, emotions, and will. The mind embraces *knowledge,* a recognition and understanding of the truth that Christ saves. The heart gives *assent,* or the settled confidence and affirmation that Christ's salvation is applicable to one's own soul. The will responds with *trust,* the personal commitment to and appropriation of Christ as the only hope for eternal salvation.

This "trust," or *fiducia,* faith's volitional component, is the crowning element of believing. It involves surrender to the object of faith. It is a personal appropriation of Christ as *both* Lord and Savior. Standard theology universally affirms this. Strong defined *fiducia* as "trust in Christ as Lord and Savior; or, in other words—to distinguish its two aspects: (*a*) Surrender of the soul, as guilty and defiled, to Christ's governance. . . . (*b*) Reception and appropriation of Christ, as the source of pardon and spiritual life."[5] Berkhof echoes Strong at

---

[4]Augustus H. Strong, *Systematic Theology* (Philadelphia: Judson, 1907), 837–38; Louis Berkhof, *Systematic Theology* (Grand Rapids, Mich.: Eerdmans, 1939), 503–5.

In *Absolutely Free!* Zane Hodges claimed I had "seriously distort[ed]" Berkhof's definition (*AF* 207). "*Assensus* is *not* an 'emotional element,'" Hodges protested. But those are, after all, Berkhof's own words. Note that Strong, for one, held an identical view. Even Ryrie agrees (*SGS* 120). By "emotional element," Strong and Berkhof meant that *assensus* goes beyond considering the object of faith in a detached and disinterested way. Berkhof wrote, "When one embraces Christ by faith, he has a deep conviction of the truth and reality of the object of faith, feels that it meets an important need in his life, and is conscious of an absorbing interest in it. . . . It is exactly the distinguishing characteristic of the knowledge of saving faith" (Berkhof, 504–5).

John Calvin defined *assensus* as "more a matter of the heart than the head, of the affection than the intellect." He equated assent with "pious affection"; see John Calvin, *Institutes of the Christian Religion,* trans. Henry Beveridge, 3:2:8 (reprint, Grand Rapids, Mich.: Eerdmans, 1966), 1:476.

[5]Strong, *Systematic Theology,* 338–39.

this point almost word for word.[6] B. B. Warfield, noting that *trust* comprises some element of commitment to its object, wrote, "We cannot be said to believe that which we distrust too much to commit ourselves to it."[7]

Saving faith, then, is the whole of my being embracing all of Christ. Faith cannot be divorced from commitment.

Radical no-lordship theology dismisses all of the above as unnecessary "psychoanalysis" of what should be a simple concept. "No one needs to be a psychologist to understand what faith is," Zane Hodges has written. "Still less do we need to resort to 'pop psychology' to explain it. It is an unproductive waste of time to employ the popular categories—intellect, emotion, or will—as a way of analyzing the mechanics of faith. Such discussions lie far outside the boundaries of biblical thought" (*AF* 30–31).

But all three elements of faith are clearly implied in our text: *knowledge:* "By faith we *understand*" (v. 3); *assent:* "faith is the *assurance* of things hoped for" (v. 1); and *trust:* "faith is . . . the *conviction* of things not seen" (v. 1). The men and women profiled in this great Hall of Faith were all fully committed—mind, heart, and soul—to the object of their faith. How could anyone familiar with this chapter ever devise a notion of faith that lacks personal commitment?

Faith is believing that God is. Hebrews 11:6, a landmark verse, gives still more insight into the nature of faith: "Without faith it is impossible to please Him, for he who comes to God must believe that He is, and that He is a rewarder of those who seek Him."

Absolutely nothing we do can please God apart from this kind of faith. Without faith, pleasing God is *impossible*. Religion, racial heritage, meritorious works—everything the Hebrews regarded as pleasing to God—is utterly futile apart from faith.

The beginning of faith is simply believing that God *is*. This certainly means far more than believing in an unnamed and unknown supreme being. The Hebrews knew God's name as I AM (Exod. 3:14). The phrase "he who comes to God must believe that He is" is a call for faith in the one God who had revealed Himself in Scripture. This verse does not ratify belief in some abstract deity—the "ground of being," the "man upstairs," Allah, the "Unknown god" of the Greek philosophers

---

[6]Berkhof, *Systematic Theology*, 505.

[7]Benjamin B. Warfield, *Biblical and Theological Studies* (Philadelphia: Presbyterian & Reformed, 1968), 402–3.

(Acts 17:23), or any of the other manmade gods. It is speaking of faith in the one God of the Bible, whose highest revelation of Himself is in the Person of His Son, the Lord Jesus Christ.

Clearly, true faith has objective substance. There *is* an intellectual content to our faith. Believing is not a mindless leap in the dark or some ethereal kind of trust apart from knowledge. There is a factual, historical, intellectual basis for our faith. Faith that is not grounded in this objective truth is no faith at all. On that, I think everyone on both sides of the lordship question is in full agreement.

But no-lordship teaching is inclined at this point to two serious errors. First, it strips faith of *everything but* the objective, academic aspect, making the exercise of faith a simple head game. Second, it tends to pare down the objective content of faith to the barest minimum, making the ground of faith so meager that one need scarcely know anything about who God is or what Christ has done. It is a minimalist approach to believing that has no warrant in Scripture.

How far will no-lordship apologists go in divesting the gospel of its essential content? A recent article in the leading no-lordship fraternity's monthly newsletter suggested that "a person can place his or her trust in Jesus Christ and Him alone without understanding precisely *how* He takes away sins." Therefore, the article stated, "it is possible to believe savingly in Christ without understanding the reality of His resurrection."[8] The man who wrote the piece maintains that neither Christ's death nor His resurrection are essential to the evangelistic message. It is enough, he says, "to present only the core truth of the gospel: namely, that whoever believes in Jesus Christ has eternal life."[9] Evidently he believes people can be saved who have never even heard that Christ died for their sins.

But the apostle Paul said, "If you confess with your mouth Jesus as Lord, and believe in your heart that God raised Him from the dead, you shall be saved" (Rom. 10:9). The resurrection was central to Paul's gospel: "I make known to you, brethren, the gospel which I preached . . . that Christ died for our sins . . . and that He was buried, and that He was raised on the third day according to the Scriptures" (1 Cor. 15:1–4). There are many false christs (Matt. 24:24). The only One who grants eternal life rose from the dead to make salvation possible. Those who worship a lesser christ cannot be saved: "If

---

[8]Bob Wilkin, "Tough Questions About Saving Faith," *The Grace Evangelical Society News* (June 1990): 1.

[9]Ibid., 4.

Christ has not been raised, then our preaching is vain, your faith also is vain" (1 Cor. 15:14).

The crucifixion and resurrection are the most vital facts of the gospel (1 Cor. 15:1–4). When Hebrews 11:6 calls for "believ[ing] that He is," it is requiring that we believe in the God of Scripture, the One who gave His Son to die and rise again. Granted, Old Testament saints did not have full revelation about Christ's death and resurrection. They were saved through their faith based on what God *had* revealed. But since that first resurrection Sunday, no one has been saved except through believing in Christ's atonement for sins and His subsequent resurrection.

So the phrase "believe that He is" speaks of faith in the God of Scripture, based on an understanding of crucial truth about Him. This is *notitia,* knowledge—the objective side of faith. But as we are seeing, there is more to saving faith.

Faith is seeking God. It is not enough just to believe that the God of the Bible exists. It is not enough to know about His promises or even intellectually believe the truth of the gospel. In order to please Him it is also necessary to "believe . . . that He is a rewarder of those who seek Him." That phrase brings together assent (*assensus*) and trust (*fiducia*) to make the picture of faith complete. *Assent* goes beyond a dispassionate observation of who God is. The assenting heart affirms the goodness of His character as "a rewarder." *Trust* applies this knowledge personally and practically by turning to God in sincere faith as a seeker of *Him*.

It is not enough merely to postulate a supreme being. It is not enough even to accept the *right* God. Real faith is not just knowing *about* God: it is *seeking* God. In fact, "seeking God" is often used as a synonym for faith in Scripture. Isaiah 55:6 is a call to faith: "Seek the Lord while He may be found; Call upon Him while He is near." God Himself told Israel, "You will seek Me and find Me, when you search for Me with all your heart" (Jer. 29:13). "For thus says the Lord to the house of Israel, 'Seek Me that you may live'" (Amos 5:4). "But seek first His kingdom and His righteousness; and all these things shall be added to you" (Matt. 6:33).

Perhaps someone will object that Hebrews 11:6 simply says we must *believe* that God rewards seekers; it doesn't say we must *be* seekers of God. But why does God reward those who seek Him? Because of their works? No, "all our righteous deeds are like a filthy garment" (Isa. 64:6). God rewards only those with faith—without faith it is impossible to please Him. This verse thus identifies seeking God as the epitome of true faith.

Seeking Him leads to finding Him fully revealed in the Lord Jesus Christ (Matt. 7:7; Luke 11:9).

The attitude described here is the antithesis of works-righteousness. Instead of trying to earn favor with God, faith pursues God Himself. Instead of bartering for God's approbation, faith follows after *Him* as the soul's greatest pleasure. Far from making faith a human work, this definition emphasizes that faith is the abandonment of seeking to please God through works—and the adherence to God, who manifests what pleases Him by His works through His people.

Faith, then, is seeking and finding God in Christ, desiring Him, and ultimately being fulfilled with Him. Another way of saying it is that faith is wholly leaning on Christ—for redemption, for righteousness, for counsel, for fellowship, for sustenance, for direction, for succor, for His lordship, and for all in life that can truly satisfy.

Notice that we have come full circle to the definition of faith suggested by the English dictionary: Faith is being satisfied with Christ. Jesus Himself said so: "I am the bread of life; he who comes to Me shall not hunger, and he who believes in Me shall never thirst" (John 6:35). There is no way a genuine believer can ultimately fail to be satisfied with Christ. After all, God Himself has declared His beloved Son fully satisfying (Matt. 3:17; 17:5). How could sincere faith deem Him something less?

How do you suppose this kind of faith behaves? The rest of Hebrews 11 gives an unequivocal answer to that question.

What Faith Does

Faith obeys. That, in two words, is the key lesson of Hebrews 11. Here we see people of faith worshiping God (v. 4); walking with God (v. 5); working for God (v. 7); obeying God (vv. 8–10); overcoming barrenness (v. 11); and overpowering death (v. 12).

Faith enabled these people to persevere to death (vv. 13–16); trust God with their dearest possessions (vv. 17–19); believe God for the future (vv. 20–23); turn away from earthly treasure for heavenly reward (vv. 24–26); see Him who is unseen (v. 27); receive miracles from the hand of God (28–30); have courage in the face of great danger (31–33); conquer kingdoms, perform acts of righteousness, obtain promises, shut the mouths of lions, quench the power of fire, escape the edge of the sword, from weakness be made strong, become mighty in war, and put foreign armies to flight (vv. 33–34). This faith has overcome death, endured torture, outlasted chains and imprisonment, withstood temptation, undergone martyrdom, and survived all manner of hardship (vv. 35–38).

And faith endures. If anything is true about Hebrews 11 faith, it is that it cannot be killed. It perseveres. It endures no matter what—holding to God with love and assurance no matter what kind of assaults the world or the forces of evil might bring against it.

No-lordship theology posits an altogether different kind of faith. No-lordship faith is a fragile, sometimes temporary, often nonworking faith. No-lordship faith is simply being convinced of something or giving credence to historical facts (*SGS* 30). No-lordship faith is confidence, trust, holding something as true—but without any commitment to the object of faith (*SGS* 118–19). No-lordship faith is the inward conviction that what God says to us in the gospel is true—that and that alone (*AF* 31). No-lordship faith is "a single, one-time appropriation of God's gift." It won't necessarily continue believing (*AF* 63). In fact, no-lordship faith might even turn into hostile unbelief (*SGS* 141).

Is faith merely the illumination of human reason, or does it transform the whole being? Some advocates of the no-lordship view resent the accusation that they see faith as merely a mental activity. But they consistently fail to define believing as anything *more* than a cognitive function. Many use the word *trust*, but when they define it, they actually describe *assent*.

Charles Ryrie, for example, cites approvingly Berkhof's section on *notitia, assensus,* and *fiducia.* He even quotes Berkhof's definition of *fiducia,* trust: "a personal trust in Christ as Savior *and Lord, including a surrender of the soul as guilty and defiled to Christ,* and a reception and appropriation of Christ as the source of pardon and a spiritual life" (*SGS* 120, emphasis added). In the same paragraph, however, Ryrie makes the curious assertion that "Berkhof does not inject or speak to the issue of the mastery of Christ over one's life." As Ryrie continues his own explanation of "trust," it becomes clear that he actually wants to abridge Berkhof to this: *Fiducia* is "a personal trust in Christ as Savior . . . and . . . as the source of pardon and [eternal] life." In fact, when Ryrie further explains what he means by "personal trust in Christ," he continually falls back on language that speaks only of believing facts: "To believe in Christ for salvation means to have confidence that He can remove the guilt of sin and give eternal life" (*SGS* 119). That is *assent,* not *trust.* Assent is the acceptance of truth *about* Christ; trust is a turning *to* Him in full self-surrender (cf. Deut. 30:10; 2 Kings 23:25; 1 Thess. 1:9). That was Berkhof's point.

Here is the typical no-lordship appeal to sinners: "trust in the gospel" (*SGS* 30), "believe in the good news" (*SGS* 39), "believe that Christ died for our sins" (*SGS* 40), "Believe that He is God and your Messiah who died and who rose from the dead" (*SGS* 96), "believe that Christ can forgive" (*SGS* 118), "believe that his death paid for all your sin" (*SGS* 119), "trust in the truth" (*SGS* 121), "believe that Someone . . . can take away sin" (*SGS* 123).

No-lordship doctrine inevitably makes the gospel *message* the object of faith, rather than the Lord Jesus Himself. Contrast the no-lordship appeals with biblical language: "Believe in the Lord Jesus, and you shall be saved" (Acts 16:31). Sinners are called to believe in *Him,* not only the facts about Him (Acts 20:21; 24:24; 26:18; Rom. 3:22, 26; Gal. 2:16, 20; 3:22, 26; Phil. 3:9). Faith certainly *includes* knowledge of and assent to the truth about Christ and His saving work. But saving faith must go beyond knowledge and assent. It is personal trust in the Savior. The call of the gospel is to trust *Him* (cf. John 5:39–40).[10] That necessarily involves some degree of love, allegiance, and surrender to His authority.

Does this mix faith and works, as some are fond of saying? Not at all. Let there be no confusion on this point. Faith is an *internal* reality with *external* consequences. When we say that faith encompasses obedience, we are speaking of the God-given *attitude* of obedience, not trying to make *works* a part of the definition of faith. God makes the believing heart an obedient heart; that is, a heart eager to obey. Faith itself is complete before one work of obedience ever issues forth.

But make no mistake—real faith will always produce righteous works. Faith is the root; works are the fruit. Because God Himself is the vinedresser, fruit is guaranteed. That's why whenever Scripture gives examples of faith—as here in Hebrews 11—faith inevitably is seen as obedient, working, and active.

No-lordship theology reasons that to be truly free from works-righteousness, faith must be free from all obedience, including an *attitude* of obedience. In no-lordship thought, it is unacceptable to require that faith include even a *willingness* to obey.[11] But willingness

---

[10]Ryrie occasionally speaks of Christ as the object of faith, but inevitably defines what he means in a way that nullifies the whole point. For example, when he says, "the object of faith or trust is the Lord Jesus Christ," he immediately counters with: "The issue about which we trust Him is His ability to forgive our sin and take us to heaven" (*SGS* 121).

[11]Charles C. Ryrie, *Balancing the Christian Life* (Chicago: Moody, 1969), 169–70.

to obey is precisely what sets genuine faith apart from hypocrisy. Warfield wrote, "It may be very fairly contended that 'preparedness to act' supplies a very good test of the genuineness of 'faith,' 'belief.' A so-called 'faith,' 'belief' on which we are not prepared to act is near to no real 'faith,' 'belief' at all. What we are convinced of, we should certainly confide in; and what we are unwilling to confide in we seem not quite sure of—we do not appear thoroughly to believe, to have faith in."[12]

Faith and unbelief are states of the heart. But they necessarily impact behavior.[13] Jesus said, "The good man out of the good treasure of his heart brings forth what is good; and the evil man out of the evil treasure brings forth what is evil; for his mouth speaks from that which fills his heart" (Luke 6:45). The state of one's heart will inevitably be revealed by its fruit. That is a key lesson to be drawn from Hebrews 11 and its chronicle of faithfulness.

----

[12]Warfield, *Biblical and Theological Studies*, 379.

[13]That faith necessarily has practical moral results is seen in the cause-and-effect statements of John 8:36–47 (emphasis added):

> "If therefore the Son shall make you free, *you shall be free indeed.* I know that you are Abraham's offspring; yet *you seek to kill Me, because My word has no place in you.* I speak the things which I have seen with My Father; *therefore you also do the things which you heard from your father.*"
>
> They answered and said to Him, "Abraham is our father."
>
> Jesus said to them, "*If you are Abraham's children, do the deeds of Abraham.* But as it is, you are seeking to kill Me, a man who has told you the truth, which I heard from God; this Abraham did not do. *You are doing the deeds of your father.*"
>
> They said to Him, "We were not born of fornication; we have one Father, even God."
>
> Jesus said to them, "*If God were your Father, you would love Me;* for I proceeded forth and have come from God, for I have not even come on My own initiative, but He sent Me. Why *do you not understand* what I am saying? *It is because you cannot hear My word.* You are of your father the devil, and *you want to do the desires of your father.* He was a murderer from the beginning, and does not stand in the truth, because there is no truth in him. Whenever he speaks a lie, he speaks from his own nature; for he is a liar, and the father of lies. But *because I speak the truth, you do not believe Me.* Which one of you convicts Me of sin? If I speak truth, why do you not believe Me? *He who is of God hears the words of God; for this reason you do not hear them, because you are not of God.*"

A key to that passage is verse 42: "If God were your Father, you would love Me." Their *saying* that God was their Father did not make it so. Their behavior and affections reflected the spiritual reality.

A crucial point must be made here. The works described in Hebrews 11 are *faith works.* These are not fleshly efforts to earn God's favor. The works described here are in no sense meritorious. They are the pure expression of believing hearts. *By faith* Abel offered a better sacrifice (v. 4). *By faith* Enoch walked with God (v. 5). *By faith* Noah built an ark (v. 7). *By faith* Abraham obeyed (v. 8). *By faith* he lived in a foreign land (v. 9). *By faith* he offered up Isaac (v. 17). *By faith* Isaac, Jacob, and Joseph persevered to the end of their lives (vv. 20–22). *By faith* Moses' parents hid him (v. 23). *By faith* Moses spurned Egypt in favor of the reproach of Christ (vv. 24–26). *By faith* he left Egypt without fear (v. 27). *By faith* he kept the Passover (v. 28). *By faith* all Israel passed through the Red Sea (v. 29). *By faith* they conquered Jericho (v. 30). *By faith* Rahab welcomed the spies in peace (v. 31).

> What more shall I say? For time will fail me if I tell of Gideon, Barak, Samson, Jephthah, of David and Samuel and the prophets, who *by faith* conquered kingdoms, performed acts of righteousness, obtained promises, shut the mouths of lions, quenched the power of fire, escaped the edge of the sword, from weakness were made strong, became mighty in war, put foreign armies to flight. Women received back their dead by resurrection; and others were tortured, not accepting their release, in order that they might obtain a better resurrection; and others experienced mockings and scourgings, yes, also chains and imprisonment. They were stoned, they were sawn in two, they were tempted, they were put to death with the sword; they went about in sheepskins, in goatskins, being destitute, afflicted, ill-treated . . . wandering in deserts and mountains and caves and holes in the ground.
>
> Hebrews 11:32–38, emphasis added

Works-righteousness? No. "All these . . . gained approval through their *faith*" (v. 39). Hebrews 12:1 identifies these people as a "great . . . cloud of witnesses surrounding us." Witnesses in what sense? They give testimony to the validity, joy, peace, satisfaction, power, and continuity of saving faith. The writer, then, calls on all to run the faith-race (vv. 1–2).

In spite of this monumental testimony to faith works, no-lordship apologists often claim that viewing works as the inevitable expression of faith is tantamount to setting up a system of works-righteousness. Zane Hodges argues this way:

> Lordship salvation cannot escape the charge that it mixes faith and works. The way it does so is succinctly stated by MacArthur: "Obedience is the inevitable manifestation of saving faith."
>
> But this is the same as saying, "Without obedience there is no justification and no heaven." Viewed from *that* standpoint, "obedience" is actually a *condition* for justification and for heaven. . . . If heaven really cannot be attained apart from obedience to God—and this is what lordship salvation teaches—then, logically, that obedience is a *condition* for getting there (*AF* 213–14).

But the folly of that line of reasoning is immediately evident. To say that works are a necessary *result* of faith is *not* the same as making works a *condition* for justification. Hodges himself surely believes all Christians will ultimately be glorified (Rom. 8:30). Would he accept the charge that he is making glorification a *condition* for justification? Presumably, both the lordship and no-lordship views agree that all believers will ultimately be conformed to the image of Christ (Rom. 8:29). We differ only on the timing. Lordship salvation maintains that the process of becoming like Christ begins at the moment of conversion and continues for all of life. The no-lordship view allows for the possibility that practical sanctification may stall short of its goal, or not even begin until this life on earth ends.

Meritorious works have nothing to do with faith. But *faith works* have everything to do with it. As we shall see in chapter 9, faith that does not produce works is dead faith, inefficacious faith. Faith that remains idle is no better than the faith the demons display (James 2:19).

Here we must close this chapter with a clear and careful distinction. Faith works are a *consequence* of faith, not a *component* of faith. As we observed earlier, faith is an entirely inward response and therefore is complete before it produces its first work. At the moment of salvation, faith *does* nothing but receive the provision of Christ. The believer himself contributes nothing meritorious to the saving process. As J. Gresham Machen stated in the quotation with which I began this chapter, "Faith is the acceptance of a gift at the hands of Christ." Better yet, faith lays hold of Christ Himself. In no sense is this an issue of works or merit.

But true faith never remains passive. From the moment of regeneration, faith goes to work. It doesn't work for divine favor. It doesn't work against God's grace, but in accord with grace. As we "work out

[our] salvation with fear and trembling" (Phil. 2:12), we discover that "it is God who is at work in [us], both to will and to work for His good pleasure" (v. 13). True faith keeps our eyes fixed on Jesus, the author and perfecter of all genuine faith (Heb. 12:2).

4

Cheap Grace?

Cheap grace means grace sold on the market like cheap-jacks' wares. . . .

Cheap grace is not the kind of forgiveness that frees us from the toils of sin. Cheap grace is the grace we bestow on ourselves.

Cheap grace is the preaching of forgiveness without requiring repentance, baptism without church discipline, Communion without confession, absolution without personal confession. Cheap grace is grace without discipleship, grace without the cross, grace without Jesus Christ, living and incarnate.

Dietrich Bonhoeffer[1]

*C*heap grace. The term itself is offensive.

"Why do you use that expression?" a friend asked. "It just seems to denigrate the grace of God. After all, grace isn't *cheap*—it's absolutely free! Isn't perfect freeness the very essence of grace?"

But "cheap grace" doesn't speak of God's grace. It is a self-imparted grace, a pseudograce. This grace is "cheap" in *value,* not cost. It is a bargain-basement, damaged-goods, washed-out, moth-eaten, second-hand grace. It is a manmade grace reminiscent of the indulgences Rome was peddling in Martin Luther's day. Cheap? The cost is actually far more than the buyer could possibly realize, though the "grace" is utterly worthless.

---

[1]Dietrich Bonhoeffer, *The Cost of Discipleship* (New York: Collier, 1959), 45–47.

The term "cheap grace" was coined by a German Lutheran pastor and Nazi resister named Dietrich Bonhoeffer. Bonhoeffer was hanged in 1945 by SS guards, but not before his writings had left their mark. Bonhoeffer's theological perspective was neo-orthodox, and evangelicalism rightly rejects much of his teaching. But Bonhoeffer spoke powerfully against the secularization of the church. He correctly analyzed the dangers of the church's frivolous attitude toward grace. After we discard the neo-orthodox teachings, we do well to pay heed to Bonhoeffer's diatribe against cheap grace:

> Cheap grace means grace as a doctrine, a principle, a system. It means forgiveness of sins proclaimed as a general truth, the love of God taught as the Christian "conception" of God. An intellectual assent to that idea is held to be of itself sufficient to secure the remission of sins. The Church which holds the correct doctrine of grace has, it is supposed, *ipso facto* a part in that grace. In such a Church the world finds a cheap covering for its sins; no contrition is required, still less any real desire to be delivered from sin. Cheap grace therefore amounts to a denial of the Incarnation of the Word of God.
>
> Cheap grace means the justification of sin without the justification of the sinner. Grace alone does everything, they say, and so everything can remain as it was before. "All for sin could not atone." The world goes on in the same old way, and we are still sinners "even in the best life" as Luther said. Well, then, let the Christian live like the rest of the world, let him model himself on the world's standards in every sphere of life, and not presumptuously aspire to live a different life under grace from his old life under sin.[2]

Cheap grace has not lost its worldly appeal since Bonhoeffer wrote those words. If anything, the tendency to cheapen grace has eaten its way into the heart of evangelical Christianity. The no-lordship movement has led the way in legitimizing and institutionalizing cheap grace in American fundamentalism. No-lordship teaching tragically misconstrues and misapplies the biblical doctrine of grace. While verbally extolling the wonders of grace, it exchanges the real item for a facsimile. This bait-and-switch tactic has confounded many sincere Christians.

No-lordship theology utterly ignores the biblical truth that grace "instruct[s] us to deny ungodliness and worldly desires and to live

---

[2]Ibid., 45–46.

sensibly, righteously and godly in the present age" (Titus 2:12). Instead, it portrays grace as a supernatural "Get Out of Jail FREE" ticket—a no-strings-attached, open-ended package of amnesty, beneficence, indulgence, forbearance, charity, leniency, immunity, approval, tolerance, and self-awarded privilege divorced from any moral demands.

Supergrace is fast becoming the most popular bandwagon in the evangelical parade. Those who make allegiance to Christ's lordship optional are leading the way. They have even begun calling their teaching "grace theology" and refer to their movement as "The Grace Movement."

Yet the "grace" they speak of alters believers' *standing* without affecting their *state*. It is a grace that calls sinners to Christ but does not bid them surrender to Him. In fact, no-lordship theologians claim grace is *diluted* if the believing sinner must surrender to Christ. The more one actually surrenders, the more grace is supposedly watered down (*SGS* 18). This is clearly not the grace of Titus 2:11–12.

No wonder Christians are confused. With so much contradictory and obviously unbiblical teaching continuing to gain popularity, we might wonder about the future of biblical Christianity.

What Is Grace?

Grace is a terribly misunderstood word. Defining it succinctly is notoriously difficult. Some of the most detailed theology textbooks do not offer any concise definition of the term. Someone has proposed an acronym: GRACE is God's Riches At Christ's Expense. That's not a bad way to characterize grace, but it is not a sufficient theological definition. One of the best-known definitions of grace is only three words: God's unmerited favor. A. W. Tozer expanded on that: "Grace is the good pleasure of God that inclines him to bestow benefits on the undeserving."[3] Berkhof is more to the point: grace is "the unmerited operation of God in the heart of man, effected through the agency of the Holy Spirit."[4]

At the heart of the term *grace* is the idea of divine favor. The Hebrew word for grace is *chēn*, used, for example, in Genesis 6:8: "Noah found favor in the eyes of the Lord." Closely related is the verb *chānan*, meaning "to show favor." In the New Testament, "grace" is a rendering of the

---

[3]A. W. Tozer, *The Knowledge of the Holy* (New York: Harper & Row, 1961), 100.

[4]Louis Berkhof, *Systematic Theology* (Grand Rapids, Mich.: Eerdmans, 1939), 427.

Greek *charis,* meaning "gracefulness," "graciousness," "favor," or "gratitude." Intrinsic to its meaning are the ideas of favor, goodness, and goodwill.

Grace is all that and more. Grace is not merely unmerited favor; it is favor bestowed on sinners who deserve wrath. Showing kindness to a stranger is "unmerited favor"; doing good to one's enemies is more the spirit of grace (Luke 6:27–36).

Grace is not a dormant or abstract quality, but a dynamic, active, working principle: "The grace of God has appeared, bringing salvation . . . and instructing us" (Titus 2:11–12). It is not some kind of ethereal blessing that lies idle until we appropriate it. Grace is God's sovereign initiative to sinners (Eph. 1:5-6). Grace is not a one-time event in the Christian experience. We stand in grace (Rom. 5:2). The entire Christian life is driven and empowered by grace: "It is good for the heart to be strengthened by grace, not by foods" (Heb. 13:9). Peter said we should "grow in the grace and knowledge of our Lord and Savior Jesus Christ" (2 Pet. 3:18).

Thus we could properly define grace as *the free and benevolent influence of a holy God operating sovereignly in the lives of undeserving sinners.*

Graciousness is an attribute of God. It is His nature to bestow grace. "He is gracious and compassionate and righteous" (Ps. 112:4). "He is gracious and compassionate, slow to anger, abounding in lovingkindness, and relenting of evil" (Joel 2:13). He is "the God of all grace" (1 Pet. 5:10); His Son is "full of grace and truth" (John 1:14); His Spirit is "the Spirit of grace" (Heb. 10:29). Berkhof observed, "While we sometimes speak of grace as an inherent quality, it is in reality the active communication of divine blessings by the inworking of the Holy Spirit, out of the fulness of Him who is 'full of grace and truth.'"[5]

Charis is found in the Greek text 155 times, 100 times in the Pauline epistles alone. Interestingly, the term itself is never used in reference to divine grace in any of the recorded words of Jesus. But grace permeated all His ministry and teaching ("The blind receive sight and the lame walk, the lepers are cleansed and the deaf hear, and the dead are raised up, and the poor have the gospel preached to them" [Matt. 11:5]; "Come to Me, all who are weary and heavy-laden, and I will give you rest" [Matt. 11:28]).

---

[5]Ibid.

Grace is a gift.[6] God "gives a greater grace. . . . [He] gives grace to the humble" (James 4:6). "Of His fulness we have all received, and grace upon grace" (John 1:16). Christians are said to be "stewards of the manifold grace of God" (1 Pet. 4:10). But that does not mean that God's grace is placed at our disposal. We do not possess God's grace or control its operation. We are subject to grace, never vice versa.

Paul frequently contrasted grace with law (Rom. 4:16; 5:20; 6:14–15; Gal. 2:21; 5:4). He was careful to state, however, that grace does not nullify the moral demands of God's law. Rather, it fulfills the righteousness of the law (Rom. 6:14–15). In a sense, grace is to law what miracles are to nature. It rises above and accomplishes what law cannot (cf. Rom. 8:3). Yet it does not annul the righteous demands of the law; it confirms and validates them (Rom. 3:31). Grace has its own law, a higher, liberating law: "The law of the Spirit of life in Christ Jesus has set you free from the law of sin and of death" (Rom. 8:2; cf. James 1:25). Note that this new law emancipates us from *sin* as well as *death*. Paul was explicit about this: "What shall we say then? Are we to continue in sin that grace might increase? May it never be! How shall we who died to sin still live in it?" (Rom. 6:1–2). Grace reigns through *righteousness* (Rom. 5:21).

There are two extremes to be avoided in the matter of grace. We must take care not to nullify grace through legalism (Gal. 2:21) or corrupt it through licentiousness (Jude 4).

Two Kinds of Grace

Theologians speak of *common grace* and *special grace*. Common grace is bestowed to mankind in general. It is the grace that restrains the full expression of sin and mitigates sin's destructive effects in human society. Common grace imposes moral constraints on people's behavior, maintains a semblance of order in human affairs, enforces a sense of right and wrong through conscience and civil government, enables men

---

[6]This is contrary to Zane Hodges' staggering claim, "It is inherently contradictory to speak here of 'grace' as the 'gift of God.' The *giving of a gift is an act* of 'grace,' but 'grace,' when viewed as a principle or basis of divine action, is never said to be a 'gift,' or part of a gift" (*AF* 219). Scripture is filled with statements that contradict that assertion: "The Lord gives grace and glory; no good thing does He withhold from those who walk uprightly" (Ps. 84:11); "He gives grace to the afflicted" (Prov. 3:34); "He gives a greater grace" (James 4:6); "God is opposed to the proud, but gives grace to the humble" (1 Pet. 5:5; cf. also Rom. 15:15; 1 Cor. 1:4; 3:10; Eph. 4:7).

and women to appreciate beauty and goodness, and imparts blessings of all kinds to all peoples. God "causes His sun to rise on the evil and the good, and sends rain on the righteous and the unrighteous" (Matt. 5:45). That is common grace.

Common grace is not redemptive. It does not pardon sin or purify sinners. It does not renew the heart, stimulate faith, or enable salvation. It can convict of sin and enlighten the soul to the truth of God. But common grace alone does not lead to eternal salvation, because the hearts of sinners are so firmly set against God (Rom. 3:10–18).

Special grace, better called *saving grace,* is the irresistible work of God that frees men and women from the penalty and power of sin, renewing the inner person and sanctifying the sinner through the operation of the Holy Spirit. Normally when the New Testament uses the term *grace,* the reference is to saving grace. Throughout this book when I speak of grace, I mean *saving* grace unless I specify otherwise.

Saving grace "reign[s] through righteousness to eternal life" (Rom. 5:21). Grace saves, sanctifies, and brings the soul to glory (Rom. 8:29–30). Every stage of the process of salvation is governed by sovereign grace. In fact, the term *grace* in the New Testament is often used as a synonym for the whole of the saving process, particularly in the Pauline epistles (cf. 1 Cor. 1:4; 2 Cor. 6:1; Gal. 2:21). Paul saw redemption as so utterly a work of God's grace that he often used the word *grace* as a blanket term to refer to the totality of salvation. Grace oversees all of salvation, beginning to end. It never stalls before concluding its work, nor does it ever botch the job.

What we're really saying is that grace is *efficacious.* In other words, grace is certain to produce the intended results. God's grace is *always* efficacious. That truth is rooted in Scripture. It was a major theme of Augustine's teaching. The doctrine of efficacious grace is the bedrock of Reformed *soteriology* (teaching about salvation).[7] Charles Hodge defined efficacious grace as "the almighty power of God."

No-lordship theology is fundamentally a denial of efficacious grace. The "grace" described in no-lordship teaching is *not* certain to accomplish its purposes—and most often, it seems, it does not. Under

---

[7]This explains why Reformed theologians universally agree on lordship salvation. Many of them consider the no-lordship arguments somewhat silly, because they correctly understand that faith, repentance, surrender, and holiness are all part of God's gracious saving work.

no-lordship grace, key parts of the process—including repentance, commitment, surrender, and even holiness—are optional aspects of the Christian experience, left up to the believer himself (cf. *SGS* 18). The believer's faith might even grind to a screeching halt. Yet no-lordship grace tells us we are not supposed to conclude that "he or she was never a believer in the first place" (*SGS* 142). Well, then, what *are* we to conclude? That saving grace is not efficacious? It is the only reasonable conclusion we *can* draw from no-lordship theology: "God's miracle of salvation in our lives, accomplished by grace through faith without works, makes ample *provision* for the lifetime of good works for which he has designed us. *But it does not guarantee this*" (*AF* 73–74, emphasis added).

One could legitimately characterize the whole lordship controversy as a dispute over efficacious grace. All points in the discussion ultimately come back to this: Does God's saving grace inevitably obtain its desired effects? If all sides could come to consensus on that one question, the debate would be settled.

Sovereign Grace

It is clear from all this that the sovereignty of God in salvation is at the heart of the lordship debate. The irony is that the so-called Grace Movement denies the whole point of grace: that it is *God* who effects the complete saving work in sinners. Redemption is *all* His work. God is wholly sovereign in the exercise of His grace; He is not subject to the human will. "For He says to Moses, 'I will have mercy on whom I have mercy, and I will have compassion on whom I have compassion.' So then it does not depend on the man who wills or the man who runs, but on God who has mercy" (Rom. 9:15–16).

Don't misunderstand; we are not idle in the process. Nor does saving grace force people to believe against their will. That is not what *irresistible grace* means. Grace is not coercion. But by transforming the heart, grace makes the believer wholly willing to trust and obey.

Scripture makes clear that every aspect of grace is God's sovereign work. He foreknows and foreordains the elect (Rom. 8:29), calls the sinner to Himself (Rom. 8:30), draws the soul to Christ (John 6:44), accomplishes the new birth (John 1:13; James 1:18), grants repentance (Acts 11:18) and faith (Rom. 12:3; Acts 18:27), justifies the believer (Rom. 3:24; 8:30), makes the redeemed holy (Eph. 2:10), and finally glorifies them (Rom. 8:30).[8] In no stage of the process is grace thwarted by human failure, dependent on human merit, or subjugated to human effort. "What then shall we say to these things? If God is for us, who is against us? He who did not spare His own Son, but delivered Him up for us all, how will He not also with Him *freely give us all things?*" (Rom. 8:30–32, emphasis added). *That's* grace.

Many people struggle with the concept of sovereign grace, but if God is not sovereign in the exercise of His grace, then it is not grace at all. If God's purposes were dependent on some self-generated response of faith or on human merit, then God Himself would not be sovereign, and salvation would not be wholly His work. If that were the case, the redeemed would have something to boast about, and grace wouldn't be grace (Rom. 3:27; Eph. 2:9).

Furthermore, because of human depravity, there is nothing in a fallen, reprobate sinner that desires God or is capable of responding in faith. Paul wrote, "There is none who understands, there is none who seeks for God; all have turned aside, together they have become useless; there is none who does good, there is not even one. Their throat is an open grave, with their tongues they keep deceiving, the poison of asps is under their lips" (Rom. 3:11–13). Note the metaphors involving death. That is the state of everyone in sin. As we shall see shortly, Scripture teaches that sinful humanity is dead in trespasses and sins (Eph. 2:1), "separate[d] from Christ, excluded from the commonwealth of

---

[8]I am not explicitly suggesting an *ordo salutis,* or order of salvation, in these comments. Much has been written on the *ordo salutis,* but it is beyond the scope of my purposes in this book to deal with the question. One of the better treatments of the issue is found in Anthony A. Hoekema, *Saved by Grace* (Grand Rapids, Mich.: Eerdmans, 1989), 14–27.

Hoekema shows that salvation is not so much a series of successive steps as a simultaneous application of several aspects of saving grace. The *ordo salutis* must be primarily a logical, not a chronological, arrangement, for in the same moment that we are regenerated we are converted, we repent, we believe, we are justified, we are sanctified, and we embark on a life of faith and obedience that will persevere unto glorification.

In the broad sense, *regeneration,* or the new birth, is a term sometimes used as a synonym for salvation (Titus 3:5; cf. John 3:3, 5, 7; 1 Pet. 1:23). In its specific, theological sense, regeneration is the work of the Holy Spirit that imparts new life to the sinner. The word is never in the New Testament used of some narrow prefaith act by God which can be separated out as an autonomous event or a stand-alone commodity. From the viewpoint of reason, regeneration *logically* must initiate faith and repentance. But the saving transaction is all a single, instantaneous event.

The crucial point to be made in respect to this is that it rules out making sanctification, consecration, Spirit baptism, or any other aspect of conversion a second-level experience. No phase of conversion is postponed or offered as a second work of grace.

Israel, and strangers to the covenants of promise, having no hope and without God in the world" (v. 12). There is no escape from such a desperate predicament, except for the sovereign intervention of God's saving grace.

By Grace Are You Saved

The classic text on salvation by grace is Ephesians 2:8–9: "For by grace you have been saved through faith; and that not of yourselves, it is the gift of God; not as a result of works, that no one should boast." Let's look at those verses in their context and try to understand better how Scripture describes the salvation that is by grace through faith in the Lord Jesus Christ.

In Ephesians 1, Paul's central point was God's sovereignty in graciously saving the elect. He wrote that God chose us (v. 4), predestined us (v. 5), guaranteed our adoption (v. 5), bestowed on us His grace (v. 6), redeemed us (v. 7), forgave us (v. 7), lavished riches of grace on us (v. 8), made known to us His will (v. 9), obtained an inheritance for us (v. 11), guaranteed that we would glorify Him (vv. 11–12), saved us (v. 13), and sealed us with the Spirit (vv. 13–14). In short, He "has blessed us with every spiritual blessing in the heavenly places in Christ" (v. 3). All of this was the work of His sovereign grace, performed not because of any good in us, but simply "according to the kind intention of His will" (v. 5, cf. v. 9) and "according to His purpose who works all things after the counsel of His will" (v. 11).

Here in the first ten verses of Ephesians 2, Paul chronicles the process of salvation from eternity past:

> And you were dead in your trespasses and sins, in which you formerly walked according to the course of this world, according to the prince of the power of the air, of the spirit that is now working in the sons of disobedience. Among them we too all formerly lived in the lusts of our flesh, indulging the desires of the flesh and of the mind, and were by nature children of wrath, even as the rest. But God, being rich in mercy, because of His great love with which He loved us, even when we were dead in our transgressions, made us alive together with Christ (by grace you have been saved), and raised us up with Him, and seated us with Him in the heavenly places, in Christ Jesus, in order that in the ages to come He might show the surpassing riches of His grace in kindness toward us in Christ Jesus. For by grace you have been saved through faith; and that not of yourselves, it is the gift of God; not as a result of works,

that no one should boast. For we are His workmanship, created in
Christ Jesus for good works, which God prepared beforehand, that
we should walk in them.

Paul's focus in those verses is solely on *God's* work in saving us, because
there is no *human* work to be considered as a part of the saving process
(vv. 8–9). These verses describe our past, present, and future as Christians: what we were (vv. 1–3), what we are (vv. 4–6, 8–9), and what we
will be (vv. 7, 10). The passage reads like a tract on lordship salvation.
The apostle Paul names six features of salvation: It is from sin (vv. 1–3),
by love (v. 4), into life (v. 5), for God's glory (vv. 6–7), through faith
(vv. 8–9), and unto good works (v. 10).

Salvation is from sin. Paul writes, "You were dead in your trespasses and sins, in which you formerly walked according to the course of
this world, according to the prince of the power of the air, of the spirit
that is now working in the sons of disobedience. Among them we too
all formerly lived in the lusts of our flesh, indulging the desires of the
flesh and of the mind, and were by nature children of wrath, even as the
rest" (2:1–3). There is perhaps no more succinct statement in Scripture
on the total depravity and lost condition of sinful mankind.

Because we were born in sin we were born to death, "for the wages
of sin is death" (Rom. 6:23). People do not become spiritually dead
because they sin; they are sinners "by nature" (v. 3) and therefore born
without spiritual life. Because we were dead to God, we were dead to
truth, righteousness, peace, happiness, and every other good thing, no
more able to respond to God than a cadaver.

One afternoon early in my ministry at Grace Church I heard a
frantic pounding on my office door. I opened the door and there was
a little boy, breathless and crying. In a panicked voice he asked, "Are
you the Reverend?" When I told him I was, he said, "Hurry! Please
come with me." It was obvious something was terribly wrong, so I ran
with him to his house, about half a block away and across the street
from our church.

Inside, the boy's mother was weeping uncontrollably. She said,
"My baby is dead! My baby is dead!" She quickly took me to a back
room. On the bed was the limp body of a tiny infant. He had evidently
died in his sleep. The body was blue and already cold to the touch. The
mother had been trying desperately to revive him, but nothing could be
done. The child was gone. There was absolutely no sign of life. The
mother tenderly held the tiny body, kissed it, gently touched its face,
spoke to it, and wept over it. But the child made no response. A crew of

paramedics arrived and tried to get the child breathing again, but it was too late. Nothing had any effect. There was no response because there was no life. Even the powerful love of a heartbroken mother could not evoke a response.

Spiritual death is exactly like that. Unregenerate sinners have no life by which they can respond to spiritual stimuli. No amount of love, beseeching, or spiritual truth can summon a response. People apart from God are the ungrateful dead, spiritual zombies, death-walkers, unable even to understand the gravity of their situation. They are lifeless. They may go through the motions of life, but they do not possess it. They are dead even while they live (cf. 1 Tim. 5:6).

Before salvation every Christian was in precisely the same predicament. None of us responded to God or to His truth. We were "dead in [our] trespasses and sins" (Eph. 2:1). "We were dead in our transgressions" (v. 5). "Trespasses and sins" and "transgressions" here do not speak of specific acts. They describe the sphere of existence of the person apart from God, the realm in which sinners live. It is the eternal night of the living dead. All its inhabitants are totally depraved.

Total depravity does not mean that every person's lifestyle is equally corrupt and wicked, or that sinners are always as bad as they can be. It means that mankind is corrupt in every regard. The unredeemed are depraved in their minds, their hearts, their wills, their emotions, and their physical beings. They are utterly incapable of anything but sin. Even if they perform humanitarian, philanthropic, or religious deeds, they do them for their own glory, not God's (cf. 1 Cor. 10:31). Sinners may not always sin as grotesquely as possible, but they cannot do anything to please God or earn His favor. Sin has tainted every aspect of their being. That is what it means to be spiritually dead.

A hundred cadavers in the morgue might be in a hundred different phases of decomposition, but they are all equally dead. Depravity, like death, is manifested in many different forms. But just as death itself has no differing degrees of intensity, so depravity is always absolute. Not all people are manifestly as evil as they could be, but all are equally dead in sins.

How do people get around in this state of spiritual death? They walk "according to the course of this world, according to the prince of the power of the air, of the spirit that is now working in the sons of disobedience" (Eph. 2:2). Satan is "the prince of the power of the air." He governs the realm of sin and death ("this world") in which the unredeemed function. It is a realm that features many different and apparently competing religions, moral systems, and standards of behavior, but ultimately they are all under the control and in the grip of the devil. "The whole world lies in the power of the evil one" (1 John 5:19).

Thus the unredeemed—whether they realize it or not—have a common lord, "the prince of the power of the air." Satan is the *archōn*, the prince. He is "the ruler of this world" and will reign until the Lord casts him out (John 12:31). All those in this realm of sin and death live under his dominion, share his nature, are conspirators in his rebellion against God, and so respond naturally to his authority. They are on the same spiritual wavelength. Jesus even calls the devil the father of those under his lordship (John 8:44).

Note that the unsaved are "by nature children of wrath" (Eph. 2:3). People are not "all God's children," as some are fond of saying. Those who have not received salvation through Jesus Christ are God's enemies (Rom. 5:10; 8:7; James 4:4), not only "sons of disobedience" but consequently "children of wrath"—objects of God's eternal condemnation.

Paul's purpose in Ephesians 2:1–3 is not to show how unsaved people live—though the teaching is valuable for that purpose—but to remind believers how they *previously* lived. All of us "*formerly* lived in the lusts of our flesh, indulging the desires of the flesh and of the mind, and were by nature children of wrath, even as the rest" (v. 3, emphasis added). The realm of sin and death is a past-tense experience for the believer. We *were* hopelessly subject to the world, the flesh, and the devil (vv. 2–3). We *formerly* walked as sons of disobedience (v. 2). We *were* dead in sins and trespasses (v. 1). Now all that is in the past.

Although we were once like the rest of mankind, by God's grace we are no longer like that. Because of His saving work in us, we are presently and eternally redeemed. We have been delivered from spiritual death, sin, alienation from God, disobedience, demon control, lust, and divine judgment (vv. 1–3). That is what saving grace accomplishes.

Salvation is by love. "But God, being rich in mercy, because of His great love with which He loved us . . . made us alive together with Christ" (vv. 4–5). God's mercy is "rich," measureless, overflowing, abundant, unlimited. Some who struggle with the concept of sovereign grace believe God is unfair to elect some and not save everyone. That is exactly opposite from right thinking. The truth is, *everyone* deserves hell. God in His grace elects to save some. *No one* would be saved apart from God's sovereign grace. The thing that keeps sinners from being reconciled to God is not a deficiency of mercy or grace on God's side of the equation. It is *sin,* and sin is a human problem. Rebellion and rejection are in the nature of every sinner.

The two words "but God" affirm that the initiative to save is all God's. Because He is rich in mercy toward us, and because of His great love for us, He intervened and provided a way by grace for us to return to Him.

God is intrinsically kind, merciful, and loving. Love is so integral to who He is that the apostle John wrote, "God is love" (1 John 4:8, 16). In His love He reaches out to sinful, corrupt, impoverished, condemned, spiritually dead human beings and blesses them with every spiritual blessing in the heavenly places in Christ (Eph. 1:3).

Not only does God love enough to forgive, but also enough to give His Son to die for the very ones who had offended Him: "God so loved the world, that He gave His only begotten Son, that whoever believes in Him should not perish, but have eternal life" (John 3:16). "Greater love has no one than this, that one lay down his life for his friends" (John 15:13). God's love for those who do not deserve it makes salvation possible and fills salvation with every mercy. It is the epitome of sovereign grace.

Salvation is unto life. "Even when we were dead in our transgressions, [God] made us alive together with Christ" (Eph. 2:5). The saving transaction begins the moment God gives spiritual life to a dead person. It is God who makes the first move. Jesus said, "No one can come to Me, unless the Father who sent Me draws him" (John 6:44). Of course! The unsaved are *dead,* incapable of any spiritual activity. Until God quickens us, we have no capacity to respond to Him in faith.

When sinners are saved, they are no longer alienated from the life of God. They become spiritually alive through a miraculous, God-wrought union with Christ. They become sensitive to God for the first time. Paul calls it "newness of life" (Rom. 6:4). Now they understand spiritual truth and desire spiritual things (1 Cor. 2:10–16). Now they have become partakers of the divine nature (2 Pet. 1:4). They can pursue godliness—"the things above"—rather than "the things that are on earth" (Col. 3:2).

This new life is "in Christ Jesus" (Eph. 2:6). He *is* our life (Col. 3:4). "We . . . live with Him" (Rom. 6:8), in the likeness of His resurrection (6:5). Our new life is actually His life lived in us (Gal. 2:20). It is utterly different from our former life and the supreme manifestation of God's sovereign grace.

Salvation is for God's glory. "[God] raised us up with Him, and seated us with Him in the heavenly places, in Christ Jesus, in order that in the ages to come He might show the surpassing riches of His grace in kindness toward us in Christ Jesus" (Eph. 2:6–7). Salvation has a particular purpose: that we might enjoy and display His glory, showing forth the riches of His grace (cf. Rom. 9:23).

Our new citizenship is in heaven (Phil. 3:20). God raises us up with Christ and seats us with Him in the heavenly places. We no longer belong to this present world or its sphere of sinfulness and rebellion. We are rescued from spiritual death and the consequences of our sin. That is pure grace.

Note that the apostle describes this heavenly life as if it were already fully accomplished. Even though we are not yet in full possession of all that God has for us in Christ, we live in His domain, just as we formerly lived in the realm of sin and death. "Heavenly places" clearly implies the full sense of God's dominion. This expression cannot be read in a way that makes His lordship optional. To dwell in the heavenly domain is to enjoy full fellowship with the Godhead. It is because we dwell in this realm that we enjoy God's protection, His day-to-day provision, all the blessings of His favor. But no one dwells there who still walks according to the course of this world, according to the prince of the power of the air, and under the control of the spirit that now works in the sons of disobedience. We are no longer "children of wrath" but "children of God" (John 1:12; 1 John 3:1) and citizens of heaven (Eph. 2:19).

Just as in the old realm of sin and death we were subject to the prince of the power of the air (v. 2), so in this new realm we follow a new Lord. Just as we were "by nature children of wrath" (v. 3) and "sons of disobedience" (v. 2), so now we are by nature "alive together with Christ" (v. 5) and "in Him" (v. 6).

God's ultimate purpose in our salvation is to exalt His sovereign grace "in order that in the ages to come He might show the surpassing riches of His grace in kindness toward us in Christ Jesus" (v. 7). So our loving Father glorifies Himself even as He blesses us. His grace is the centerpiece of His glory. From the first moment of salvation throughout "the ages to come," we never stop benefiting from His grace and goodness to us. At no point does grace stop and human effort take over.[9]

Salvation is through faith. "For by grace you have been saved through faith; and that not of yourselves, it is the gift of God; not as a

---

[9]A major flaw in no-lordship theology is its tendency to make grace operative in justification only and make works the ground of sanctification. Zane Hodges teaches that "God's gift of life" and the "potential" for sanctification are "absolutely free" gifts of grace. "But from there on" growth, fruitfulness, and practical sanctification require arduous human effort (*AF* 74).

result of works, that no one should boast" (2:8–9). Faith is our *response,* not the *cause* of salvation. Even faith is "not of ourselves"; it is included in "the gift of God."

Some no-lordship advocates object to this interpretation.[10] They point out that "faith" (*pistis*) is feminine, while "that" (*touto*) is neuter. Grammatically, the pronoun "that" has no clear antecedent. It refers not to the noun, *faith,* but more likely to the (understood) act of believing. It could possibly refer to the whole of salvation.

Either way, the meaning is inescapable: Faith is God's gracious gift. Jesus explicitly affirmed this truth: "No one can come to Me, unless it has been granted him from the Father" (John 6:65). Faith is also spoken of as a divine gift in Acts 3:16 ("The faith which comes through Him has given him this perfect health in the presence of you all"), Philippians 1:29 ("To you it has been granted for Christ's sake, not only to believe in Him, but also to suffer for His sake"), and 2 Peter 1:1 ("Simon Peter, a bond-servant and apostle of Jesus Christ, to those who have received a faith of the same kind as ours").[11]

"Not by works" is not contrasting faith versus repentance, faith versus commitment, or faith versus surrender. In fact, the issue here is not as simple as faith versus circumcision or faith versus baptism. The contrast is between *divine grace* and *human merit.*

Human effort cannot bring salvation. We are saved by grace alone through faith alone in Christ alone. When we relinquish all hope except faith in Christ and His finished work on our behalf, we are acting by the faith that God in His grace supplies. Believing is therefore the first act of an awakened spiritual corpse; it is the new man drawing his first breath. Because faith is unfailing, the spiritual man keeps on breathing.

Obviously, if salvation is entirely by God's grace, it cannot be as a result of works. Human effort has nothing to do with gaining or sustaining it (cf. Rom. 3:20; Gal. 2:16). No one should boast, as if we had any part in bringing it about (cf. Rom. 3:27; 4:5; 1 Cor. 1:31).

But we cannot stop here, for there is one more crucial point in Paul's line of reasoning. It is the principal thesis to which he has been building.

---

[10]Charles Ryrie may be an exception to the rule on this point. In one place, he acknowledges that "the whole of salvation, including faith, is the gift of God" (*SGS* 96). Unfortunately, he mentions this crucial reality only as "an interesting sidelight" and does not deal with the implications of it in his system.

[11]Contrast Hodges' declaration: "The Bible never affirms that saving faith per se is a gift" (*AF* 219).

Salvation is unto good works. "We are His workmanship, created in Christ Jesus for good works, which God prepared beforehand,
that we should walk in them" (2:10). That is a verse no-lordship theology cannot adequately explain. Many no-lordship books have simply
ignored it. Verses 8 and 9 may seem to fit easily into the no-lordship
system. But without verse 10 we do not have the full picture of what
Paul is saying about our salvation.

It cannot be overemphasized that works play no role in *gaining*
salvation. But good works have everything to do with *living out* salvation. No good works can *earn* salvation, but many good works *result*
from genuine salvation. Good works are not necessary to *become* a disciple, but good works are the necessary *marks* of all true disciples. God
has, after all, ordained that we should walk in them.

Note that before we can do any good work for the Lord, He does
His good work in us. By God's grace we become "*His* workmanship,
created in Christ Jesus for good works." The same grace that made us
alive with Christ and raised us up with Him enables us to do the good
works unto which He has saved us.

Note also that it is God who "prepared" these good works. We get
no credit for them. Even *our* good works are works of *His* grace. In the
previous chapter we called them "faith works." It would also be appropriate to call them "grace works." They are the corroborating evidence
of true salvation. These works, like every other aspect of divine salvation,
are the product of God's sovereign grace.

Good deeds and righteous attitudes are intrinsic to who we are as
Christians. They proceed from the very nature of one who lives in the
realm of the heavenlies. Just as the unsaved are sinners by nature, the
redeemed are righteous by nature. Paul told the Corinthians that God's
abundant grace provided an overflowing sufficiency that equipped them
"for every good deed" (2 Cor. 9:8). He told Titus that Christ "gave
Himself for us, that He might redeem us from every lawless deed and
purify for Himself a people for His own possession, *zealous for good
deeds*" (Titus 2:14, emphasis added).

Remember that Paul's primary message here is *not* evangelistic. He
is writing to believers, many of whom had come to Christ years earlier.
His point is not to tell them how *to be* saved, but to remind them of how
they *were* saved, so that they could see how grace is meant to operate in
the lives of the redeemed. The phrase "we are His workmanship" is the
key to this whole passage.

The Greek word for "workmanship" is *poiema*, from which we get
poem. Our lives are like a divinely written sonnet, a literary masterpiece.

From eternity past, God designed us to be conformed to the image of His Son (Rom. 8:29). All of us are still imperfect, unfinished works of art being carefully crafted by the divine Master. He is not finished with us yet, and His work will not cease until He has made us into the perfect likeness of His Son (1 John 3:2). The energy He uses to accomplish His work is grace. Sometimes the process is slow and arduous; sometimes it is immediately triumphant. Either way, "I am confident of this very thing, that He who began a good work in you will perfect it until the day of Christ Jesus" (Phil. 1:6).

Cheap grace? No way. Nothing about true grace is cheap. It cost God His Son. Its value is inestimable. Its effects are eternal. But it *is* free—"freely bestowed on us in the Beloved" (Eph. 1:6)—and "it abounds to many" (Rom. 5:15), elevating us into that heavenly realm where God has ordained that we should walk.

5

The Necessity of
Preaching Repentance

> Our ears have grown accustomed to hearing men told
> to "accept Jesus as your personal Saviour," a form of words
> which is not found in Scripture. It has become an empty
> phrase. These may be precious words to the Christian—"per-
> sonal Saviour." But they are wholly inadequate to instruct a
> sinner in the way to eternal life. They wholly ignore an essen-
> tial element of the Gospel, namely repentance. And that nec-
> essary ingredient of Gospel preaching is swiftly fading from
> evangelical pulpits, though the New Testament is filled with
> it. . . .
>   Paul confronted the intellectuals of Mars' Hill by preach-
> ing, "God now commandeth all men everywhere to repent"
> (Acts 17:30). This was no optional note on the apostolic
> trumpet. It was the melody, the theme of their instructions to
> sinners. Merely to talk about "accepting a personal Saviour"
> eliminates this crucial imperative.
>
>   Walter Chantry[1]

*O*ver the past five years or so, I have had opportunities to minister in
many of the nations that we used to call "Iron Curtain" countries. There
I have encountered a surprisingly vigorous evangelical church—solidly
biblical, doctrinally orthodox, and *alive.* Western Christians generally do

---

[1]Walter Chantry, *Today's Gospel: Authentic or Synthetic?* (Edinburgh: Banner of Truth,
1970), 48–49.

not comprehend or appreciate the vitality of Eastern European churches without visiting them firsthand. The churches are full—often uncomfortably packed—with crowds standing outside looking through windows. The people are earnest in their commitment to Christ in a way that is rare among Western Christians. Their services are worshipful, subdued, yet intensely passionate. Spontaneous weeping is as common as laughter. Prayer for the lost and personal evangelism are on the hearts and minds of these people more than social activities and sports. The focus of their message to the world is a clear call to repentance.

Eastern European Christianity typically refers to new Christians as "repenters." When someone comes to Christ, fellow believers say the new Christian has "repented." Usually new believers are given the opportunity to stand before the church and verbalize their repentance. In nearly every church service I have attended in the former Soviet Union, at least one new convert has made a public confession of repentance.

It is entirely biblical for the church to make repentance the chief feature of its message to the unsaved world. After all, the gospel calls people to come to the One who can deliver them from *sin*. People who don't feel guilt and want to be delivered from the power and penalty of sin wouldn't even want a deliverer.

Did you realize that our Lord's Great Commission demands that we preach repentance? Luke alone of all the Gospels records the *content* of the message Jesus commanded His disciples to preach: "that repentance for forgiveness of sins should be proclaimed in His name to all the nations" (Luke 24:47). As we shall shortly see, repentance was the substance of the church's message to a hostile world throughout the Book of Acts.

The Bible is clear: Repentance is at the heart of the gospel call. Unless we are preaching repentance we are not preaching the gospel our Lord has charged us to preach. If we fail to call people to turn from their sins, we are not communicating the same gospel the apostles proclaimed.

The Western church has subtly changed the thrust of the gospel. Instead of exhorting sinners to repent, evangelicalism in our society asks the unsaved to "accept Christ." That makes sinners sovereign and puts Christ at their disposal. In effect it puts Christ on trial and hands the judge's robes and gavel to the inquirer—precisely opposite of what should be. Ironically, people who *ought* to be concerned about whether Christ will accept them are being told by Christians that it is the sinner's prerogative to "accept Christ." This modified gospel depicts conversion as "a decision for Christ" rather than a life-transforming change of heart involving genuine faith, repentance, surrender, and rebirth unto newness of life.

A. W. Tozer wrote,

> The formula "Accept Christ" has become a panacea of universal application, and I believe it has been fatal to many. . . .
>
> The trouble is that the whole "Accept Christ" attitude is likely to be wrong. It shows Christ [appealing] to us rather than us to Him. It makes Him stand hat-in-hand awaiting our verdict on Him, instead of our kneeling with troubled hearts awaiting His verdict on us. It may even permit us to accept Christ by an impulse of mind or emotions, painlessly, at no loss to our ego and no inconvenience to our usual way of life.
>
> For this ineffectual manner of dealing with a vital matter we might imagine some parallels; as if, for instance, Israel in Egypt had "accepted" the blood of the Passover but continued to live in bondage, or the prodigal son had "accepted" his father's forgiveness and stayed on among the swine in the far country. Is it not plain that if accepting Christ is to mean anything there must be moral action that accords with it?[2]

The "moral action" Tozer was referring to is repentance.

Repentance in the Lordship Debate

Repentance is no more a meritorious work than its counterpart, faith. It is an *inward* response. Genuine repentance pleads with the Lord to forgive and deliver from the burden of sin and the fear of judgment and hell. It is the attitude of the publican who, fearful of even looking toward heaven, smote his breast and cried, "God, be merciful to me, the sinner!" (Luke 18:13). Repentance is not merely behavior reform. But because true repentance involves a change of heart and purpose, it inevitably *results* in a change of behavior.

Like faith, repentance has intellectual, emotional, and volitional ramifications. Berkhof describes the *intellectual* element of repentance as "a change of view, a recognition of sin as involving personal guilt, defilement, and helplessness." The *emotional* element is "a change of feeling, manifesting itself in sorrow for sin committed against a holy God." The *volitional* element is "a change of purpose, an inward turning away from sin, and a disposition to seek pardon and cleansing."[3]

---

[2] A. W. Tozer, *That Incredible Christian* (Harrisburg, Pa.: Christian Publications, 1964), 18.

[3] Louis Berkhof, *Systematic Theology* (Grand Rapids, Mich.: Eerdmans, 1939), 486.

Each of those three elements is deficient apart from the others. Repentance is a response of the total person; therefore some speak of it as total surrender.

Obviously, that view of repentance is incompatible with no-lordship theology. What do no-lordship teachers say about repentance? They do not fully agree among themselves.

Some radical no-lordship protagonists simply deny that repentance has any place in the gospel appeal: "Though genuine repentance *may* precede salvation . . . , it *need not* do so. And because it is not essential to the saving transaction as such, it is in no sense a condition for that transaction" (*AF* 146). This view hinges on making the "saving transaction" nothing more than forensic *justification* (God's gracious declaration that all the demands of the law are fulfilled on behalf of the believing sinner through the righteousness of Jesus Christ). This single-faceted "saving transaction" does not even bring the sinner into a right relationship with God. Thus the radical no-lordship view offers this peculiar formula: "If the issue is simply, 'What must I do to be saved?' the answer is to believe on the Lord Jesus Christ (Ac 16:31). If the issue is the broader one, 'How can I get on harmonious terms with God?' the answer is 'repentance toward God and faith toward our Lord Jesus Christ' (Ac 20:21)" (*AF* 146).

The insinuations underlying those statements are staggering. How or why would anyone who is unrepentant raise the question, "What must I do to be saved?" What would such a person be seeking salvation *from?* In what sense is salvation a separate issue from "get[ting] on harmonious terms with God"? Is it possible to obtain eternal salvation with no sense of the gravity of one's own sin and alienation from God? That is the implication of radical no-lordship teaching.

But the predominate no-lordship view on repentance is simply to redefine repentance as a change of mind—not a turning from sin or a change of purpose. This view states, "In both the Old and New Testaments *repentance* means 'to change one's mind'" (*SGS* 92). "Is repentance a condition for receiving eternal life? Yes, if it is repentance or changing one's mind about Jesus Christ. No if it means to be sorry for sin or even resolve to turn from sin" (*SGS* 99). Repentance by that definition is simply a synonym for the no-lordship definition of faith. It is simply an intellectual exercise.[4]

---

[4]Though Ryrie, to his credit, *does* acknowledge that repentance "effects some change in the individual" (*SGS* 157), he takes such great pains to describe repentance as *only* an intellectual activity that he seems to contradict himself.

Note that the no-lordship definition of repentance *explicitly* denies the emotional and volitional elements in Berkhof's description of repentance. No-lordship repentance is *not* "be[ing] sorry for sin or even resolv[ing] to turn from sin." It means simply "changing one's mind about his former conception of God and disbelief in God and Christ" (*SGS* 98). Again, one could experience that kind of "repentance" without any understanding of the gravity of sin or the severity of God's judgment against sinners. It is a remorseless, hollow, pseudorepentance.

Repentance in the Bible

Does the no-lordship definition of repentance square with Scripture? It clearly does not. It is true that sorrow from sin is not repentance. Judas felt remorse, but he didn't repent (Matt. 27:3). Repentance is not just a resolve to do better; everyone who has ever made New Year's resolutions knows how easily human determination can be broken. Repentance certainly is not *penance,* an activity performed to try to atone for one's own sins.

But neither is repentance a solely intellectual issue. Surely even Judas changed his mind; what he didn't do was turn from his sin and throw himself on the Lord for mercy. Repentance is not just a change of *mind;* it is a change of *heart.* It is a spiritual turning, a total about-face. Repentance in the context of the new birth means turning from sin to the Savior. It is an inward response, not external activity, but its fruit will be evident in the true believer's behavior (Luke 3:8).

It has often been said that repentance and faith are two sides of the same coin. That coin is called *conversion.* Repentance turns from sin to Christ, and faith embraces Him as the only hope of salvation and righteousness. That is what conversion means in simple terms.

Faith and repentance are distinct concepts, but they cannot occur independently of each other. Genuine repentance is *always* the flip side of faith; and true faith accompanies repentance. "The two cannot be separated."[5]

Isaiah 55:1–13, the classic Old Testament call to conversion, shows both sides of the coin. Faith is called for in several ways: "Come to the waters . . . buy wine and milk without money and without cost" (v. 1). "Eat what is good, and delight yourself in abundance" (v. 2). "Listen, that you may live" (v. 3). "Seek the Lord while He may be found; call upon Him while He is near" (v. 6).

---

[5]Berkhof, *Systematic Theology,* 487.

But the passage also enjoins repentance: "Let the wicked forsake his way, and the unrighteous man his thoughts; And let him return to the Lord" (v. 7).

As that verse demonstrates, the issue in repentance is moral, not merely intellectual. What repentance calls for is not only a "change of mind" but a turning away from the love of sin. A leading New Testament dictionary emphasizes that the New Testament concept of repentance is *not* predominately intellectual. "Rather the decision by the whole man to turn around is stressed. It is clear that we are concerned neither with a purely outward turning nor with a merely intellectual change of ideas."[6] Another principal theological dictionary defines repentance as:

> radical conversion, a transformation of nature, a definitive turning from evil, a resolute turning to God in total obedience (Mk. 1:15; Mt. 4:17; 18:3). . . . This conversion is once-for-all. There can be no going back, only advance in responsible movement along the way now taken. It affects the whole man, first and basically the centre of personal life, then logically his conduct at all times and in all situations, his thoughts, words and acts (Mt. 12:33 ff. par.; 23:26; Mk. 7:15 par.). The whole proclamation of Jesus . . . is a proclamation of unconditional turning to God, of unconditional turning from all that is against God, not merely that which is downright evil, but that which in a given case makes total turning to God impossible. . . . It is addressed to all without distinction and presented with unmitigated severity in order to indicate the only way of salvation there is. *It calls for total surrender, total commitment to the will of God.* . . . It embraces the whole walk of the new man who is claimed by the divine lordship. It carries with it the founding of a new personal relation of man to God. . . . It awakens joyous obedience for a life according to God's will.[7]

Repentance in the Gospels

One argument against repentance that is invariably found in no-lordship books goes like this: The Gospel of John, perhaps the one book in Scripture whose purpose is most explicitly evangelistic (John 20:31),

---

[6] *The New International Dictionary of New Testament Theology,* ed. Colin Brown (Grand Rapids, Mich.: Zondervan, 1967), s.v. "conversion" (1:358).

[7] *Theological Dictionary of the New Testament,* ed. Gerhard Kittel (Grand Rapids, Mich.: Eerdmans, 1967), s.v. "metanoia" (4:1002–3, emphasis added).

never once mentions repentance. If repentance were so crucial to the gospel message, don't you suppose John would have included a call to repent?

Lewis Sperry Chafer wrote, "The Gospel by John, which is written to present Christ as the object of faith unto eternal life, does not once employ the word *repentance*."[8] Chafer suggested that the Fourth Gospel would be "incomplete and misleading if repentance must be accorded a place separate from, and independent of, believing. No thoughtful person would attempt to defend [repentance as a condition of salvation] against such odds, and those who have thus undertaken doubtless have done so without weighing the evidence or considering the untenable position which they assume."[9]

More recently, Charles Ryrie has written,

> It is striking to remember that the Gospel of John, the Gospel of belief, never uses the word *repent* even once. And yet John surely had many opportunities to use it in the events of our Lord's life which he recorded. It would have been most appropriate to use *repent* or *repentance* in the account of the Lord's conversation with Nicodemus. But *believe* is the word used (John 3:12, 15). So if Nicodemus needed to repent, *believe* must be a synonym; else how could the Lord have failed to use the word *repent* when talking with him? To the Samaritan harlot, Christ did not say repent. He told her to ask (John 4:10), and when her testimony and the Lord's spread to other Samaritans, John recorded not that they repented but that they believed (verses 39, 41–42). And there are about fifty more occurrences of "believe" or "faith" in the Gospel of John, but not one use of "repent." The climax is John 20:31: "These have been written that you may believe . . . and that believing you may have life in His name" (*SGS* 97–98).

But no one camps on this point more fiercely than Zane Hodges:

> One of the most striking facts about the doctrine of repentance in the Bible is that this doctrine is totally absent from John's gospel. There is not even so much as one reference to it in John's twenty-one chapters! Yet one lordship writer states: "No evangelism that omits the message of repentance can properly be called the gospel,

---

[8]Lewis Sperry Chafer, *Systematic Theology*, 8 vols. (Dallas: Seminary Press, 1948), 3:376.

[9]Ibid., 3:376–77.

for sinners cannot come to Jesus Christ apart from a radical change of heart, mind, and will."[10]

This is an astounding statement. Since John's Gospel *does* omit the message of repentance, are we to conclude that its gospel is not the biblical gospel after all?

The very idea carries its own refutation. The fourth evangelist explicitly claims to be doing evangelism (John 20:30–31). It is not the theology of the gospel of John that is deficient; it is the theology found in lordship salvation. Indeed, the desperate efforts of lordship teachers to read repentance into the fourth gospel show plainly that they have identified their own fundamental weakness. Clearly, the message of John's gospel is complete and adequate without any reference to repentance whatsoever (*AF* 146–47).

Hodges suggests that the apostle John was purposely *avoiding* the subject of repentance (*AF* 149). He finds in the Gospel of John

> not a word—not a syllable—about repentance. And if ever there was a perfect place for the evangelist to inject this theme into his gospel, this is the place.
>
> But his silence is deafening! . . .
>
> The silence of chapter one persists to the very end of the book. The fourth gospel says nothing at all about repentance, much less does it connect repentance in any way with eternal life.
>
> This fact is the death knell for lordship theology. Only a resolute blindness can resist the obvious conclusion: *John did not regard repentance as a condition for eternal life.* If he did, he would have said so. After all, that's what his book is all about: obtaining eternal life (*AF* 148).

What are we to think of this suggestion? Is the apostle John's "silence" on repentance really a death knell for the lordship position?

Hardly. H. A. Ironside responded to this issue more than fifty years ago. He wrote:

> The arrangement of the four Gospels is in perfect harmony. In the Synoptics [Matthew, Mark, and Luke] the call is to repent. In John the emphasis is laid upon believing. Some have thought that there is inconsistency or contradiction here. But we need to remember that John wrote years after the older Evangelists, and with

---

[10]Hodges at this point is quoting from my book, *The Gospel According to Jesus* (Grand Rapids, Mich.: Zondervan, 1988), 167.

the definite object in view of showing that Jesus is the Christ, the Son of God, and that, believing, we might have life through His Name. He does not simply travel over ground already well trodden. Rather, he adds to and thus supplements the earlier records, inciting to confidence in the testimony God as given concerning His Son. He does not ignore the ministry of repentance because he stresses the importance of faith. On the contrary, he shows to repentant souls the simplicity of salvation, of receiving eternal life, through a trusting in Him who, as the true light, casts light on every man, thus making manifest humanity's fallen condition and the need of an entire change of attitude toward self and toward God.[11]

Zane Hodges' assertion that "the fourth gospel says nothing at all about repentance" (*AF* 148) is demonstrably false. It is true that John does not use the word *repentance,* but as we observed in the previous chapter, our Lord did not use the word *grace.* One suspects no-lordship theologians would recoil from any suggestion that the doctrine of grace was missing from Jesus' teaching.

Repentance is woven into the very fabric of the Gospel of John, though the word itself is never employed. In the account of Nicodemus, for example, repentance was clearly suggested in Jesus' command to be "born again" (John 3:3, 5, 7). Repentance was the point of the Old Testament illustration our Lord gave Nicodemus (vv. 14–15). In John 4, the woman at the well *did* repent, as we see from her actions in verses 28–29.

Isn't repentance included by implication in the following Johannine descriptions of saving faith?

> *John 3:19–21:* And this is the judgment, that the light is come into the world, and men loved the darkness rather than the light; for their deeds were evil. For everyone who does evil hates the light, and does not come to the light, lest his deeds should be exposed. But he who practices the truth comes to the light, that his deeds may be manifested as having been wrought in God.
>
> *John 10:26–28:* But you do not believe, because you are not of My sheep. My sheep hear My voice, and I know them, and *they follow Me;* and I give eternal life to them (emphasis added).
>
> *John 12:24–26:* Truly, truly, I say to you, unless a grain of wheat falls into the earth and dies, it remains by itself alone; but if it dies, it bears much fruit. He who loves his life loses it; and he who

---

[11]H. A. Ironside, *Except Ye Repent* (Grand Rapids, Mich.: Zondervan, 1937), 37–38.

hates his life in this world shall keep it to life eternal. If anyone serves
Me, let him follow Me; and where I am, there shall My servant also
be; if anyone serves Me, the Father will honor him.

To say that John called for a faith that excluded repentance is to
grossly misconstrue the apostle's concept of what it means to be a believer. Although John never uses *repent* as a verb, the verbs he *does* employ are even stronger. He teaches that all true believers love the light
(3:19), come to the light (3:20–21), obey the Son (3:36), practice the
truth (3:21), worship in spirit and truth (4:23-24), honor God (5:22–
24), do good deeds (5:29), eat Jesus' flesh and drink His blood (6:48–
66), love God (8:42, cf. 1 John 2:15), follow Jesus (10:26–28), and
keep Jesus' commandments (14:15). Those ideas hardly concur with
no-lordship salvation! All of them presuppose repentance, commitment,
and a desire to obey.

As those terms suggest, the apostle was careful to describe conversion as a complete turnabout. To John, becoming a believer meant resurrection from death to life, a coming out of darkness and into light,
abandoning lies for the truth, exchanging hatred for love, and forsaking
the world for God. What are those but images of radical conversion?

Loving God is the expression John uses most frequently to describe
the believer's demeanor. How can sinners begin to love God apart from
genuine repentance? What does *love* imply, anyway?

Finally, remember that it is the Gospel of John that outlines the
Holy Spirit's ministry of conviction toward the unbelieving world (John
16:8–11). Of what does the Holy Spirit convict unbelievers? Of "sin,
righteousness, and judgment" (John 16:8). Wouldn't it seem that the
Holy Spirit's ministry of convicting people of sin and its consequences
has the specific purpose of laying the groundwork for repentance?

Repentance underlies all John's writings. It is *understood,* not necessarily explicit. His readers were so familiar with the apostolic message
that he didn't need to dwell on the issue of repentance. John was emphasizing different facets of the gospel message than those highlighted
by Matthew, Mark, and Luke. But he most assuredly was not writing to
contradict them! His aim certainly was not to devise a no-lordship doctrine of salvation.

In fact, John's purpose was exactly the opposite. He was showing
that Jesus is *God* (e.g., 1:1–18; 5:18; 12:37–41). John's readers clearly
understood the implication of *that:* If Jesus is God and we must receive
Him as God (John 1:12), our first duty in coming to Him is to repent
(cf. Luke 5:8).

Repentance in Apostolic Preaching

Even the most cursory study of the preaching in Acts shows that the gospel according to the apostles was a clarion call to repentance. At Pentecost, Peter concluded his sermon—a clear lordship message—with this: "Therefore let all the house of Israel know for certain that God has made Him both Lord and Christ—this Jesus whom you crucified" (Acts 2:36). The message penetrated his listeners' hearts, and they asked Peter what response was expected of them. Peter said plainly, "Repent, and let each of you be baptized in the name of Jesus Christ for the forgiveness of your sins" (v. 38).

Note that he made no mention of faith. That was implied in the call to repentance. Peter was not making baptism a condition of their salvation; he simply outlined the first step of obedience that should follow their repentance (cf. 10:43–48). Peter's audience, familiar with the ministry of John the Baptist—understood baptism as an external corroboration of sincere repentance (cf. Matt. 3:5–8). Peter was not asking them to perform a meritorious act, and the whole of biblical teaching makes that clear.

But the message he gave them that day was a straightforward command to repent. As the context of Acts 2 shows, the people who heard Peter understood that he was demanding unconditional surrender to the Lord Jesus Christ.

In Acts 3 we encounter a similar scene. Peter and John had been used of the Lord to heal a lame man at the Temple gate (vv. 1–9). When a crowd gathered, Peter began to preach to them, rehearsing how the Jewish nation had killed their own Messiah. His conclusion was precisely the same as it had been at Pentecost: "*Repent therefore and return,* that your sins may be wiped away, in order that times of refreshing may come from the presence of the Lord; and that He may send Jesus, the Christ appointed for you, whom heaven must receive until the period of restoration of all things about which God spoke by the mouth of His holy prophets from ancient time" (vv. 19–21, emphasis added). The King James Version says, "Repent . . . and be converted, that your sins may be blotted out." Again, Peter's meaning was unmistakable. He was calling for a radical, 180-degree turning from sin. That is repentance.

In Acts 4, the day after Peter and John had been instrumental in the healing the lame man, they were brought before the Sanhedrin, the ruling body of Israel. Boldly, Peter said, "Let it be known to all of you, and to all the people of Israel, that by the name of Jesus Christ the Nazarene, whom you crucified, whom God raised from the dead—by this name this man stands here before you in good health. He is the stone which was rejected by you, the builders, but which became the very corner stone. And there is salvation in no one else; for there is no other name under heaven that has been given among men, by which we must be saved" (Acts 4:10–12). While there is no mention of the word *repentance* there, it was Peter's obvious message to these rulers. They had rejected and killed their rightful Messiah. Now they needed to do an about-face: turn from the heinous sin they had committed, and turn to the One whom they had sinned against. He alone could grant them salvation.

When Peter was called of God to proclaim the gospel to Cornelius and his household, the message had a different emphasis: "that through His name everyone who believes in Him receives forgiveness of sins" (Acts 10:43).

But did Peter overlook the issue of repentance in his ministry to Cornelius? Not at all. It is evident that Cornelius *was* repentant. When Peter later recounted the incident to the church at Jerusalem, the church leaders responded, "Well then, God has granted to the Gentiles also *the repentance that leads to life.*" (Acts 11:18, emphasis added). Obviously the entire Jerusalem church understood repentance as tantamount to a saving response.

No-lordship advocates usually gravitate to Acts 16:30–31 to find support for their view that repentance is not essential in the call to saving faith. There the apostle Paul answered the Philippian jailer's famous question, "Sirs, what must I do to be saved?" What did Paul tell him? Simply, "Believe in the Lord Jesus, and you shall be saved, you and your household." Evidently Paul did not call the jailer to repentance.

But wait. Is that a fair conclusion to draw from this passage? No, it is not. The jailer knew very well the cost of being a Christian (vv. 23–24). He was also obviously prepared to repent. He was about to take his own life when Paul stopped him (vv. 25–27). He had clearly come to the end of himself. Moreover, Paul gave him a more extensive gospel presentation than is recorded for us in Acts 16:31. Verse 32 says "they spoke the word of the Lord to him together with all who were in his house." Ultimately the jailer *did* repent. He proved his repentance by his deeds (vv. 33–34). This passage cannot be used to prove that Paul preached the gospel without calling sinners to repentance.

Repentance was always at the heart of Paul's evangelistic preaching. He confronted the pagan philosophers of Athens and proclaimed, "Having overlooked the times of ignorance, God is now declaring to men that all everywhere should repent" (Acts 17:30). In his farewell message to the elders of Ephesus, Paul reminded them, "I did not shrink from declaring to you anything that was profitable, and teaching you publicly and from house to house, solemnly testifying to both Jews and Greeks of *repentance toward God and faith in our Lord Jesus Christ*" (Acts 20:20–21, emphasis added). Later, when he was hauled before King Agrippa, Paul defended his ministry with these words: "I did not prove disobedient to the heavenly vision, but kept declaring . . . even to the Gentiles, that they should repent and turn to God, performing deeds appropriate to repentance" (Acts 26:19–20).

Clearly, from the beginning of the Book of Acts to the end, repentance was the central appeal of the apostolic message. The repentance they preached was not merely a change of mind about who Jesus was. It was a turning from sin (3:26; 8:22) and a turning toward the Lord Jesus Christ (20:21). It was the kind of repentance that results in behavioral change (26:20). The apostolic message was nothing like the no-lordship gospel that has gained popularity in our day.

I am deeply concerned as I watch what is happening in the church today. Biblical Christianity has lost its voice. The church is preaching a gospel designed to soothe rather than confront sinful individuals. Churches have turned to amusement and show business to try to win the world. Those methods may seem to draw crowds for a season. But they're not *God's* methods, and therefore they are destined to fail. In the meantime, the church is being infiltrated and corrupted by professing believers who have never repented, never turned from sin, and therefore, never really embraced Christ as Lord *or* Savior.

We must return to the message God has called us to preach. We need to confront sin and call sinners to repentance—to a radical break from the love of sin and a seeking of the Lord's mercy. We must hold up Christ as Savior *and* Lord, the one who frees His people from the penalty *and* power of sin. That is, after all, the gospel He has called us to proclaim.

6

Just by Faith

The difference between Rome and the Reformation can be seen in these simple formulas:

Roman view
faith + works = justification

Protestant view
faith = justification + works

Neither view eliminates works. The Protestant view eliminates human merit. It recognizes that though works are the evidence or fruit of true faith they add or contribute nothing to the meritorious basis of our redemption.

The current debate over "Lordship/salvation" must be careful to protect two borders. On the one hand it is important to stress that true faith yields true fruit; on the other hand it is vital to stress that the only merit that saves us is the merit of Christ received by faith alone.

R. C. Sproul[1]

*I*n the 1500s a fastidious monk, who by his own testimony "hated God," was studying Paul's epistle to the Romans. He couldn't get past the first half of Romans 1:17: "[In the gospel] is the righteousness of God revealed from faith to faith" (KJV). He wrote:

[1]R. C. Sproul, "Works or Faith?" *Tabletalk* (May 1991): 6.

> I greatly longed to understand Paul's Epistle to the Romans and nothing stood in the way but that one expression, "the [righteousness] of God," because I took it to mean that justice whereby God is just and deals justly in punishing the unjust. My situation was that, although an impeccable monk, I stood before God as a sinner troubled in conscience, and I had no confidence that my merit would assuage him. Therefore I did not love a just and angry God, but rather hated and murmured against him. Yet I clung to the dear Paul and had a great yearning to know what he meant.[2]

One simple biblical truth changed that monk's life—and ignited the Protestant Reformation. It was the realization that God's righteousness could become the sinner's righteousness—and that could happen through the means of faith alone. Martin Luther found the truth in the same verse he had stumbled over, Romans 1:17: "Therein is the righteousness of God revealed from faith to faith: as it is written, *the just shall live by faith*" (KJV, emphasis added). Luther had always seen "the righteousness of God" as an attribute of the sovereign Lord by which He judged sinners—not an attribute sinners could ever possess. He described the breakthrough that put an end to the dark ages:

> I saw the connection between the justice of God and the statement that "the just shall live by his faith." Then I grasped that the justice of God is that righteousness by which through grace and sheer mercy God justifies us through faith. Thereupon I felt myself to be reborn and to have gone through open doors into paradise. The whole of Scripture took on a new meaning, and whereas before the "justice of God" had filled me with hate, now it became to me inexpressibly sweet in greater love. This passage of Paul became to me a gate to heaven.[3]

Justification by faith was the great truth that dawned on Luther and dramatically altered the church. It is also the doctrine that brings equilibrium to the lordship position. Critics usually claim that lordship salvation is salvation by works. Justification by faith is the answer to that charge.

Because Christians are justified by faith alone, their standing before God is not in any way related to personal merit. Good works and practical holiness do not provide the grounds for acceptance with God. God

---

[2]Cited in Roland Bainton, *Here I Stand* (New York: Abingdon, 1950), 65.
[3]Ibid.

receives as righteous those who believe, not because of any good thing He sees in them—not even because of His own sanctifying work in their lives—but solely on the basis of *Christ's* righteousness, which is reckoned to their account. "To the one who does not work, but believes in Him who justifies the ungodly, his faith is reckoned as righteousness" (Rom. 4:5). That is justification.

Declared Righteous: What Actually Changes?

In its theological sense, justification is a forensic, or purely legal, term. It describes what God *declares* about the believer, not what He *does to change* the believer. In fact, justification effects no actual change whatsoever in the sinner's nature or character. Justification is a divine judicial edict. It changes our status only, but it carries ramifications that guarantee other changes will follow. Forensic decrees like this are fairly common in everyday life.

When I was married, for example, Patricia and I stood before the minister (my father) and recited our vows. Near the end of the ceremony, my father declared, "By the authority vested in me by the state of California, I now pronounce you man and wife." Instantly we were legally husband and wife. Whereas seconds before we had been an engaged couple, now we were married. Nothing inside us actually changed when those words were spoken. But our status changed before God, the law, and our family and friends. The implications of that simple declaration have been lifelong and life-changing (for which I am grateful). But when my father spoke those words, it was a legal declaration only.

Similarly, when a jury foreman reads the verdict, the defendant is no longer "the accused." Legally and officially he instantly becomes either guilty or innocent—depending on the verdict. Nothing in his actual nature changes, but if he is found not guilty he will walk out of court a free man in the eyes of the law, fully justified.

In biblical terms, justification is a divine verdict of "not guilty—fully righteous." It is the reversal of God's attitude toward the sinner. Whereas He formerly condemned, He now vindicates. Although the sinner once lived under God's wrath, as a believer he or she is now under God's blessing. Justification is more than simple pardon; pardon alone would still leave the sinner without merit before God. So when God justifies He imputes divine righteousness to the sinner (Rom. 4:22–25). Christ's own infinite merit thus becomes the ground on which the believer stands before God (Rom. 5:19; 1 Cor. 1:30; Phil.

3:9). So justification elevates the believer to a realm of full acceptance and divine privilege in Jesus Christ.

Therefore because of justification believers not only are perfectly free from any charge of guilt (Rom. 8:33) but also have the full merit of Christ reckoned to their personal account (Rom. 5:17). At justification we are adopted as sons and daughters (Rom. 8:15); we become fellow heirs with Christ (v. 17); we are united with Christ so that we become one with Him (1 Cor. 6:17); and we are henceforth "in Christ" (Gal. 3:27) and He in us (Col. 1:27). Those are all forensic realities that flow out of justification.

How Justification and Sanctification Differ

Justification is distinct from sanctification because in justification God does not *make* the sinner righteous; He *declares* that person righteous (Rom. 3:28; Gal. 2:16). Justification *imputes* Christ's righteousness to the sinner's account (Rom. 4:11b); sanctification *imparts* righteousness to the sinner personally and practically (Rom. 6:1–7; 8:11–14). Justification takes place outside sinners and changes their standing (Rom. 5:1–2); sanctification is internal and changes the believer's state (Rom. 6:19). Justification is an event, sanctification a process. The two must be distinguished but can never be separated. God does not justify whom He does not sanctify, and He does not sanctify whom He does not justify. Both are essential elements of salvation.

Why differentiate between them at all? If justification and sanctification are so closely related that you can't have one without the other, why bother to define them differently?

That question is crucial to the lordship debate. It was also the central issue between Rome and the Reformers in the sixteenth century.

Justification in Roman Catholic Doctrine

Roman Catholicism blends its doctrines of sanctification and justification. Catholic theology views justification as an infusion of grace that *makes* the sinner righteous. In Catholic theology, then, the ground of justification is something made good within the sinner—not the imputed righteousness of Christ.

The Council of Trent, Rome's response to the Reformation, pronounced anathema on anyone who says "that the [sinner] is justified by faith alone—if this means that nothing else is required by way of cooperation in the acquisition of the grace of justification."[4] The Catholic council ruled that "Justification . . . is not remission of sins merely, but also the sanctification and renewal of the inward man, through the voluntary reception of the grace, and of the gifts, whereby man of unjust becomes just."[5] So Catholic theology confuses the concepts of justification and sanctification and substitutes the righteousness of the believer for the righteousness of Christ.

This difference between Rome and the Reformers is no example of theological hair-splitting. The corruption of the doctrine of justification results in several other grievous theological errors. If sanctification is included in justification, then justification is a process, not an event. That makes justification progressive, not complete. One's standing before God is then based on subjective experience, not secured by an objective declaration. Justification can therefore be experienced and then lost. Assurance of salvation in this life becomes practically impossible because security can't be guaranteed. The ground of justification ultimately is the sinner's own continuing present virtue, not Christ's perfect righteousness and His atoning work.

Those issues were fiercely debated in the Reformation, and the lines were clearly drawn. Reformed theology to this day upholds the biblical doctrine of justification by faith against the Roman view of justification by works/merit.

Justification in Reformation Teaching

Advocates of no-lordship theology often suggest that lordship salvation has more in common with Roman Catholicism than with Reformation teaching. One outspoken advocate of the radical no-lordship view has repeatedly voiced alarm that lordship salvation is "not paving the road back to Wittenberg but, rather, paving the road back to Rome."[6]

The suggestion ignores both church history and the real issues in the contemporary lordship debate. No advocate of lordship theology I

---

[4]Henry Bettenson, ed., *Documents of the Christian Church* (New York: Oxford, 1963), 263.

[5]Philip Schaff, ed., *The Creeds of Christendom,* 3 vols. (reprint, Grand Rapids, Mich.: Baker, 1983), 3:94.

[6]Earl Radmacher, "First Response to 'Faith According to the Apostle James' by John F. MacArthur, Jr.," *Journal of the Evangelical Theological Society* 33/1 (March 1990): 40.

know of denies the doctrine of justification by faith. Rather, lordship theology represents a refusal to disengage justification and sanctification. On that we are in full accord with every significant Reformer.

Reformation teaching was clear on this issue. Calvin, for example, wrote,

> Christ . . . justifies no man without also sanctifying him. These blessings are conjoined by a perpetual and inseparable tie. Those whom he enlightens by his wisdom he redeems; whom he redeems he justifies; whom he justifies he sanctifies. But as the question relates only to justification and sanctification, to them let us confine ourselves. Though we distinguish between them they are both inseparably comprehended in Christ. Would ye then obtain justification in Christ? You must previously possess Christ. But you cannot possess him without being made a partaker of his sanctification: for Christ cannot be divided. Since the Lord, therefore, does not grant us the enjoyment of these blessings without bestowing himself, he bestows both at once, but never one without the other. Thus it appears how true it is that we are justified not without, and yet not by works, since in the participation of Christ, by which we are justified, is contained not less sanctification than justification.[7]

Elsewhere, discussing James 2:21–22 ("Was not Abraham our father justified by works, when he offered up Isaac his son on the altar? You see that faith was working with his works, and as a result of the works, faith was perfected"), Calvin added,

> It appears certain that he is speaking of the manifestation, not of the imputation of righteousness, as if he had said, Those who are justified by true faith prove their justification by obedience and good works, not by a bare and imaginary semblance of faith. In one word, he is not discussing the mode of justification, but requiring that the justification of believers shall be operative. And as Paul contends that men are justified without the aid of works, so James will not allow any to be regarded as justified who are destitute of good works. Due attention to the scope will thus disentangle every doubt; for the error of our opponents lies chiefly in this, that they think James is defining the mode of justification, whereas his only object is to destroy the depraved security of those who vainly pretended faith as an excuse for their contempt of good works. Therefore, let

---

[7]John Calvin, *Institutes of the Christian Religion,* trans. Henry Beveridge, 3:16:1 (reprint, Grand Rapids, Mich.: Eerdmans, 1966), 2:99.

them twist the words of James as they may, they will never extract out of them more than the two propositions: That an empty phantom of faith does not justify, and that the believer, not contented with such an imagination, manifests his justification by good works.[8]

Martin Luther championed justification by faith as passionately as any Reformer. Did he believe sanctification was optional? Not at all. When some of Luther's associates began to teach *antinomianism* (the idea that behavior is unrelated to faith, or that Christians are not bound by any moral law), he opposed them. He called their teaching "the crassest error," designed to "grind me under foot and throw the gospel into confusion." Such teaching, according to Luther, "kick[s] the bottom out of the barrel" of God's saving work.[9]

Someone reported to Luther that one of these men, Jacob Schenck, "had preached carnal license and had taught: 'Do what you please. Only believe and you will be saved.'"[10]

> Luther replied, "This is a wicked disjunction. Turn the matter about: 'Dear fellow, believe in God, and then afterward, when you are reborn, are a new man, etc., do whatever comes to hand.' The fools don't know what faith is. They suppose it's just a lifeless idea. . . . It's impossible to be reborn of God and yet [continuously] sin, for these two things contradict each other.[11]

Although many more examples could be given, I'll just mention one other. The Formula of Concord, the definitive Lutheran statement of faith, written in 1576, dealt extensively with the relationship between justification and the believer's obedience. This document reveals that the questions at the heart of the contemporary lordship controversy were also on the minds of the Reformers. The Formula of Concord, like every other significant Protestant creed, refused to divorce justification from sanctification, though it underscored the distinction between the two.

According to this creed, "the renewing of man . . . is rightly distinguished from the justification of faith." The Formula stated

---

[8]Ibid., 2:115.

[9]Martin Luther, *Table Talk*, in *Luther's Works*, ed. Helmut T. Lehman, trans. Theodore G. Tappert, 55 vols. (Philadelphia: Fortress, 1967), 54:248.

[10]Ibid., 54:289–90.

[11]Ibid., 54:290.

explicitly that "antecedent contrition [repentance] and subsequent new obedience do not appertain to the article of justification before God."[12]

But it immediately added, "Yet we are not to imagine any such justifying faith as can exist and abide with a purpose of evil. . . . But after that man is justified by faith, then that true and living faith works by love [Gal. 5:6], and *good works always follow justifying faith, and are most certainly found together with it.*"[13]

The Formula of Concord repudiated the teaching that *justify* means "[to] become in very deed righteous before God." But it also condemned the notion "that faith is such a confidence in the obedience of Christ as can abide and have a being even in that man who is void of true repentance, and in whom it is not followed by charity [love], but who contrary to conscience perseveres in sins."[14]

The well-known Reformation epigram is "Faith alone justifies, but not the faith that is alone." F. W. Robertson adds, "Lightning alone strikes, but not the lightning which is without thunder."[15] On these matters the principal Reformers all agreed. Only the antinomians taught that true faith might fail to produce good works.

Justification in the Lordship Debate

Contemporary no-lordship doctrine is nothing but latter-day antinomianism. Although most no-lordship advocates object to that term,[16] it is a fair characterization of their doctrine.

Zane Hodges misses the point when he calls *antinomianism* "Reformed theology's favorite 'cuss word.'"[17] He writes,

---

[12]Schaff, *The Creeds of Christendom,* 3:117–18.

[13]Ibid., 3:118 (emphasis added).

[14]Ibid., 3:119.

[15]Cited in Augustus H. Strong, *Systematic Theology* (Philadelphia: Judson, 1907), 875.

[16]J. Kevin Butcher, "A Critique of *The Gospel According to Jesus,*" *Journal of the Grace Evangelical Society* (Spring 1989): 28. Butcher believes that by describing Chafer, Ryrie, and Hodges as antinomian, I am implying "that these men (as well as the view they represent) are only concerned with populating heaven, showing a disdain for holiness and a consistent Christian walk." But that is not what the term *antinomian* means, as the discussion on these pages shows.

[17]Zane Hodges, "Calvinism Ex Cathedra," *Journal of the Grace Evangelical Society* (Autumn 1991): 68.

We could define "Antinomianism" in the way the American Heritage Dictionary (2nd College Edition, 1985) does as "holding that faith alone is necessary for salvation." If that were what was meant by the term, I would be quite comfortable with it. Unfortunately, because "Antinomianism" implies to many minds a disregard for moral issues, I must reject this designation. I urge my Reformed counterparts to drop this term because of its pejorative, and often unfair, connotations and overtones. But I will not hold my breath waiting for them to do so![18]

It is important to understand the term *antinomianism* in its theological sense. I do not use the word to be derogatory. To say someone is antinomian is not necessarily to say that person spurns holiness or condones ungodliness. Most antinomians vigorously appeal for Christians to walk in a manner worthy of their calling; but at the same time they minimize the relationship between obedience and faith. Antinomians typically believe Christians *should* yield to the lordship of Christ; they just do not believe surrender is a binding requirement in the gospel call to faith. Antinomians do not necessarily despise the law of God; they simply believe it is irrelevant to saving faith. They suggest that obedience to the righteous principles of the law might not become a pattern in the Christian's life (cf. Rom. 8:4; 10:4). In short, antinomianism is the belief that allows for justification without sanctification.

Antinomianism makes obedience elective. While most antinomians strongly *counsel* Christians to obey (and even urge them to obey), they do not believe obedience is a necessary consequence of true faith. Zane Hodges, for example, includes a chapter on obedience entitled "The Choice Is Yours" (*AF* 117–26). The leading theologian of the no-lordship movement has written, "The unsaved person has only one course of action—to serve sin and self, or to leave God out of his life—while the believer has an option. He may serve God, and as long as he is in a human body he may also choose to leave God out and live according to the old nature."[19] Clearly, no-lordship theology *does* make obedience optional. And that is what makes no-lordship theology antinomian.

---

[18]Ibid., 69.

[19]Charles C. Ryrie, *Balancing the Christian Life* (Chicago: Moody, 1969), 35. The context of this quotation is a section arguing that believers have two natures. Ryrie suggests that carnality can be a continued state of existence for the Christian (ibid., 170–73). When he speaks of those who "choose to leave God out and live according to the old nature" he is clearly speaking of something more than temporary failure.

This kind of antinomianism tends to see justification by faith as the whole of God's saving work. Antinomians minimize sanctification or even render it noncompulsory. Antinomian discussions of salvation typically omit any consideration of practical holiness. They emphasize justification by faith and Christian freedom to such an extreme that they become unbalanced, fearful of talking about personal righteousness, obedience, the Law of God, or anything but the purely forensic aspects of salvation.

No-lordship theology is classic antinomianism. There is no way around that fact. Because it is important to understand the no-lordship view in the context of Reformation teaching, we cannot avoid the term *antinomianism,* even though proponents of no-lordship teaching find it offensive. Their view is, after all, firmly in the tradition of historic antinomianism.[20]

One other point must be made about the no-lordship tendency to downplay sanctification. Most no-lordship advocates acknowledge the necessity for *some* degree of sanctification. Dr. Ryrie concedes that "every Christian will bear spiritual fruit. Somewhere, sometime, somehow. Otherwise the person is not a believer. Every born-again individual will be fruitful. Not to be fruitful is to be faithless, without faith, and therefore without salvation" (*SGS* 45).

Even Zane Hodges has lately affirmed that "some measure or degree of sanctification *will* indeed result from justification [and] that final sanctification *is* an inevitable result of justification."[21]

But those disclaimers must be understood in context. Ryrie, for example, is quick to add that some believers' "fruit" may be so meager

---

[20]There are many parallels between modern no-lordship theology and the other forms of antinomianism that have emerged from time to time in church history. These include, for example, the teachings of Johann Agricola, whom Luther condemned, and the Sandemanian cult that flourished in Scotland in the 1700s.

[21]Hodges, "Calvinism Ex Cathedra," 67. In a footnote Hodges implies that he expressed this same view in *Absolutely Free!* (213–15). But in *Absolutely Free!* Hodges never made such an assertion. Turning to the section of *Absolutely Free!* Hodges cites, we find that, ironically, he begins by condemning me for writing, "Obedience is the inevitable manifestation of saving faith" (*AF* 213). He concludes incongruously by stating, "We must add that there is no need to quarrel with the Reformers' view that where there is justifying faith, works will undoubtedly exist too" (*AF* 215). But that is precisely the view Hodges *is* arguing against! Hodges concludes that it is only "a reasonable assumption," that works will follow faith. And such works might be invisible to a human observer: "God alone may be able to detect the fruits of regeneration in some of His children" (215).

and so fleeting as to be invisible to everyone around them (*SGS* 45). Elsewhere Ryrie seems to suggest that *practical* sanctification is by no means guaranteed. He quotes Romans 8:29–30 ("Whom He foreknew, He also predestined to become conformed to the image of His Son, that He might be the first-born among many brethren; and whom He predestined, these He also called; and whom He called, these He also justified; and whom He justified, these He also glorified"). "But what of sanctification?" Ryrie asks.

> Nowhere does it appear in Paul's list in Romans 8:29–30. Only predestination, calling, justification, and glorification. Could it be that Paul didn't want to base our guarantee of ultimate glorification on our personal sanctification? Assuredly it does not rest on that, for the many sons who will be glorified will have exhibited varying degrees of personal holiness during their lifetimes. Yet all, from the carnal to the most mature, will be glorified (*SGS* 150).

Ryrie outlines three facets of sanctification—*positional sanctification*, "an actual position that does not depend on the state of one's growth and maturity"; *progressive sanctification*, or practical holiness; and *ultimate sanctification*, perfect holiness that will be realized in heaven (*SGS* 151). It is clear that Ryrie views the first and third aspects of sanctification as guaranteed. But he evidently believes *practical* sanctification can be forfeited or bypassed, for he makes room for "believers" who fall into utter carnality and permanent unbelief (*SGS* 141).

Hodges holds a similar view. If anything, his tendency to depreciate the practical aspect of sanctification is more pronounced than Ryrie's. Hodges' most extensive book on the lordship debate, *Absolutely Free!* omits any discussion of sanctification as a doctrine.[22] What Hodges does make clear from the beginning to the end of his book is that no measure of practical holiness is guaranteed in the life of a child of God.

Although no-lordship doctrine may give lip service to the necessity of sanctification, it seems certain that most no-lordship proponents do not really believe *practical* sanctification goes hand-in-hand with justification.

---

[22]In my reading of *Absolutely Free!* I could not find a single occurrence of the words *sanctify* or *sanctification*, except in one quotation from my book. Nor is sanctification dealt with in either of Hodges' other major works on the lordship issue, *The Gospel under Siege* (Dallas: Redención Viva, 1981) and *Grace in Eclipse* (Dallas: Redención Viva, 1985). Hodges evidently views practical holiness and growth in grace as purely the *believer's* work (*AF* 117–26). We shall deal with the issue of sanctification at length in chapter 7.

That is, in fact, the fundamental point no-lordship advocates want to make. They have dismembered the biblical doctrine of salvation by severing justification from sanctification.[23] They are left with a crippled antinomianism that cannot guarantee any measure of holiness in the Christian experience. Therefore they have utterly missed the point of the biblical doctrine of justification by faith as it is closely related to sanctification.

Justification in the New Testament

Justification is the heart and soul of New Testament soteriology. Realizing that is the case, a friend asked me why my book *The Gospel According to Jesus* had virtually no discussion of justification. The reason is that Jesus Himself had very little to say explicitly about justification by faith. That doctrine was first expounded in its fullness by the apostle Paul. In his epistle to the Romans, it is a major theme.

The first half of Romans divides naturally into three parts. Paul begins by showing that all men and women have sinned against God's perfect righteousness. This is his theme throughout the opening chapters of the book: "There is none righteous, not even one" (3:10). Beginning in 3:21 through the end of chapter 5, he explains in detail the doctrine of justification by faith. "Therefore having been justified by faith, we have peace with God through our Lord Jesus Christ" (5:1). In chapters 6 through 8 he expounds the doctrine of sanctification. "That the requirement of the Law might be fulfilled in us, who do not walk according to the flesh, but according to the Spirit" (8:4).

So Paul talks about sin, saving faith, and sanctification. Or, as a friend of mine has said, Romans 1:1–3:20 speaks of *God's righteousness defied* by a sinful world. Romans 3:21–5:21 shows *God's righteousness supplied* for believing sinners. Chapters 6 through 8 focus on *God's righteousness applied* in the lives of the saints.

Justification by faith is the means through which God's righteousness is *supplied* on behalf of believing sinners. I wish there were space in this book for a full exposition of these crucial chapters (Romans 3–5), which make up the core of biblical truth about justification. But that

---

[23]R. T. Kendall, whom Hodges frequently cites for support, is explicit about this: "It is true that sanctification was not a prerequisite for glorification, or Paul would have placed it in line with 'calling' and 'justification' (Romans 8:30)." R. T. Kendall, *Once Saved, Always Saved* (Chicago: Moody, 1983), 134. Note the similarity between Kendall's statement and the paragraph quoted above from Ryrie (*SGS* 150).

would require multiple chapters, so instead we will focus only on one section, Paul's main illustration of justification by faith—Abraham—found in Romans 4.

Here Paul writes,

> What then shall we say that Abraham, our forefather according to the flesh, has found? For if Abraham was justified by works, he has something to boast about; but not before God. For what does the Scripture say? "And Abraham believed God, and it was reckoned to him as righteousness." Now to the one who works, his wage is not reckoned as a favor, but as what is due. But to the one who does not work, but believes in Him who justifies the ungodly, his faith is reckoned as righteousness.
>
> Romans 4:1–5

Several crucial truths rise from this text.

True salvation cannot be earned by works. There are, after all, only two kinds of religion in all the world. Every false religion ever devised by mankind or by Satan is a *religion of human merit*. Pagan religion, humanism, animism, and even false Christianity all fall into this category. They focus on what people must *do* to attain righteousness or please the deity.

Biblical Christianity alone is the *religion of divine accomplishment*. Other religions say, "Do this." Christianity says, "It is done" (cf. John 19:30). Other religions require that the devout person supply some kind of merit to atone for sin, appease deity, or otherwise attain the goal of acceptability. Scripture says Christ's merit is supplied on behalf of the believing sinner.

The Pharisees in Paul's day had turned Judaism into a religion of human achievements. Paul's own life before salvation was one long and futile effort to please God through personal merit. He had been steeped in the Pharisaic tradition, "a Pharisee, a son of Pharisees" (Acts 23:6), "a Hebrew of Hebrews; as to the Law, a Pharisee; as to zeal, a persecutor of the church; as to the righteousness which is in the Law, found blameless" (Phil 3:5–6). Paul understood the religious culture of his day as well as anyone. He knew that the Pharisees revered Abraham as the father of their religion (John 8:39). So he singled him out to prove that justification before God is by faith in what God has accomplished.

By showing Abraham as the ultimate example of justification by faith, Paul was setting Christian doctrine against centuries of rabbinic tradition. By appealing to the Old Testament Scriptures, Paul was showing that Judaism had moved away from the most basic truths affirmed by all believing Jews since Abraham himself. He was seeking to anchor the church so that it would not follow the drift of Israel.

Abraham's faith was the foundation of the Jewish nation and the basis for God's covenant with His chosen people. For the Pharisees' tradition to be at odds with Abraham was unthinkable. But, as Paul was about to prove, Abraham did not practice the Pharisees' religion of merit.

Boasting is excluded. If people could earn justification by works, they would indeed have something to boast about. The doctrine of justification by faith is therefore a humbling truth. We do not merit salvation. We cannot be good enough to please God. There is no room in God's redemptive plan for human pride. Even Abraham, the father of the faith, had no reason to glory in himself: "If Abraham was justified by works, he has something to boast about; but not before God. For what does the Scripture say? 'And Abraham believed God, and it was reckoned to him as righteousness'" (Rom. 4:2–3).

Paul was quoting Genesis 15:6: "[Abraham] believed in the Lord; and He reckoned it to him as righteousness." That single Old Testament verse is one of the clearest statements in all of Scripture about justification. The word *reckoned* shows the forensic nature of justification. In Romans 4, *reckoned* is translated from the Greek word *logizomai,* a term used for accounting and legal purposes. It speaks of something put down to an account.

This reckoning was a one-sided transaction. God designated righteousness to Abraham's spiritual account. Abraham *did* nothing to earn it. Even his faith was not meritorious. Faith is never said to be the *ground* for justification, only the channel through which justifying grace is received. Abraham believed God, and so God imputed righteousness to his account.

Again, the forensic nature of justification is clearly evident: "Now to the one who works, his wage is not reckoned as a favor, but as what is due. To the one who does not work, but believes in Him who justifies the ungodly, his faith is reckoned as righteousness" (vv. 4–5). Those who attempt to earn justification by *doing* something will find a huge debt on their ledger. Those who receive God's gift by grace through faith have an infinitely sufficient asset applied to their account.

Faith, then, means the end of any attempt to earn God's favor through personal merit. God saves only those who do not trust in themselves—those who trust "Him who justifies the ungodly." Therefore, until a person confesses that he is ungodly, that person cannot be saved, because he still trusts in his own goodness. That is what Jesus meant when He said, "I have not come to call the righteous but sinners to repentance" (Luke 5:32). Those who are righteous in their own eyes have no part in God's redemptive work of grace. Consequently, those who are saved know they have nothing to boast about.

Justification brings the blessing of forgiveness. In verses 6 through 8 Paul quotes David as support for the idea of righteousness by imputation: "David also speaks of the blessing upon the man to whom God reckons righteousness apart from works: 'Blessed are those whose lawless deeds have been forgiven, and whose sins have been covered. Blessed is the man whose sin the Lord will not take into account.'" Paul is quoting from Psalm 32:1–2. The blessedness David refers to is salvation.

Notice that David speaks of both a positive and a negative accounting: righteousness is reckoned to the believer; sin is not taken into account. Justification has both positive and negative elements: the reckoning of righteousness to the individual, and the forgiveness of sins. This forgiveness would not be possible if our sin had not been paid for by the sacrifice of Christ's own blood. His death paid the price so "PAID" can be written on the believer's spiritual invoice (cf. Col. 2:14).

As our sin was imputed to Christ (1 Pet. 2:24), so His righteousness is imputed to the believer. No other payment or reimbursement is required.

Abraham was not justified by circumcision. Paul anticipated the question that Jews would be asking themselves at this point in his argument: *If Abraham was justified by his faith alone, why did God demand circumcision of Abraham and all his descendants?*

Most Jews in New Testament times were thoroughly convinced that circumcision was the unique mark that set them apart as God's chosen people. They also believed it was the means by which they became acceptable to God. In fact, circumcision was considered such a mark of God's favor that many rabbis taught that no Jew could be sent to hell unless God first reversed his circumcision.

Genesis 17:10–14 records God's instructions that circumcision was to be a mark of God's covenant with Abraham and his descendants. On the basis of that passage the rabbis taught that circumcision itself was the means of getting right with God. But as Paul carefully points out, Abraham was not made righteous by his circumcision. When God commanded him to be circumcised he had *already* been declared righteous:

Is this blessing then upon the circumcised, or upon the uncircumcised also? For we say, "Faith was reckoned to Abraham as righteousness." How then was it reckoned? While he was circumcised, or
uncircumcised? Not while circumcised, but while uncircumcised;
and he received the sign of circumcision, a seal of the righteousness
of the faith which he had while uncircumcised, that he might be the
father of all who believe without being circumcised, that righteousness might be reckoned to them, and the father of circumcision to
those who not only are of the circumcision, but who also follow in
the steps of the faith of our father Abraham which he had while
uncircumcised.

Romans 4:9–12

The chronology of Genesis proves that Abraham was declared righteous
long before he observed God's command to be circumcised. At
Abraham's circumcision he was ninety-nine years old and Ishmael was
thirteen (Gen. 17:24–25). But when Abraham was justified (15:6),
Ishmael had not even been conceived (16:2–4). At Ishmael's birth
Abraham was eighty-six (16:16). So Abraham was justified at least *fourteen years* before his circumcision. When Abraham was declared righteous he was actually no different from an uncircumcised Gentile.

Circumcision and other external rituals—including baptism, penance, holy orders, marriage, celibacy, extreme unction, fasting, prayer,
or whatever—are no means to justification. Abraham was in God's covenant and under His grace long before he was circumcised, whereas
Ishmael, although circumcised, was never in the covenant. Circumcision, a sign of man's need for spiritual cleansing, was only a mark of the
covenant relationship between God and His people.

Paul had already stated in Romans 2:28–29: "For he is not a Jew
who is one outwardly; neither is circumcision that which is outward in
the flesh. But he is a Jew who is one inwardly; and circumcision is that
which is of the heart, by the Spirit, not by the letter; and his praise is not
from men, but from God." Only justification by faith makes someone a
son of Abraham (4:12).

Abraham was not justified by the law. "For the promise to
Abraham or to his descendants that he would be heir of the world was
not through the Law, but through the righteousness of faith. For if
those who are of the Law are heirs, faith is made void and the promise
is nullified; for the Law brings about wrath, but where there is no law,
neither is there violation" (4:13–15).

Again the chronology of Scripture proves Paul's point beyond dispute. Obviously, the law was not revealed to Moses until more than half

a millennium *after* Abraham lived. Abraham clearly did not become righteous by means of the law.

Justification has never been through ritual *or* law. God's law "is holy, and the commandment is holy and righteous and good" (Rom. 7:12; cf. Gal. 3:21). But the law has never been a means of salvation. "For as many as are of the works of the Law," that is, seek to justify themselves on the basis of keeping the law, "are under a curse; for it is written, 'Cursed is everyone who does not abide by all things written in the book of the law, to perform them'" (Gal. 3:10). The law demands perfection. But the only way to obtain perfect righteousness is by imputation—that is, being justified by faith.

The purpose of the law was to reveal God's perfect standards of righteousness. At the same time, it sets a standard that is impossible for sinful humans to live up to. That should show us our need for a Savior and drive us to God in faith. Thus the law is a "tutor to lead us to Christ, that we may be justified by faith" (Gal. 3:24).

God has never recognized any righteousness but the righteousness of faith. The law cannot save because the law only brings wrath. The more someone seeks justification through the law, the more that person proves his or her sinfulness, and the more judgment and wrath is debited to that person's account (cf. Rom. 4:4).

Then comes the climax.

Abraham was justified by God's grace. "For this reason it is by faith, that it might be in accordance with grace, in order that the promise may be certain to all the descendants, not only to those who are of the Law, but also to those who are of the faith of Abraham, who is the father of us all, (as it is written, 'A father of many nations have I made you') in the sight of Him whom he believed, even God, who gives life to the dead and calls into being that which does not exist" (4:16–17).

The gist of this entire passage is stated in verse 16: "*it is by faith, that it might be in accordance with grace.*" The dynamic of justification is God's grace. Abraham's faith was not in itself righteousness. Faith is only *reckoned* for righteousness. Justification is wholly a work of God's grace.

Again, we see here the purely forensic nature of justification: God "calls into being that which does not exist." The King James Version says that He "calleth those things which be not as though they were." That is a fascinating statement about God.

If you or I were to declare "things that [are] not as though they were," we would be lying. God can do it because He is God, and His decrees carry the full weight of divine sovereignty. God spoke, and the worlds were created. "What is seen was not made out of things which are visible" (Heb. 11:3). He spoke things that were not, and behold! They were. He can call people, places, and events into existence solely by His divinely sovereign decrees. He can declare believing sinners righteous even though they are not. That is justification.

But justification never occurs alone in God's plan. It is always accompanied by sanctification. God does not declare sinners righteous legally without making them righteous practically. Justification is not just a legal fiction. When God declares someone righteous, He will inevitably bring it to pass. "Whom He justified, these He also glorified" (Rom. 8:30). When justification occurs, the process of sanctification begins. Grace always encompasses both.

As we shall see in chapter 7, Paul clearly taught both truths. He did not end with a discussion of justification and forget the matter of sanctification. The salvation he described in his epistle to the Roman church was not a single-faceted, merely forensic reckoning. But the forensic element—justification—was without doubt the footing on which Paul based the whole of Christian experience.

7

Free from Sin, Slaves of Righteousness

> You cannot receive Christ as your justification only, and then, later, decide to refuse or to accept Him as your sanctification. He is one and indivisible, and if you receive Him at all, at once He is made unto you "wisdom and righteousness and sanctification and redemption." You cannot receive Him as your Saviour only, and later decide to accept or refuse Him as your Lord; for the Saviour is the Lord who by His death has [bought] us and therefore owns us. Sanctification is nowhere taught or offered in the New Testament as some additional experience possible to the believer. It is represented rather as something which is already within the believer, something which he must realise more and more and in which he must grow increasingly.
>
> D. Martyn Lloyd-Jones[1]

A dear friend of mine once ministered in a church where he encountered a retired layman who thought of himself as a Bible teacher. The fellow would seize every opportunity to teach or testify publicly, and his message was always the same. He would talk about how "positional truth" had given him new enthusiasm for the Christian faith.

The "positional truth" he spoke of included the perfect righteousness of Christ that is imputed to believers at justification. The man also

---

[1]Cited in Iain H. Murray, *D. Martyn Lloyd-Jones: The First Forty Years* (Edinburgh: Banner of Truth, 1982), 375.

loved to point out that all Christians are seated with Christ in heavenly places (Eph. 2:6) and hidden with Christ in God (Col. 3:3). He was eager to remind his fellow Christians that we all stand before God as "a chosen race, a royal priesthood, a holy nation, a people for God's own possession" (1 Pet. 2:9). Those "positional" realities *are* true of all genuine Christians, regardless of our level of spiritual maturity. Our unassailable standing in Christ is one of the most precious truths of Christian doctrine.

But this particular man, obsessed with "positional truth," lived a deplorable life. He was a drunkard. He was addicted to cigarettes. He was ill tempered and arrogant. He was unloving to his wife. He had created division and strife in several churches over the years. He was completely undisciplined in almost every way. My friend once visited the man's home, and signs of his ungodly lifestyle were all over the house.

To this man, "positional truth" evidently meant truth that has no practical ramifications. He had wrongly concluded that since our *position* in Christ isn't altered by our *practice*, Christians really needn't be bothered about their sins. He evidently believed he could be assured of the promises of the Christian life even though none of the practical fruits of faith were evident in his walk. In short, he loved the idea of justification but seemed to give scant attention to sanctification. My friend rightly encouraged him to examine whether he was truly in Christ (2 Cor. 13:5).

Nowhere in Scripture do we find positional righteousness set against righteous behavior, as if the two realities were innately disconnected. In fact, the apostle Paul's teaching was diametrically opposed to the notion that "positional truth" means we are free to sin. After two and a half chapters of teaching about "positional" matters, Paul wrote, "What shall we say then? Are we to continue in sin that grace might increase? May it never be!" (Rom. 6:1–2). In stark contrast to the man who concluded that sin must be OK since our practice doesn't alter our position, Paul taught that our position *does* make a difference in our practice: "How shall we who died to sin still live in it?" (v. 2).

What is no-lordship theology but the teaching that those who have died to sin can indeed live in it? In that regard, no-lordship teaching rests on the same foundation as the doctrine of the "positional truth" zealot I have just described. It separates justification from sanctification.

Second-Blessing Spirituality?

No-lordship theology demands a two-level approach to the Christian experience. Because of the presupposition that faith has nothing to do with surrender, no-lordship teaching about obedience and spiritual maturity must begin with a postconversion experience of personal consecration to God. This is analogous to "deeper life" theology, which in turn echoes the Wesleyan idea of a "second blessing," or second work of grace.

Charles Ryrie is candid about the no-lordship approach to spirituality:

> Before any lasting progress can be made on the road of spiritual living, the believer must be a dedicated person. Although this is not a requirement for salvation, it is the basic foundation for sanctification. As we have pointed out, *dedication is a complete, crisis commitment of self for all of the years of one's life.* Such dedication may be triggered by some problem or decision that has to be faced, but it concerns a person, the child of God, not an activity or ambition or plan for the future. A dedicated person will have dedicated plans and ambitions; but dedicated plans do not necessarily require or guarantee dedication of the planner.
>
> *Dedication is a break with one's own control over his life and a giving of that control to the Lord.* It does not solve all the problems immediately and automatically, but *it does provide the basis for solution, growth and progress in the Christian life.*[2]

Dr. Ryrie includes a diagram that illustrates how he views typical progress in the Christian life. It is a line that rises and falls to show the peaks and valleys of the Christian life, always with an upward trend. What is significant about the diagram is that the line is flat—indicating no growth whatsoever—between the point of conversion and the "crisis" of dedication. Only *after* dedication does practical sanctification begin.

According to no-lordship theology, it seems, conversion alone does not "provide the basis for . . . growth and progress in the Christian life" or "the basic foundation for sanctification." A second-level experience is necessary before practical sanctification can even begin. Thus no-lordship theology divides Christians into two groups—the haves and the have-nots. The terminology is slightly different, but this theology is nothing but a repackaging of second-blessing sanctification. It sends Christians on a futile quest for an experience to supply what they already possess—if they are truly believers.

---

[2]Charles C. Ryrie, *Balancing the Christian Life* (Chicago: Moody, 1969), 186–87 (emphasis added).

More than a century ago J. C. Ryle correctly analyzed the chief fallacy of every two-step approach to spirituality:

> Sudden, instantaneous leaps from conversion to consecration I fail to see in the Bible. I doubt, indeed, whether we have any warrant for saying that a man can possibly be converted without being consecrated to God! More consecrated he doubtless can be, and will be as his grace increases; but if he was not consecrated to God in the very day that he was converted and born again, I do not know what conversion means. . . .
>
> I have sometimes thought, while reading the strong language used by many about "consecration" that those who use it must have had previously a singularly low and inadequate view of "conversion," if indeed they knew anything about conversion at all. In short, I have almost suspected that when they were "consecrated," they were in reality converted for the first time!
>
> . . . By all means let us teach that there is more holiness to be attained and more of heaven to be enjoyed upon earth than most believers now experience. But I decline to tell any converted man that he needs a second conversion.[3]

All no-lordship teaching hinges on a two-stage theory of the Christian life. Stage one, conversion, is receiving Christ as Savior. Stage two, consecration, is surrendering to Him as Lord. In between is usually a period of time during which the "carnal Christian" lives like a pagan before he or she makes the "decision" to become a "disciple."[4] One needs only to listen to testimonies to see how pervasive this teaching has become in American evangelicalism: "I received Christ as my Savior at age seven, and didn't make Him Lord until I was in my thirties."

I am convinced that such testimonies reflect people's misinterpretation of their own experiences. There are many degrees of sanctification; hence many levels of commitment to Christ. But no one who truly has trusted Christ for salvation is *un*committed in principle to Christ's lordship, and no one who perpetually lives in conscious and purposeful rebellion against Him can truly claim to trust Him.

As I have pointed out, God justifies no one whom He does not sanctify. No second work of grace is necessary for those who have been

---

[3]J. C. Ryle, *Holiness* (reprint, Durham, England: Evangelical Press, reprint), xxv.

[4]Hence Zane Hodges writes, "The rich young ruler was not ready for a life [of reliance on Jesus' lordship], but the born-again disciples of the Son of God were" (*AF* 189).

born again. The apostle Peter could not have stated it more clearly: "His divine power has granted to us *everything pertaining to life and godliness,* through the true knowledge of Him who called us by His own glory and excellence" (2 Pet. 1:3, emphasis added). Sanctification is not a second-level experience entered into sometime after conversion. Paul addressed the Corinthians as "*those who have been sanctified* in Christ Jesus, saints by calling, *with all who in every place call upon the name of our Lord Jesus Christ,* their Lord and ours" (1 Cor. 1:2, emphasis added). He re-minded them, "By [God's] doing you are in Christ Jesus, who became to us wisdom from God, and righteousness and sanctification, and re-demption" (v. 30). He told the Thessalonians, "God has chosen you from the beginning for salvation through sanctification by the Spirit and faith in the truth" (2 Thess. 2:13).

If the *positional* aspects of God's truth are applicable to a life, His *practical* sanctifying work will also be operative in that same life.

What Is Sanctification?

Sanctification is the continuous operation of the Holy Spirit in believers, making us holy by conforming our character, affections, and behavior to the image of Christ. Justification is a one-time *event;* sanc-tification is an ongoing *process.* Justification frees us from the *guilt* of sin, sanctification from the *pollution* of sin. As we are seeing, one is as much a necessary part of God's saving work as the other.

Note this crucial distinction: At justification we surrender the *prin-ciple* of sin and self-rule. In sanctification we relinquish the *practice* of specific sins as we mature in Christ. Total surrender to Christ's lordship does not mean that we make all of life's decisions as a prerequisite to conversion (cf. *SGS* 49). It does not demand that we give up all our sins before we can be justified. It is not "the commitment of the years of one's life on earth" (*SGS* 118, cf. 106–7, 120, 123). It means that when we trust Christ for salvation we settle the issue of who is in charge. At salvation we surrender to Christ in principle, but as Christians we will surrender in practice again and again. This practical outworking of His lordship is the process of sanctification.

There *is* an immediate aspect of sanctification that is simultaneous with justification: "Such were some of you; but you were washed, but you were sanctified, but you were justified in the name of the Lord Jesus Christ, and in the Spirit of our God" (1 Cor. 6:11). This once-for-all aspect of sanctification is undoubtedly what the apostle had in view when he addressed the Corinthians as "those who *have been* sanctified"

(1:2). This initial, immediate aspect is sometimes referred to as "positional sanctification" (*SGS* 151).

But sanctification, unlike justification, is not a one-time, legal declaration. It is an experiential separation from sin that begins at salvation and continues in increasing degrees of practical holiness in one's life and behavior. Sanctification may be observable in greater or lesser degrees from believer to believer. But it is not optional, nor is it separable from the other aspects of our salvation.

Perhaps the writer to the Hebrews stated the necessity of practical sanctification most succinctly: "Pursue peace with all men, and the sanctification without which no one will see the Lord" (Heb. 12:14). The context shows that verse is speaking of holy behavior, practical righteousness, not just a positional or forensic holiness (vv. 11, 12, 13, 15, 16).

To Work, or Not to Work?

In Romans 4:5 ("But to the one who does not work, but believes in Him who justifies the ungodly, his faith is reckoned as righteousness") Paul's point was that God's righteousness is reckoned to people who believe, not to people who try to earn divine favor by religious ritual or self-righteous works. He was *not* suggesting, as many do today, that a believer who has been declared righteous might fail to produce good works. In no way does this verse erect a barrier—or even suggest a separation—between justification and sanctification.

In fact, following the progression of Paul's argument in Romans 3–8, we find he deals with precisely this issue. As we noted in chapter 6, Romans 3 and 4 describe the legal aspect of justification, God's reckoning by which a believing sinner is declared fully righteous. Romans 5 explains how guilt or righteousness can be imputed to one person because of the obedience or disobedience of another.

In Romans 6 the apostle turns to the practical aspect of God's righteousness—sanctification. He is teaching that God's righteousness, granted by faith to every believer, has both judicial and practical implications. There are not two *kinds* of righteousness—only two *aspects* of divine righteousness. Righteousness is a single package; God does not declare someone righteous whom He does not also make righteous. Having begun the process, He will continue it to ultimate glorification (Rom. 8:29–30; cf. Phil. 1:6).

Dr. B. B. Warfield saw this as the whole point of Romans 6:

> The whole sixth chapter of Romans . . . was written for no other purpose than to assert and demonstrate that justification and sanctification are indissolubly bound together; that we cannot have the one without having the other; that, to use its own figurative language, dying with Christ and living with Christ are integral elements in one indisintegrable salvation. To wrest these two things apart and make separable gifts of grace of them evinces a confusion in the conception of Christ's salvation which is nothing less than portentous. It forces from us the astonished cry, Is Christ divided? And it compels us to point afresh to the primary truth that we do not obtain the benefits of Christ apart from, but only in and with His Person; and that when we have Him we have all.[5]

Sanctification is so much an essential part of salvation that the term is commonly used in Scripture as a synonym for salvation (cf. Acts 20:32; 26:18; 1 Cor. 1:2, 30; 6:11; 2 Thess. 2:13; Heb. 2:11; 10:14; 1 Pet. 1:2).

A Closer Look at Romans 6

As Paul finished his discussion of justification, he extolled the grace of God. "The Law came in that the transgression might increase; but where sin increased, grace abounded all the more, that, as sin reigned in death, even so grace might reign through righteousness to eternal life through Jesus Christ our Lord" (Rom. 5:20–21). If the increased presence of sin means grace abounds all the more, an obvious question comes to mind: "Are we to continue in sin that grace might increase?" (6:1). After all, if justification means we are instantly declared perfectly righteous, what real difference does it make whether we sin or not? If our sin only accents the grace of God, why not sin even more?

---

[5]Benjamin B. Warfield, *Perfectionism* (Philadelphia: Presbyterian & Reformed, 1958), 356–57. Warfield went on to say: "This crass separation of sanctification from justification, as if it was merely an additional gift of grace to be sought and obtained for itself—instead of, as it is, an inseparable component part of the one salvation that belongs to all believers—lays the foundation, of course, for that circle of ideas which are summed up in the phrase, 'the Second Blessing.' These are far from wholesome. Among them may be mentioned, for example, the creation of two different kinds of Christians, a lower and a higher variety" (ibid., 357–58). Of course, the two-classes-of-Christians error underlies all no-lordship teaching. See further discussion of this in chapter 8.

Paul anticipated that such questions would be raised. He answers them in depth by making several key points about how sanctification operates.

Sanctification is inseparably linked to justification. Paul attacks the notion that justification is the sum of God's work in salvation: "What shall we say then? Are we to continue in sin that grace might increase? May it never be! How shall we who died to sin still live in it? Or do you not know that all of us who have been baptized into Christ Jesus have been baptized into His death? Therefore we have been buried with Him through baptism into death, in order that as Christ was raised from the dead through the glory of the Father, so we too might walk in newness of life" (Romans 6:1–4).

Evidently Paul had already encountered considerable opposition to the doctrine of justification by faith. Certainly his Jewish audiences would have been unable to conceive of pleasing God by any means other than strict adherence to the rabbinic law. In their system, legalism epitomized godliness (cf. Acts 15:1–29). To legalistic Jews, justification by faith sounded like antinomianism. To teach that salvation is God's work, not ours, was an affront to their haughty egos. The notion that God's grace abounds where sin thrives hit at the heart of their system (cf. Luke 18:11–12). Because they didn't understand grace, they could think of only one alternative to legalism: antinomianism. They reasoned that if salvation is all by grace, and grace glorifies God, and God delights in justifying the ungodly, then why not sin more? After all, ungodliness only allows God to demonstrate His grace in greater measures.

That, by the way, was precisely the theology of Rasputin, religious adviser to the ruling family of Russia nearly a hundred years ago. He taught that man's sin glorifies God. The greater man's sin, the more God is glorified in giving grace. Therefore he encouraged people to sin with abandon. Those who suppress their sin suppress God's ability to show His glory, according to Rasputin. His teaching contributed to the downfall of Russia.

In the mid-seventeenth century an English sect known as the Ranters taught a similar doctrine. They encouraged immorality and indulgence, believing God is glorified by showing grace. Puritan Richard Baxter opposed their teaching.

Paul himself had already confronted similar ideas. In Romans 3:5–6 he cited the argument of those who claimed God was unrighteous to punish sin since our unrighteousness demonstrates His righteousness. Then he condemned those who had accused the apostles of teaching pragmatic antinomianism ("Let us do evil that good may come" [Rom. 3:8]).

We see that antinomianism has been a threat from the earliest days of the church. Jude wrote, "Certain persons have crept in unnoticed, those who were long beforehand marked out for this condemnation, ungodly persons who turn the grace of our God into licentiousness and deny our only Master and Lord, Jesus Christ" (Jude 4). Jude was describing early antinomians.

In Romans 6, Paul says justification by faith makes no place for antinomianism. He attacks the antinomians without yielding an inch of ground to the legalists. He would neither abandon God's grace to accommodate legalism nor abandon God's righteousness to accommodate libertinism. According to Paul, true holiness is as much a gift of God as is the new birth and the spiritual life it brings. The life that is void of holiness has no claim to justification.

"Are we to continue in sin that grace might increase?" The Greek word translated "continue" speaks of habitual persistence. Paul was not asking whether believers might fall into sin; he was ruling out intentional, willful, constant sinning as a routine of life.

Put in theological terms, this is the summary question: Can justification truly exist apart from sanctification? Paul's answer is emphatically no.

To be alive in Christ is to be dead to sin. "May it never be!" (6:2) is an accurate translation. But the King James Version captures the force of Paul's exclamation: "God forbid!" The very suggestion that sin in the Christian's life might in any way glorify God was abhorrent to Paul. "How shall we who died to sin still live in it?"

Christians have died to sin. It is therefore inconceivable to Paul that we might continue to live in the sin from which we were delivered by death. Only a corrupt mind using perverted logic could argue that continuing in sin magnifies God's grace. It is self-evident that death terminates life; it is equally obvious that death to sin must end a life of unbroken transgression.

"Died to sin" (Gk., *apothnēskō*) speaks of a historical fact referring to our death in the death of Christ. Because we are "in Christ" (6:11; 8:1), and He died in our place (5:6–8), we are counted dead with Him. We are therefore dead to sin's penalty and dominion. Death is permanent. Death and life are incompatible. So the person who has died to sin cannot continue living in iniquity. Certainly we can commit sins, but we do not live anymore in the dimension of sin and under sin's rule (cf. 8:2–4). Sin is contrary to our new disposition. "No one who is born of

God practices sin," according to John, "because His seed abides in him; and he cannot sin, because he is born of God" (1 John 3:9). It is not merely that we *should not* continue to live in unbroken sin but that we *cannot*.

Dying to sin implies an abrupt, irreversible, wholesale break with the power of sin. This schism with sin is the immediate, once-for-all aspect of sanctification we spoke of earlier. It is the past tense of sanctification out of which all practical holiness proceeds.

The phrase "we who died to sin" does not describe an advanced class of Christians. Paul is speaking here of all believers. His point is that a justified life must be a sanctified life. Practical holiness is as much God's work as any other element of redemption. When we are born again, God not only declares us righteous, but He also begins to cultivate righteousness in our lives. Thus salvation is not only a forensic declaration; it is a miracle of conversion, of transformation. There is no such thing as a true convert to Christ who is justified but who is not being sanctified. There is no gap between justification and sanctification. Dr. Donald Grey Barnhouse wrote,

> Although justification is not sanctification, justification is intended to produce sanctification. Holiness is to be the touchstone of the Christian life. Christ came in order to save his people from their sins (Matt. 1:21); they were not to be saved in the midst of their sins and then lie down in them again. Though men seek to pervert the gospel, the Christian must not be drawn aside to any position other than that which demands holiness and which leads to holiness. . . .
>
> Justification and sanctification are as inseparable as a torso and a head. You can't have one without the other. God does not give "gratuitous righteousness" apart from newness of life. While justification, in its action, has nothing to do with sanctification, it does not follow that sanctification is not necessary. "Without holiness no man shall see the Lord" (Heb. 12:14). Holiness starts where justification finishes, and if holiness does not start, we have the right to suspect that justification never started either.[6]

As the sinful, unregenerate person cannot help manifesting his or her true character, neither can the regenerate person.

So it is impossible to be alive in Christ and still be alive to sin.

---

[6]Donald G. Barnhouse, *Romans,* 4 vols. (Grand Rapids, Mich.: Eerdmans, 1961), 3:2:10–12.

Our union with Christ guarantees a changed life. Death to sin is a result of the believer's union with Christ. "Do you not know that all of us who have been baptized into Christ Jesus have been baptized into His death? Therefore we have been buried with Him through baptism into death, in order that as Christ was raised from the dead through the glory of the Father, so we too might walk in newness of life. For if we have become *united with Him* in the likeness of His death, certainly we shall be also in the likeness of His resurrection" (vv. 3–5, emphasis added).

Elsewhere Paul says we become new creatures "in Christ" (2 Cor. 5:17). He means that our union with Christ is the basis of our sanctification. It spells both the end of the old and the start of the new.

"In Christ" is one of Paul's favorite phrases (cf. Rom. 8:1; 12:5; 16:7; 1 Cor. 1:2; Col. 1:28). Because we are "in Christ Jesus" He has become to us "wisdom from God, and righteousness and sanctification, and redemption" (1 Cor. 1:30). Our life is hid with Christ in God (Col. 3:3). We are buried with Him by baptism into death (Rom. 6:4; Col. 2:12). We are one body in Him (Rom. 12:5). Christ is our life (Col. 3:4). Christ is in us, the hope of glory (Col. 1:27). Those verses describe the absolute identification with Christ that is the essential characteristic of the elect. We are indivisibly linked in a spiritual sphere of new life.

That unfathomable truth is why Paul so strongly rebuked the sexual immorality of some in the Corinthian church: "Do you not know that your bodies are members of Christ? Shall I then take away the members of Christ and make them members of a harlot? May it never be!" (1 Cor. 6:15).

To be "in Christ" is not only to believe some truths *about* Him, but rather to be united *to* Him inseparably as the source of our eternal life, as both the "author *and perfecter* of faith" (Heb. 12:2, emphasis added). To be "in Him" is to be in the process of sanctification.

We are united with Christ specifically in His death and resurrection (Rom. 6:3–10). This truth is far too wonderful for us to comprehend fully, but the main idea Paul wants to convey here is that we died with Christ so that we might have life through Him and live like Him. Paul's stress is not on the *immorality* of continuing to live the way we did before we were saved, but on the *impossibility* of it. The whole purpose of our union in Christ's death and resurrection with Christ is so that "we too might walk in newness of life" (v. 4). How could we continue in the realm of sin?

So the certain consequence of our union in Christ's death to sin and His resurrection to life is that we will share in His holy walk. "If we have become united with Him in the likeness of His death, certainly we shall be also in the likeness of His resurrection." As our old self died, a new creation was born (cf. 2 Cor. 5:17). Bishop Handley Moule wrote, "It is a thing not to be thought of that the sinner should accept justification—and live to himself. It is a moral contradiction of the very deepest kind, and cannot be entertained without betraying an initial error in the man's whole spiritual creed."[7]

In Christ we are not the same people we were before salvation. "Our old self was crucified with Him, that our body of sin might be done away with, that we should no longer be slaves to sin" (Rom. 6:6). Elsewhere Paul wrote, "I have been crucified with Christ; and it is no longer I who live, but Christ lives in me; and the life which I now live in the flesh I live by faith in the Son of God, who loved me, and delivered Himself up for me" (Gal. 2:20). Our new life as Christians is not an amended old life but a divinely bestowed new life that is of the same nature as Christ's very own. It is what our Lord spoke of when He promised abundant life (John 10:10).

Nor is Paul describing a dualistic, schizophrenic Christian. The old man—the unregenerate person that was "in Adam" (cf. 1 Cor. 15:22; Rom. 5:14–15)—is dead. We are to "lay aside" that crucified, dead, and corrupt old self (Eph. 4:22), and "put on the new self, which in the likeness of God has been created in righteousness and holiness of the truth" (v. 24). It is true of every genuine believer that our old self is dead. "Those who belong to Christ Jesus have crucified the flesh with its passions and desires" (Gal. 5:24). If the old self *isn't* dead, conversion hasn't occurred. Paul reminded the Colossians that they had *already* "laid aside the old self with its evil practices, and . . . put on the new self who is being renewed to a true knowledge according to the image of the One who created him" (Col. 3:9–10).

As we shall note in chapter 8, Christians sin because of the vestiges of sinful flesh, not because they have the same old active sinful nature. Certainly we sin, but when we sin it is contrary to our nature, not because we have two dispositions—one sinful and one not. "Our old self was crucified with Him, that our body of sin might be done away with" (Rom. 6:6).

---

[7]Handley Moule, *The Epistle to the Romans* (London: Pickering & Inglis, n.d.), 160–61.

That does not mean our sinful tendencies are annihilated. The Greek word translated "done away with" literally means "to render inoperative, invalidate." Sin has lost its dominating control over us. Obviously we all struggle with sinful propensities. Death to the sinful self does not mean death to the flesh and its corrupted inclinations. Because of the pleasures of sin and the weakness of our remaining flesh, we often yield to sin.

The tyranny and penalty of sin have been nullified, but sin's potential for expression has not yet been fully removed. Our human weaknesses and instincts make us capable of succumbing to temptation (as we shall see in chapter 8 when we study Romans 7:14–25). We are, in short, new creations—holy and redeemed but wrapped in grave clothes of unredeemed flesh. We are like Lazarus, who came forth from the grave still wrapped from head to foot in his burial garments. Jesus instructed those standing nearby to "unbind him, and let him go" (John 11:44).

So the apostle admonishes believers, "we should no longer be slaves to sin" (Rom. 6:6). The translation leaves the meaning somewhat ambiguous. Is Paul suggesting that it is optional as to whether we live as slaves to sin or not? Is he implying that we have a choice—that Christians can still be enslaved to sin? Verses 17–18 answer that question with no ambiguity: "Though you were slaves of sin, you *became obedient* from the heart to that form of teaching to which you were committed, and having *been freed* from sin, you *became slaves of righteousness*" (emphasis added). Every verb in those two verses underscores the truth that our slavery to sin is already broken by Christ and is henceforth a thing of the past. Verse 22 confirms it: "Having been freed from sin and enslaved to God, you derive your benefit [lit., "fruit"], resulting in sanctification, and the outcome, eternal life."

So in verse 6, the phrase "should no longer be slaves of sin" clearly means that believers *can* no longer be slaves of sin. No genuine Christian lives in bondage to sin. Those who have died in Christ are free from such slavery (v. 7). Paul even uses the analogy of marriage (Rom. 7:1–4), making the point that the first husband has died, so we are no longer obligated to him, but we have been freed and joined to a new husband, namely Christ, "that we might bear fruit for God" (v. 4).

Peter taught precisely the same thing: "Therefore, since Christ has suffered in the flesh arm yourselves also with the same purpose, because he who has suffered in the flesh has ceased from sin, so as to live the rest of the time in the flesh no longer for the lusts of men, but for the will of God" (1 Pet. 4:1–2).

Faith is the means by which we conquer sin. The series of verbs in Romans 6—"know" (vv. 3, 6, 9), "reckon" (v. 11, KJV), and "yield" (v. 13 KJV)—speak of faith. In fact, they perfectly parallel the three essential elements of faith we listed in chapter 3: know (*notitia*), reckon (*assensus*), and yield (*fiducia*). Paul is challenging the Romans to apply their faith more diligently, to take off the old grave clothes and live the new life to the fullness of Christ's righteousness and glory: "Consider yourselves to be dead to sin, but alive to God in Christ Jesus. Therefore do not let sin reign in your mortal body that you should obey its lusts, and do not go on presenting the members of your body to sin as instruments of unrighteousness; but present yourselves to God as those alive from the dead, and your members as instruments of righteousness to God. For sin shall not be master over you, for you are not under law, but under grace" (6:11–14). That sums up the life of faith.

Our spiritual death to sin and resurrection into new life with Christ are the underpinning of our sanctification. We need to know and believe that we are not what we used to be. We must see that we are not remodeled sinners but reborn saints. We must grasp the truth that we are no longer under sin's tyranny. The dawn of faith is *knowledge* of these spiritual realities. "My people are destroyed for lack of knowledge. Because you have rejected knowledge, I also will reject you" (Hos. 4:6).

Reckoning takes the believer's response one step further: "Consider yourselves to be dead to sin, but alive to God in Christ Jesus" (Rom. 6:11). "Consider," or "reckon" (KJV), in that verse comes from the same Greek term, *logizomai,* which we saw in Romans 4:3 ("Abraham believed God, and it was *reckoned* to him as righteousness"). It is an accounting term meaning "calculate," or "figure." In this context it takes the believer's faith beyond mere knowledge. To "reckon" here means to have unreserved confidence, to affirm a truth from the heart, as opposed to knowing it intellectually.

Yielding goes even beyond that and involves the believer's will. Paul writes, "Do not let sin reign in your mortal body that you should obey its lusts, and do not go on presenting the members of your body to sin as instruments of unrighteousness; but *present* [*yield,* KJV] yourselves to God as those alive from the dead, and your members as instruments of righteousness to God" (Rom. 6:12–13).

Sin is still a powerful force, but it is no longer master over the Christian. Sin is like a deposed but angry monarch, determined to reign again in our lives. It still occupies some territory, but not the capital city. Paul says we are not to yield to sin, but we must yield instead to God.

This is an act of trust. "This is the victory that has overcome the world—our faith" (1 John 5:4). So even our sanctification is by faith.

Grace guarantees victory over sin. Because salvation is forever, our immortal souls are eternally beyond sin's reach. But sin *can* attack Christians in their mortal bodies. Even our bodies will someday be glorified and forever be out of sin's reach, but as long as this life lasts we are subject to corruption and death. "This perishable must put on the imperishable, and this mortal must put on immortality" (1 Cor. 15:53). Until then our mortal bodies are still subject to sin. That is why "we . . . groan within ourselves, waiting eagerly for our adoption as sons, the redemption of our body" (Rom. 8:23).

Therefore Paul says, "Do not go on presenting the members of your body to sin as instruments of unrighteousness; but present yourselves to God as those alive from the dead, and your members as instruments of righteousness to God" (Rom. 6:13). This parallels Romans 12:1: "I urge you therefore, brethren, by the mercies of God, to present your *bodies* a living and holy sacrifice, acceptable to God, which is your spiritual service of worship" (Rom. 12:1, emphasis added), and "I buffet my *body* and make it my slave, lest possibly, after I have preached to others, I myself should be disqualified" (1 Cor. 9:27, emphasis added).

Many interpreters have been tripped up by the verb tenses in Romans 6:12–13. "Do not let sin reign" and "do not go on presenting" are present active imperative verbs. They are contrasted with an aorist imperative, "but present yourselves to God." At first glance it seems the apostle could be saying "*Stop* letting sin reign and *stop* yielding your members to sin, but submit yourselves to God" implying that these people were Christians who had never surrendered to Christ's lordship.

But the context clearly indicates otherwise. Paul also reminds them, "you became obedient from the heart" (v. 17); "you became slaves of righteousness" (v. 18); and "[you were] freed from sin and enslaved to God." These are not people who have never surrendered. Here, and in Romans 12:1–2, Paul was simply encouraging them to keep surrendering in practice what they had already surrendered in principle. He was calling for decisive, deliberate surrender in their lives right now.

Is the outcome in doubt? Certainly not. In verse 14 Paul offers these assuring words: "Sin shall not be master over you, for you are not under law, but under grace." The Christian is no longer under the condemning power of God's law but is now under the redeeming power of His grace. It is in the power of that grace, by faith, that the Lord now calls him to live.

Freedom from sin enslaves us to righteousness. Paul returns to the question of antinomianism:

> What then? Shall we sin because we are not under law but under grace? May it never be! Do you not know that when you present yourselves to someone as slaves for obedience, you are slaves of the one whom you obey, either of sin resulting in death, or of obedience resulting in righteousness? But thanks be to God that though you were slaves of sin, you became obedient from the heart to that form of teaching to which you were committed, and having been freed from sin, you became slaves of righteousness.
>
> Romans 6:15–18

Freedom from the law means freedom from sin's bondage and freedom from the law's penalty—not freedom from moral restraint. Grace does not mean we have permission to do as we please; it means we have the power to do what pleases God. The mere suggestion that God's grace gives us license to sin is self-contradictory, for the very purpose of grace is to free us from sin. How can we who are the recipients of grace continue in sin?

"May it never be!" is the same powerful and unequivocal denial Paul gave in verse 2. This truth needs no proof; it is self-evident: "Do you not know?" implies that *everyone* should understand something so basic. What could be more obvious? When you present yourselves to someone as slaves for obedience, you are slaves of the one whom you obey! There are only two choices. If our lives are characterized by sin, then we are sin's slaves. If we are characterized by obedience, then we are slaves of righteousness (vv. 16–18). Either way, we are not our own masters.

It is equally true that "no one can serve two masters; for either he will hate the one and love the other, or he will hold to one and despise the other. You cannot serve God and mammon" (Matt. 6:24). You cannot serve God and sin. Those who think they are Christians but are enslaved to sin are sadly deceived. We cannot have two contradictory natures at the same time. We cannot live in two opposing spiritual domains simultaneously. We cannot serve two masters. We are either slaves of sin by natural birth, or slaves of righteousness by regeneration. We can't be both in the Spirit and in the flesh (cf. Rom. 8:5–9).

Paul is not teaching the Romans that they *ought to be* slaves of righteousness. He is reminding them that they *are* slaves of righteousness. He told the Colossians the same thing: "Although you were formerly alienated and hostile in mind, engaged in evil deeds, yet He has now reconciled you in His fleshly body through death, in order to present you before Him holy and blameless and beyond reproach" (Col. 1:21–22). For the Christian, the life of unrighteousness and hostility toward God is in the *past*. No true believer will continue indefinitely in disobedience, because sin is diametrically opposed to our new and holy nature. Real Christians cannot endure perpetually sinful living.

Paul thus reminds the Romans that they are no longer enslaved to sin: "Thanks be to God that though you were slaves of sin, you became obedient from the heart to that form of teaching to which you were committed," (v. 17). Paul is not speaking about a legalistic or mechanical show of righteousness: "You became obedient from the heart." Grace transforms a person's innermost being. A person whose heart has not been changed is not saved. The hallmark of grace is an obedient heart.

Again, we must be clear: Obedience does not produce or maintain salvation, but it is the inevitable characteristic of those who are saved. The desire to know and obey God's truth is one of the surest marks of genuine salvation. Jesus made it clear that those who obey His word are the true believers (cf. John 8:31; 14:21, 23, 24; 15:10).

Slaves of sin—unbelievers—are free from righteousness (Rom. 6:20). Christians, on the other hand, are free from sin and enslaved to God through faith in Jesus Christ (v. 22). The inevitable benefit is sanctification, and the ultimate outcome is eternal life (v. 22). This promise sums up the whole point of Romans 6: God not only frees us from sin's penalty (justification), but He frees us from sin's tyranny as well (sanctification).

Nevertheless, though we are no longer subject to sin's dominion, all of us struggle desperately with sin in our lives. How that can be and what we can do about it is the subject of chapter 8.

8

The Death Struggle with Sin

The form that sanctification takes is conflict with the indwelling sin that constantly assaults us. The conflict, which is lifelong, involves both resistance to sin's assaults and the counterattack of mortification, whereby we seek to drain the life out of this troublesome enemy.

J. I. Packer[1]

A man who has long championed no-lordship doctrine wrote me to object to my teaching on the gospel. I invited him to lunch, thinking a personal conversation might help us understand one another better. He was a fellow pastor in a large church, and I believed we would have much in common, even though we disagreed at this very basic level.

We met, and I felt our dialogue was beneficial. Though neither of us changed our views on the gospel, we were able to clarify misunderstandings on both sides.

Several months after our lunch meeting I was saddened to read a news report disclosing that his church had asked him to step down because he was guilty of sexual immorality. He had been living a double life for more than ten years, and now his sin and unfaithfulness were shamefully exposed.

Was his tolerance of that sin solely the result of his theology? Perhaps not. Certainly other pastors who do not espouse the no-lordship

---

[1]J. I. Packer, *Hot Tub Religion* (Wheaton: Tyndale, 1987), 172.

view have morally disqualified themselves. Conversely, many who hold the no-lordship view manage to avoid falling into sordid sin.

But turn the question around: Was his theology an accommodation to his sinful lifestyle? It surely might have been. This much is certain: No-lordship theology would have a soothing effect on a professing Christian trying to rationalize long-term immorality. Instead of subjecting conscience and behavior to the most intense self-examination, he could find reassurance in the idea that, after all, many Christians are permanently "carnal." Surely the belief that repentance is optional would encourage someone who wants to claim Christ while justifying a life of unrepentant sin. Certainly preaching that constantly touts "grace" but never features law could help someone like that find comfort while sinning. No-lordship doctrine is a perfect fit for anyone trying to justify cold-hearted religion.

By no means do I intend to imply that everyone who holds the no-lordship view lives an immoral life. Obviously that is not the case. Nor am I saying that these people *advocate* unrighteous living. I do not know of a single no-lordship teacher who would openly condone sinful behavior. In fact, the opposite is true: No-lordship preachers often feature strong appeals for holiness. One of the main goals of no-lordship preaching is to convince "carnal believers" to become "spiritual believers." So appeals for obedience and surrender are quite common in no-lordship preaching, except in evangelistic messages. Fortunately, most no-lordship teachers live a better theology than they say they believe.

But I do believe that many people who purposefully allow unrepentant and unconfessed sin in their lives also adopt no-lordship doctrine because it allows them to have the solace of "assurance" in the midst of sinful rebellion.

And I do believe that no-lordship theology tends to undermine holiness, even though this is not the intent of no-lordship teachers. It does so by offering salvation from hell but not salvation from sin. It does so by removing the moral ramifications from faith and repentance. It does so by making obedience to God optional. It does so by promising assurance even to people who live in perpetual carnality.

The Myth of the Carnal Christian

Almost all no-lordship theology leans heavily on the notion that there are three classes of humanity: unsaved people, spiritual Christians, and carnal Christians. This was one of the planks in the no-lordship platform that was laid by Lewis Sperry Chafer. Chafer popularized the carnal-Christian idea in his 1918 book, *He That Is Spiritual.*[2] Chafer's friend C. I. Scofield included a similar scheme in one of the notes in *The Scofield Reference Bible.*

In recent years the idea of the carnal Christian has been disseminated through a series of tracts and booklets published by Campus Crusade for Christ. The Campus Crusade literature features a diagram with three circles representing the three classes of humanity. At the center of each circle is a throne. The non-Christian has self on the throne with Christ outside the circle. The carnal Christian has "invited" Christ into the circle but keeps self enthroned. The spiritual Christian puts Christ on the throne, with self at the foot of the throne. The tract challenges carnal Christians to become spiritual. Millions of these pamphlets have been distributed worldwide over the past thirty years or so. They are undoubtedly the most widely read single bit of no-lordship literature and have helped influence multitudes to accept the carnal-spiritual Christian dichotomy as biblical.

But the whole idea is based on a misunderstanding of 1 Corinthians 2:14–3:3:

> A natural man does not accept the things of the Spirit of God; for they are foolishness to him, and he cannot understand them, because they are spiritually appraised. But he who is spiritual appraises all things, yet he himself is appraised by no man. For who has known the mind of the Lord, that he should instruct Him? But we have the mind of Christ.
>
> And I, brethren, could not speak to you as to spiritual men, but as to men of flesh, as to babes in Christ. I gave you milk to drink, not solid food; for you were not yet able to receive it. Indeed, even now you are not yet able, for you are still fleshly. For since there is jealousy and strife among you, are you not fleshly, and are you not walking like mere men?

In that passage the apostle Paul was rebuking the Corinthians for their unchristlike behavior. The church was dividing into factions, some saying

---

[2]Lewis Sperry Chafer, *He That Is Spiritual* (New York: Our Hope, 1918). In *The Gospel According to Jesus* I described Chafer's book and B. B. Warfield's critique of it. Warfield's review in *The Princeton Theological Review* (April 1919): 322–27, was full of sound reason and biblical insight. It reads like a thorough critique of modern no-lordship theology. If Chafer and those who were influenced by him had interacted seriously with Warfield on these issues, perhaps twentieth-century American evangelicalism might have been spared a lot of confusion and false teaching.

"I am of Paul," and others, "I am of Apollos" (1 Cor. 3:4). Paul told them their divisive behavior was unworthy of Christians: "You are still fleshly [Gk. *sarkikos*, 'pertaining to the flesh, carnal']. For since there is jealousy and strife among you, are you not fleshly, and are you not walking like mere men?"

Clearly Paul was accusing the Corinthians of behaving like non-Christians. Factions were not the only problem at Corinth. The believers there were tolerating an incestuous relationship that a "so-called brother" (5:11) was carrying on with his father's wife. Some were drunk and disorderly in the communion service (11:17–22). Christians were taking one another to court (6:1–8). They were abusing the gift of tongues (14:23), and women were being unruly in their corporate worship services (14:33).

But in 1 Corinthians 2:14–3:3 Paul was most certainly *not* defining two classes of Christians, or three classes of humanity. Paul clearly distinguished between "the natural man" and "he who is spiritual" (2:14–15)—between the unsaved person and the Christian. He recognized that all Christians are capable of carnal behavior. But never in any of his epistles did the apostle address two classes of believers.

In Romans 8, Paul's contrast was between "the mind set on the flesh" (non-Christians) and "the mind set on the Spirit" (v. 6) (Christians); between "those who are in the flesh" (v. 8—non-Christians) and those who are "in the Spirit" (v. 9—Christians). His meaning is unmistakable, for he spells it out explicitly in verse 9: "You are not in the flesh but in the Spirit, if indeed the Spirit of God dwells in you. But if anyone does not have the Spirit of Christ, he does not belong to Him."

So according to Paul, *all* Christians are spiritual. As we shall see, Paul also recognized that all believers behave carnally at times. That is what he was rebuking the Corinthians for.

These Corinthian Christians were obviously immature; that's why Paul called them "babes in Christ" (3:1). But, unlike many so-called carnal Christians today, they were not indifferent to spiritual things. In fact, their allegiance to particular leaders and their abuse of the gifts reflected a misplaced zeal. These Christians clearly had spiritual desires, no matter how imperfectly they pursued them.

Note also that Paul did not urge the Corinthians to seek some second-level experience. He did not counsel them to "make Christ Lord" or dedicate themselves once and for all. On the contrary, he told them, "You are not lacking in any gift, awaiting eagerly the revelation of our Lord Jesus Christ, who shall also confirm you to the end, blameless in the day of our Lord Jesus Christ" (1:7–8).

Still, Paul had no tolerance for those willfully acting carnally. When he learned of the incestuous man's sin, for example, he instructed the Corinthians "to deliver such a one to Satan for the destruction of his flesh, that his spirit may be saved in the day of the Lord Jesus" (5:5). Note how the apostle spoke of those in the church who are immoral, covetous, idolaters, revilers, drunkards, or swindlers. He did not call them *carnal Christians* but *so-called brothers* (5:11). He instructed the Corinthians not even to eat with such people. Clearly he knew such sins—persistent, willful, inveterate sins of lifestyle—called one's profession of faith into question. Paul corrected the church's lenient attitude toward this sinning man and others of his ilk. Evidently the Corinthians routinely accepted such people, perhaps as second-class Christians—just as evangelicals today accept them. Paul, however, commanded the church to discipline them (5:9–13), which would provide insight into whether they were natural, unredeemed people associating with believers, or spiritual people behaving carnally.

How Far Can Christians Go in Sinning?

I recently read a book about Christians and sin that began with an unusual account. The author of this book was acquainted with a pastor who had been sent to prison for robbing fourteen banks to finance his dalliances with prostitutes! The author was fully convinced the bank-robbing Lothario was a true Christian, and so he wrote a book to explore how such a thing could be possible.

Call me old-fashioned, but I think it is fair to raise the question of whether someone who regularly robs banks to pay for illicit sex is truly saved! That man's sin was secretly his lifestyle. There is every reason to believe that he would still be committing his crimes today if he had not been caught. Can we concede that this "so-called brother" is a genuine Christian, just because he was once an evangelical pastor?

True, we cannot judge the man's heart, but we *must* judge his behavior (1 Cor. 5:12). "Or do you not know that the unrighteous shall not inherit the kingdom of God? Do not be deceived; neither fornicators, nor idolaters, nor adulterers, nor effeminate, nor homosexuals, nor thieves, nor the covetous, nor drunkards, nor revilers, nor swindlers, shall inherit the kingdom of God" (1 Cor. 6:9–11). In those verses the apostle Paul was describing sins of chronic behavior, sins that color one's whole character. A predilection for such sins reflects an unregenerate heart. Paul reminded the Corinthians, "Such *were* some of you; *but you were washed, but you were sanctified, but you were justified* in the name of the Lord Jesus Christ, and in the Spirit of our God" (v. 12, emphasis added).

But wait. Doesn't Scripture include examples of believers who committed gross sin? Didn't David commit murder and adultery and allow his sin to go unconfessed for at least a year? Wasn't Lot characterized by worldly compromise in the midst of heinous sin? Yes, those examples prove that genuine believers are capable of the worst imaginable sins. But David and Lot cannot be made to serve as examples of "carnal" believers, whose whole lifestyle and appetites are no different from unregenerate people.

David, for example, *did* repent thoroughly of his sin when Nathan confronted him, and he willingly accepted the Lord's discipline (2 Sam. 12:1–23). Psalm 51 is an expression of David's deep repentance at the end of this sordid episode in his life. The point, after all, is that this was merely one episode in David's life. He was certainly not predisposed to that kind of sin. In fact, 1 Kings 15:5 says, "David did what was right in the sight of the Lord, and had not turned aside from anything that He commanded him all the days of his life, *except in the case of Uriah the Hittite*" (emphasis added).

Lot is a different case. Not much is known about him from the Old Testament account, but what *is* recorded about him is disappointing. He was a pathetic example of compromise and disobedience. On the eve of Sodom's destruction when he should have fled the city, "he hesitated" (Gen. 19:16). The angelic messengers had to seize his hand and put him outside the city. Near the end of his life, his two daughters got him drunk and committed incest with him (Gen. 19:30–38). Lot certainly *did* seem to have a proclivity for sins of compromise and worldliness.

Yet the inspired New Testament writer tells us Lot was "oppressed by the sensual conduct of unprincipled men (for by what he saw and heard that righteous man, while living among them, felt his righteous soul tormented day after day with their lawless deeds)" (2 Pet. 2:8). He hated sin and desired righteousness. He had respect for holy angels—evidence of his fear of God (Gen. 19:1–14). He obeyed God by not looking back at Sodom when God's judgment rained down (cf. v. 26).

Lot was certainly not "carnal" in the sense that he lacked spiritual desires. Though he lived in a wicked place, he was not wicked himself. His soul was "tormented," vexed, grieved, tortured with severe pain at the sight of the evil all around him. Evidently his conscience did not become seared; he "felt his righteous soul tormented day after day" with the evil deeds of those around him. Though he lived in Sodom, he never became a Sodomite. Those who use him as an illustration of someone who is saved but utterly carnal miss the point of 2 Peter 2:8.

What is the lesson of Lot's life as Peter saw it? Verse 9 sums it up: "The Lord knows how to rescue the godly from temptation, and to keep the unrighteous under punishment for the day of judgment."

In Lot's case, one means the Lord used to rescue him from temptation was severe chastisement. Lot lost his home; his wife was killed by divine judgment; and his own daughters disgraced and debased him. He paid a terrible price for his sin, being "tormented day after day." If Lot proves anything, it is that true believers cannot sin with impunity.

God always chastens and disciplines His children who sin. If they do *not* experience chastening, they are not truly His children, but spiritual bastards. Hebrews 12:7–8 explicitly states this: "What son is there whom his father does not discipline? But if you are without discipline, of which all have become partakers, then you are illegitimate children and not sons." The specific purpose for which He disciplines us is "for our good, that we may share His holiness" (Heb. 12:10).

All of that flies in the face of the notion that millions of Christians live in a state of unbroken carnality. If these people are true children of God, why are they not constantly under His discipline?

Chief of Sinners

Perhaps the classic example of a sinning believer is the apostle Paul.

Paul? Yes. The more he matured in Christ, the more the apostle became aware of his own sinfulness. When he wrote his first epistle to the Corinthians, he referred to himself as "the least of the apostles . . . not fit to be called an apostle, because I persecuted the church of God" (1 Cor. 15:9). A few years later, when he wrote to Ephesus, he called himself "the very least of all saints" (Eph. 3:8). Near the end of his life, when he wrote to Timothy, Paul spoke of himself as "foremost of all [sinners]" (1 Tim. 1:15).

This was not clever posturing on Paul's part. He was extremely sensitive to sin in his life and painfully honest about his own struggle with sin. He grieved over his sin and battled against it constantly. Yet he was one of the greatest saints who ever lived.

How can that be? Wouldn't you think that someone of Paul's stature would be an example of victory over sin? He was. Yet he called himself a "wretched man" and "chief of sinners"? Yes. Can both things be true at once? Absolutely. In fact, the more saintly we become, the more sensitive to sin we become.

Martin Luther noted the paradox of sin in every believer's life and coined a Latin expression: *simul justus et peccator* ("just and sinful at the same time"). Every true believer wrestles with this dilemma. Our justification is complete and perfect; therefore our standing before God is faultless. But our sanctification will not be perfect until we are glorified. It is the prize of our high calling in Christ (Phil. 3:14). Paul wrote, "Not that I have already obtained it, or have already become perfect, but I press on in order that I may lay hold of that for which also I was laid hold of by Christ Jesus" (v. 12). Here on earth, our practice will never match our position, no matter how earnestly we pursue sanctification.

But pursue it we will if we are truly born again, for God Himself guarantees our perseverance in righteousness: "May the God of peace Himself sanctify you entirely; and may your spirit and soul and body be preserved complete, without blame at the coming of our Lord Jesus Christ" (1 Thess. 5:23). He "is able to keep you from stumbling, and to make you stand in the presence of His glory blameless with great joy" (Jude 24).

The classic passage on Paul's personal struggle against sin is Romans 7:14–25:

> We know that the Law is spiritual; but I am of flesh, sold into bondage to sin. For that which I am doing, I do not understand; for I am not practicing what I would like to do, but I am doing the very thing I hate. But if I do the very thing I do not wish to do, I agree with the Law, confessing that it is good. So now, no longer am I the one doing it, but sin which indwells me. For I know that nothing good dwells in me, that is, in my flesh; for the wishing is present in me, but the doing of the good is not. For the good that I wish, I do not do; but I practice the very evil that I do not wish. But if I am doing the very thing I do not wish, I am no longer the one doing it, but sin which dwells in me. I find then the principle that evil is present in me, the one who wishes to do good. For I joyfully concur with the law of God in the inner man, but I see a different law in the members of my body, waging war against the law of my mind, and making me a prisoner of the law of sin which is in my members. Wretched man that I am! Who will set me free from the body of this death? Thanks be to God through Jesus Christ our Lord! So then, on the one hand I myself with my mind am serving the law of God, but on the other, with my flesh the law of sin.

Wretched Man That I Am!

Many expositors have wondered how that passage can logically follow the great declarations in Romans 6 that believers are dead to sin (Rom. 6:2), crucified with Christ so that our body of sin might be done away with (v. 6), freed from sin (v. 7), not under law, but under grace (v. 14), and slaves of righteousness (v. 18).

Some have proposed that in Romans 7 Paul was describing his life *before Christ*. They suggest that verse 14 is the key: "I am carnal, sold under sin."

Others believe Paul was describing his life *as a carnal Christian*, before he surrendered to Christ's lordship. They point out that Paul says, "I joyfully concur with the law of God in the inner man, but I see a different law in the members of my body." They believe Paul's frequent use of the personal pronoun here reveals that this is the internal conflict of a selfish, self-righteous person, someone who is trying to become righteous in the power of his own flesh. Often "deeper life" teachers will cite this passage, urging Christians to "get out of Romans 7 and into Romans 8" in their experience with God.

But a study of the text reveals that this is neither the experience of an unbeliever nor the expression of a "carnal" Christian.[3] It was Paul's experience at the time he wrote it. Though he was one of the most spiritual saints who ever lived, he struggled with personal sin the same as all of us. Though he was used mightily of God, he battled sin and temptation. "Therefore let him who thinks he stands take heed lest he fall. No temptation has overtaken you but such as is common to man" (1 Cor. 10:12–13).

How do we know Paul was saved when he experienced what this passage describes? The change in verb tenses between verses 13 and 14 provides the first clue. In Romans 7:7–13 Paul was recounting his life

---

[3]"The best commentators in every era of the church have almost invariably applied the seventh chapter of Romans to advanced believers. The commentators who do not take this view have been, with a few bright exceptions, the Romanists, the Socinians and the Arminians. Against them is arrayed the judgement of almost all the Reformers, almost all the Puritans and the best modern evangelical divines. . . . While I ask no man to call the Reformers and Puritans 'masters,' I do ask people to read what they say on this subject, and answer their arguments, if they can. This has not been done yet! . . . Let us remember that there is a great fact which cannot be got over: on one side stand the opinions and interpretation of Reformers and Puritans, and on the other the opinions and interpretation of Romanists, Socinians and Arminians. Let that be distinctly understood." J. C. Ryle, *Holiness* (reprint, Durham, England: Evangelical Press, 1979), xxii.

before conversion and remembering the conviction he felt when he stood face-to-face with the law of God. The verbs in those verses are all in the past tense. In verses 14–25, however, the verbs are in the present tense. These verses describe the battle with sin that was Paul's present experience.

Furthermore, Paul writes, "I delight in the law of God after the inward man" (Rom. 7:22). In verse 25 he adds, "I myself with my mind am serving the law of God." No non-Christian could make that claim. "The mind set on the flesh is hostile toward God; for it does not subject itself to the law of God, for it is not even able to do so" (Rom. 8:7).

Paul further describes his often-thwarted desire to obey God: "I am not practicing what I would like to do, but I am doing the very thing I hate. . . . The wishing is present in me, but the doing of the good is not. For the good that I wish, I do not do. . . . I find then the principle that evil is present in me, the one who wishes to do good" (7:15, 18–19, 21). But back in Romans 3 Paul said that the unsaved person has no such longing to do the will of God: "There is none who understands, there is none who seeks for God. . . . There is none who does good, there is not even one. . . . There is no fear of God before their eyes" (vv. 11–12, 18). The person described in Romans 7:14–25 can only be a redeemed person.

This is no carnal Christian or someone with a low degree of sanctification. Paul's repeated use of the personal pronoun in this context emphasizes that this was his own personal experience. The verb tenses show that he did not consider himself past this stage. The conflict he describes here was one he knew well—even as an advanced Christian. God's sanctifying work in his heart is clearly evident. He says he hates sin (v. 15). He loves righteousness (vv. 19, 21). He delights in the law of God from his heart (v. 22). He thanks God for the deliverance that is his in Christ (v. 25). Those are all responses of a mature Christian, in this case a seasoned apostle; not someone floundering in the throes of a desperate state of established carnality. In fact, it is the description of a godly man whose occasional sin feels like a constant thing when set against the backdrop of his holy longings.

Romans 7:14–25 thus describes the human side of the sanctifying process. We must not set it against Romans 8, as some do, imagining that these chapters describe two separate stages of Christian growth. They simply give two different perspectives on sanctification. Romans 7 is the human perspective; Romans 8 is the divine perspective. Romans 7 is Paul's own testimony of how it is to live as a Spirit-controlled, spiritually grounded believer. He loved the holy law of God with his whole heart, yet he found himself wrapped in human flesh and unable to fulfill it the way his heart wanted to. Are there Christians anywhere who are so spiritual that they can testify to a life lived above this level? Or so carnal that they live below the level of Romans 8?

All true believers should be living at precisely this level, struggling with the tension Paul describes between an ever-increasing hunger for righteousness on the one hand, and a growing sensitivity to sin on the other. Though the degree of sin will vary depending on one's level of spiritual maturity, sin in the genuine believer should always make him or her feel the conflict Paul describes in these verses.

Though some *have* tried to claim they live above Romans 7, they only reveal their own insensitivity to the pervasive effects of sin in the flesh. If they would honestly measure themselves against God's standards of righteousness, they would realize how far they fall short. The closer we get to God, the more we see our own sin. Only immature, fleshly, and legalistic persons can live under the illusion that they measure up well by God's standards. The level of spiritual insight, brokenness, contrition, and humility that characterize the person depicted in Romans 7 are marks of a spiritual and mature believer, who before God has no trust in his own goodness and achievements.

So Romans 7 is not the cry of a carnal Christian who cares not for righteousness, but the lament of a godly Christian who, at the height of spiritual maturity, nevertheless finds himself unable to live up to the holy standard. It is also the experience of every genuine believer at every stage of spiritual development.

I am fleshly, but the law is good. Look closely at Paul's lament: "We know that the Law is spiritual; but I am of flesh, sold into bondage to sin. For that which I am doing, I do not understand; for I am not practicing what I would like to do, but I am doing the very thing I hate. But if I do the very thing I do not wish to do, I agree with the Law, confessing that it is good. So now, no longer am I the one doing it, but sin which indwells me" (Rom. 7:14–17).

Justification by faith apart from the works of the law in no way implies that the law is evil. The law is spiritual. It comes from the Spirit of God. It is a reflection of His "holy and righteous and good" nature (v. 12).

But there is a barrier that prevents every believer from always obeying God's law: our carnal or fleshly nature. Note that Paul says, "I am *of* flesh"; he doesn't say he is "*in* the flesh." Here the *flesh* (Gk., *sarx*) is not a reference to the physical body, or even a "part" of our person like the body, but the principle of human frailty—especially our sinful selfishness—which remains with us after salvation until we are ultimately glorified. "Those who are in the flesh cannot please God" (8:8). "In the flesh" is descriptive of an unregenerate condition (7:5). Christians are not "in the flesh."

Nevertheless, the flesh is still in us. We are made "of flesh"; that is, we are human. And that is the problem: "I know that nothing good dwells in me, that is, in my flesh. . . . On the one hand I myself with my mind am serving the law of God, but on the other, with my flesh the law of sin" (7:18, 25). *Flesh,* used in this context, refers to our fallenness. It taints all the facets of the total person—including our mind, emotions, and body. This residual fallenness—the flesh—is what drags us repeatedly into sin, although we hate and despise sin.

That is what Paul meant in verse 14 when he said, "I am of flesh, sold into bondage to sin." That phrase "sold into bondage to sin" at first seems to pose a problem, as does a similar phrase in verse 23: "prisoner of the law of sin which is in my members." Is Paul contradicting what he said in Romans 6:14: "Sin shall not be master over you, for you are not under law, but under grace"? No, "sold into bondage to sin" doesn't mean Paul actively committed himself to sinning. He was only acknowledging that his flesh kept dragging him back into committing the very sins he hated.

This is the state of every true believer. We are no longer related to our former father, the devil (John 8:44); we no longer love the world (1 John 2:15); and we are no longer sin's slaves—but our flesh is still subject to sin's deceit and still attracted by many of its allurements. Yet as Christians we cannot be happy with our sin, because it is contrary to who we are in Christ and we know it grieves our Lord.

Sin grieves the Holy Spirit (Eph. 4:30), dishonors God (1 Cor. 6:19–20), keeps our prayers from being answered (1 Pet. 3:12), causes good things from God to be withheld (Jer. 5:25), robs us of the joy of our salvation (Ps. 51:12), inhibits spiritual growth (1 Cor. 3:1), brings chastisement from the Lord (Heb. 12:5–7), prevents us from being fit vessels for the Lord to use (2 Tim. 2:21), pollutes Christian fellowship (1 Cor. 10:21), and can even endanger our physical life and health (1 Cor. 11:29–30). No wonder true Christians hate sin.

One unbeliever, upon hearing the truth of justification by faith, commented, "If I believed that salvation is free through faith alone, I would believe and then take my fill of sin." The person witnessing to him wisely replied, "How much sin do you think it would take to fill a true Christian to satisfaction?" A person who has not lost any of his appetite for sin—and acquired instead a hunger for the things of God—has not been truly converted. "What are our tastes and choices and likings and inclinations? This is the great testing question."[4]

Here Paul confirms that the appetites and desires of the true believer's inner man are governed by the law of God: "I joyfully concur with the law of God in the inner man, but I see a different law in the members of my body, waging war against the law of my mind, and making me a prisoner of the law of sin which is in my members" (7:22–23).

The wishing is present in me, but the doing of the good is not. Every true Christian can echo Paul's lament. We concur that God's law is good. We desire to obey it. Yet we cannot rid ourselves of sin. We are bound hand and foot by our own human frailty. Sin is in our very members. Self-righteous people deceive themselves into thinking they are moral and good, but Romans 7 shows that a true Christian led by the Spirit will not. The more spiritual Christian is all the more aware of indwelling sin. The sin in our members cannot win all the time—and it will ultimately fail to defeat us—but it perpetually frustrates our attempts to obey God perfectly.

Paul says, "Nothing good dwells in me, that is, in my flesh" (v. 18). There's a big difference between surviving sin and reigning sin: Sin no longer reigns in us (6:18–19), but it does survive in us (7:20). Galatians 5:17 says, "The flesh sets its desire against the Spirit, and the Spirit against the flesh; for these are in opposition to one another, so that you may not do the things that you please." Romans 7 simply describes that battle in its hideous detail. But Galatians 5:16 tells us how to win: "Walk by the Spirit, and you will not carry out the desire of the flesh." The Holy Spirit gives us victory.

But that victory seems to come with frustrating languor. In verses 18–19 Paul writes, "The wishing is present in me, but the doing of the good is not. For the good that I wish, I do not do; but I practice the very evil that I do not wish." He is not saying he is incapable of doing *anything* right. He is saying that his *desire* to obey is always greater than his own *ability* to obey. This is the pattern of spiritual growth: As our hatred for sin increases and our capacity for victory over sin is enlarged, our frustration with the remnants of sin in the flesh is also intensified. In other words, our sensitivity to indwelling sin is inversely proportional to our experience of victory. The more we defeat sin in our lives, the more aware of its presence we become.

---

[4]Ryle, *Holiness*, 30.

Here is the crucial point: Paul was not saying he had a bent toward sinning. Just the opposite is true. His inclination was toward righteousness. He was simply frustrated by the pull of his sinful flesh.

Again, this is not the testimony of a someone living in a carelessly "carnal" state. In his heart Paul longed for righteousness, hungered to obey God, loved the law of God, and wanted to do good. That is the direction of every true Christian, regardless of where we are in the sanctifying process.

I joyfully concur with the law. "I find then the principle that evil is present in me, the one who wishes to do good. For I joyfully concur with the law of God in the inner man, but I see a different law in the members of my body, waging war against the law of my mind, and making me a prisoner of the law of sin which is in my members" (vv. 21–23).

It was not Paul's conscience that was bothering him. He was not lamenting some unforgiven sin or describing a defiant refusal to follow the Lord. What troubled him was his inner man, recreated in the likeness of Christ and indwelt by His Spirit. That inner person, having seen something of the true holiness, goodness, and glory of God's law, was grieved at the least infraction or falling short of it. In glaring contrast to his preconversion self-satisfaction (cf. Phil. 3:6), Paul now realized how wretchedly short of God's perfect law he lived, even as a Spirit-indwelt believer and an apostle of Jesus Christ.

That spirit of humble contrition is a mark of every true disciple of Christ, who cries out, "Lord, I can't be all you want me to be. I am unable to fulfill your perfect, holy, and glorious law." In great frustration and remorse we must sorrowfully confess with Paul, "I am not always practicing what I would like to do."

Paul delighted in God's law. The phrase "in the inner man" could be translated, "from the bottom of my heart." Emanating from the depths of his soul, Paul had a great love for the law of God. His inner man, the part that "is being renewed day by day" (2 Cor. 4:16) and "strengthened with power through [God's] Spirit" (Eph. 3:16), resonated with God's law. The source of his problems was the principle of frailty and fallenness that is inherent in human nature.

The author of Psalm 119 experienced the same conflict Paul did. His psalm reflects his deep longing for the things of God. Here are some sample expressions of the psalmist's desire for God's law:

- Verses 81–83: "My soul languishes for Thy salvation; I wait for Thy word. My eyes fail with longing for Thy word, while I say, "When wilt Thou comfort me?" Though I have become like a wineskin in the smoke, I do not forget Thy statutes."

- Verse 92: "If Thy law had not been my delight, then I would have perished in my affliction."
- Verse 97: "O how I love Thy law! It is my meditation all the day."
- Verse 113: "I hate those who are double-minded, but I love Thy law."
- Verse 131: "I opened my mouth wide and panted, for I longed for Thy commandments."
- Verse 143: "Trouble and anguish have come upon me; yet Thy commandments are my delight."
- Verse 163: "I hate and despise falsehood, but I love Thy law."
- Verse 165: "Those who love Thy law have great peace, and nothing causes them to stumble."
- Verse 174: "I long for Thy salvation, O Lord, and Thy law is my delight."

The measure of spirituality the psalmist expresses is intimidating. Clearly he was captivated by an overwhelming love for the things of God. That is why the last verse in Psalm 119 is so surprising: "I have gone astray like a lost sheep; seek Thy servant, for I do not forget Thy commandments" (v. 176). You might think that a person with such an intense love for God's law would not experience the failure of going astray spiritually. But that is the conflict all believers experience.

Why do we sin? Because God didn't do a good enough job when He saved us? Because He gave us a new nature that isn't complete yet? Because we're not prepared for heaven yet and still need to earn our way in?

No, because sin is still present in our flesh.

On the one hand . . . but on the other . . . "Wretched man that I am! Who will set me free from the body of this death? Thanks be to God through Jesus Christ our Lord! So then, on the one hand I myself with my mind am serving the law of God, but on the other, with my flesh the law of sin" (Rom. 7:24–25).

Paul thus lets out a final wail of distress and frustration. Again, he echoes the psalmist: "Out of the depths I have cried to Thee, O Lord. Lord, hear my voice! Let Thine ears be attentive to the voice of my supplications. If Thou, Lord, shouldst mark iniquities, O Lord, who could stand? But there is forgiveness with Thee, that Thou mayest be feared. I wait for the Lord, my soul does wait, and in His word do I hope" (Ps. 130:1–5).

Paul was surely in a similar frame of mind when he said, "Who will set me free from the body of this death?" But Paul answers his own question: "I thank God through Jesus Christ, our Lord" (v. 25). Paul was assured of ultimate triumph over the sin in his own flesh: "I consider that the sufferings of this present time are not worthy to be compared with the glory that is to be revealed to us. For the anxious longing of the creation waits eagerly for the revealing of the sons of God" (8:18–19). The final phase of our salvation is guaranteed: "Whom He justified, these He also glorified" (8:30). "This perishable must put on the imperishable, and this mortal must put on immortality. . . . But thanks be to God, who gives us the victory through our Lord Jesus Christ" (1 Cor. 15:53, 57). "Indeed while we are in this tent, we groan, being burdened, because we do not want to be unclothed, but to be clothed, in order that what is mortal may be swallowed up by life" (2 Cor. 5:4). "We eagerly wait for a Savior, the Lord Jesus Christ; who will transform the body of our humble state into conformity with the body of His glory" (Phil. 3:20–21). Ours is a triumphant hope!

Yet for now the battle goes on. Full deliverance awaits glorification. Victory here and now is only possible bit by bit as we mortify the deeds of the body through the power of the Holy Spirit: "Therefore consider the members of your earthly body as dead to immorality, impurity, passion, evil desire, and greed, which amounts to idolatry" (Col. 3:5). "For if you are living according to the flesh, you must die; but if by the Spirit you are putting to death the deeds of the body, you will live" (Rom. 8:13).

We are bound to be frustrated by our inability to experience holiness to the degree we desire. That is the inevitable experience of every true saint of God. Because of our flesh we can never in this life achieve the level of holiness to which we aspire. "We ourselves, having the first fruits of the Spirit, even we ourselves groan within ourselves, waiting eagerly for our adoption as sons, the redemption of our body" (Rom. 8:23). But that hope only further inflames our aspirations to holiness.

"Beloved, now we are children of God, and it has not appeared as yet what we shall be. We know that, when He appears, we shall be like Him, because we shall see Him just as He is. Everyone who has this hope fixed on Him purifies himself, just as He is pure" (1 John 3:2–3).

9

The Faith That *Doesn't* Work

Sanctification . . . is the invariable result of that vital union with Christ which true faith gives to a Christian. "He that abideth in Me, and I in him, the same bringeth forth much fruit" (John 15:5). The branch which bears no fruit is no living branch of the vine. The union with Christ which produces no effect on heart and life is a mere formal union, which is worthless before God. The faith which has not a sanctifying influence on the character is no better than the faith of devils. It is a "dead faith, because it is alone." It is not the gift of God. It is not the faith of God's elect. In short, where there is no sanctification of life, there is no real faith in Christ. True faith worketh by love. It constrains a man to live unto the Lord from a deep sense of gratitude for redemption. It makes him feel that he can never do too much for Him that died for him. Being much forgiven, he loves much. He whom the blood cleanses walks in the light. He who has real lively hope in Christ purifieth himself even as He is pure (James 2:17–20; Titus 1:1; Gal. 5:6; 1 John 1:7; 3:3).

J. C. Ryle[1]

A tract written by one of the most extreme defenders of no-lordship salvation seeks to explain redemption: "Even at your best, you can never earn or deserve a relationship with God. Only the object of your faith,

---

[1]J. C. Ryle, *Holiness* (reprint, Durham, England: Evangelical Press, 1979), 17.

Jesus Christ, has the merit." I agree with that. It is the clear teaching of
Scripture (Titus 3:5–7).

But the same tract also says, "Your personal sins are not an issue to
God." When the author attempts to explain *faith* in practical terms, he
says this: "You respond to God the Father by simply forming the words
privately in your mind, 'I believe in Christ.'"[2]

All of that adds up to a notion of faith that is little more than a
mental gambit. The "faith" that tract describes is not much more than
a cursory nod of the head. It is bare *intellectual assent.*

As I noted in chapter 3, many no-lordship apologists resent being
accused of portraying faith as mere mental acquiescence. Dr. Ryrie, for
example, calls it a straw-man argument.

> Being convinced of something or putting one's trust in the Gos-
> pel could hardly be said to be a casual acceptance of something.
> When a person gives credence to the historical facts that Christ
> died and rose from the dead and the doctrinal fact that this was for
> his sins, he is trusting his eternal destiny to the reliability of those
> truths. . . . Make no mistake, non-lordship people do *not* say
> what [this] straw man . . . alleges they say (*SGS* 30).

But many no-lordship people *do* say precisely what Ryrie denies they say.
Zane Hodges, for example, practically concedes that "intellectual assent" adequately describes his idea of faith. He is uncomfortable with
that phrase's "prejudicial connotation," but he doggedly defends its
gist. *Assent,* he points out, simply means "meaningful agreement." The
negative undertone, Hodges suggests, is caused by modifiers like *mental* or *intellectual.* Though they mean "nothing more than 'of or pertaining to the intellect,'" he says, they are often taken to imply
"detachment and personal disinterest" (*AF* 30). "In this context we
should discard words like mental or intellectual altogether," Hodges
adds. "The Bible knows nothing about an intellectual faith as over
against some other kind of faith (like emotional or volitional). What the
Bible does recognize is the obvious distinction between faith and unbelief!" (*AF* 30).

How does Hodges describe faith? "What faith really is, in biblical
language, is receiving the testimony of God. It is the *inward conviction*

---

[2]R. B. Thieme, Jr., "A Matter of Life [and] Death: The Gospel of Jesus Christ" (Hous-
ton: Thieme Bible Ministries, 1990), 10–12.

that what God says to us in the gospel is true. That—and that alone—is saving faith" (*AF* 31, emphasis in original).[3]

Is that an adequate characterization of what it means to believe? Is faith totally passive? Is it true that people know intuitively whether their faith is real? Do all genuinely saved people have full assurance? Cannot someone be deceived into thinking he is a believer when in fact he is not? Can a person *think* he believes yet not truly believe? Is there no such thing as spurious faith?

Scripture plainly and repeatedly answers those questions. The apostles saw counterfeit faith as a very real danger. Many of the epistles, though addressed to churches, contain warnings that reveal the apostles' concern over church members they suspected were not genuine believers. Paul, for example, wrote to the Corinthian church, "Test yourselves to see if you are in the faith; examine yourselves! Or do you not recognize this about yourselves, that Jesus Christ is in you—unless indeed you fail the test?" (2 Cor. 13:5). Peter wrote, "Therefore, brethren, be all the more diligent to make certain about His calling and choosing you; for as long as you practice these things, you will never stumble" (2 Pet. 1:10).

Evidently there were some in the very early church who flirted with the notion that faith could be some kind of static, inert, inanimate assent to facts.[4] The Book of James, probably the earliest New Testament epistle, specifically confronts this error. James sounds almost as if he were writing to twentieth-century no-lordship advocates. He says people *can* be deluded into thinking they believe when in fact they do not, and he says the single factor that distinguishes bogus faith from the real thing is the righteous behavior inevitably produced by authentic faith.

These are the questions the lordship debate must ultimately answer: Is it enough to know and understand and assent to the facts of the gospel—even holding the "*inward conviction*" that these truths apply to me personally—and yet *never* shun sin or submit to the Lord Jesus? Is a

---

[3]By emphasizing the words "inward conviction" and underscoring them with the phrase "that—and that alone," Hodges is explicitly rejecting the concept that faith inevitably produces righteous behavior. In contrast, the Reformers had a saying: "Faith alone saves, but the faith that saves is *never* alone."

[4]"Probably as a reaction from justification by works of the law a fallacy had sprung up among the Jewish Christians that faith in Christ existing as an inactive principle, a mere speculative belief, would suffice without works. St. James shows what an impossible position this is." Arthur Carr, "The General Epistle of St. James," *Cambridge Greek Testament for Schools and Colleges* (Cambridge: Cambridge University Press, 1896), 35.

person who holds that kind of belief guaranteed eternal life? Does such a hope constitute faith in the sense Scripture uses the term?

James is expressly teaching that it does not. Real faith, he says, will no doubt produce righteous behavior. The true character of saving faith may be examined in light of the believer's works. This is consistent with all Old Testament and New Testament soteriology. One enters into salvation by grace through faith (Eph. 2:8–9). Faith is by nature turned and toned toward obedience (Acts 5:32; Rom. 1:5, 2:8, 16:26), so good works are inevitable in the life of one who truly believes. These works have no part in bringing about salvation (Eph. 2:9; Rom. 3:20, 24; 4:5; Titus 3:5), but they show that salvation is indeed present (Eph. 2:10; 5:9; 1 John 2:5).

"It is evident that there is faith and FAITH," Roy Aldrich wrote in reference to James 2. "There is nominal faith and real faith. There is intellectual faith and heart faith. There is sensual faith and there is spiritual faith. There is dead faith and there is vital faith. There is traditional faith which may fall short of transforming personal faith. There is a faith that may be commended as orthodox and yet have no more saving value than the faith of demons."[5] James attacks all brands of "faith" that fall short of the biblical standard. What I and others have sometimes termed "mental acquiescence" or "intellectual assent," James characterizes as mere hearing, empty profession, demonic orthodoxy, and dead faith.

Mere Hearing

James wrote, "Prove yourselves doers of the word, and not merely hearers who delude themselves" (1:22). James uses a substantive (*pōietai*) "doers of the word," or "Word-doers" instead of a straightforward imperative ("do the word"). He is describing characteristic behavior, not occasional activity. It is one thing to fight; it is something else to be a soldier. It is one thing to build a shed; it is something else to be a builder. James is not merely challenging his readers to *do the Word;* he is telling them real Christians are *doers of the Word.* That describes the basic disposition of those who believe unto salvation.

Hearing is important, as James has emphasized in 1:19–21. Faith comes by hearing (Rom. 10:17). However, actual faith must be something *more* than mere hearing. Hearing is a means, not an end. The end is faith, which results in obedience.

---

[5]Roy L. Aldrich, "Some Simple Difficulties of Salvation," *Bibliotheca Sacra* 111/442 (April-June 1954): 167.

True believers cannot be hearers only. The Greek word for "hearer" (v. 22) is *akroatēs,* a term used to describe students who audited a class. An auditor usually listens to the lectures, but is permitted to treat assignments and exams as optional. Many people in the church today approach spiritual truth with an auditor's mentality, receiving God's Word only passively. But James' point, shown by his illustrations in verses 23–27, is that merely hearing God's Word results in worthless religion (v. 26). In other words, mere hearing is no better than unbelief or outright rejection. In fact, it's worse! The hearer-only is enlightened but unregenerate. James is reiterating truth he undoubtedly heard first-hand from the Lord Himself. Jesus warned powerfully against the error of hearing without doing (Matt. 7:21–27), as did the apostle Paul (Rom. 2:13–25).

James says hearing without obeying is self-deception (v. 22). The Greek term for "delude" (*paralogizomai*) means "to reason against." It speaks of skewed logic. Those who believe it is enough to hear the Word without obeying make a gross miscalculation. They deceive themselves. Robert Johnstone wrote,

> Knowing that the study of divine truth, through reading the Bible, giving attendance on the public ordinances of grace, and otherwise, is a most important duty,is, indeed, the road leading toward the gate of everlasting life,they allow themselves, through man's natural aversion to all genuine spirituality, to be persuaded by the wicked one that this is the sum of all Christian duty, and itself the gate of life, so that in mere "hearing" they enter in, and all is well with them. To rest satisfied with the means of grace, without yielding up our hearts to their power as means, so as to receive the grace and exhibit its working in our lives, is manifestly folly of the same class as that of a workman who should content himself with possessing tools, without using them,madness of the same class as that of a man perishing with hunger, who should exult in having bread in his hands, without eating it,but folly and madness as immeasurably greater than these, as the "work of God" (John vi. 29) transcends in importance the work of an earthly artisan, and "life with Christ in God" the perishable existence of earth.[6]

James gives two illustrations that contrast hearers-only with obedient hearers.

---

[6]Robert Johnstone, *Lectures Exegetical and Practical on the Epistle of James* (reprint, Minneapolis: Klock & Klock, 1978), 144.

The mirror. "For if anyone is a hearer of the word and not a doer, he is like a man who looks at his natural face in a mirror; for once he has looked at himself and gone away, he has immediately forgotten what kind of person he was. But one who looks intently at the perfect law, the law of liberty, and abides by it, not having become a forgetful hearer but an effectual doer, this man shall be blessed in what he does" (1:23–25).

"Not a doer" is literally "a not-doer," or someone whose disposition is to hear without doing. Contrary to some commentators, "looks . . . in a mirror" does not describe a hasty or casual glance. The verb (*katanoeō*) means "to look carefully, cautiously, observantly." "The man carefully studies his face and becomes thoroughly familiar with its features. [He] listens to the Word, apparently not momentarily but at length, so that he understands what he hears. He knows what God expects him to do. Any failure to respond cannot be blamed on lack of understanding."[7] James' point is not that this man failed to look long enough, or intently enough, or sincerely enough—but that he turned away without taking any action. "He has immediately forgotten what kind of person he was" (v. 24). This passage is reminiscent of the unproductive soils in Matthew 13. The person who hears the Word does not have the proper heart response. Therefore that which has been sown cannot bear fruit.

The point is twofold. First, James is illustrating *the urgency of actively obeying the Word*. If you don't deal with what you see while you are looking into the mirror, you will forget about it later. By Monday morning you may forget the impact of Sunday's sermon. By this afternoon, this morning's readings might be a dim memory. If you do not make the necessary responses while God is convicting your heart, you will probably not get around to it. The image reflected in the mirror of God's Word will soon fade.

Second, and more pointedly, James is illustrating *the utter uselessness of passively receiving the Word*. Verse 21 spoke of how we are to receive the Word: "Therefore putting aside all filthiness and all that remains of wickedness, in humility receive the word implanted, which is able to save your souls." The conjunction *but* at the beginning of verse 22 is equivalent to *moreover*, or *now*, implying that what follows is not a contrast but an amplification of the command in verse 21. In other words, James is saying it is wonderful to be receptive to the Word—to hear with approval and agreement—but that is not enough.

---

[7]Donald W. Burdick, "James," in *The Expositor's Bible Commentary,* ed. Frank E. Gaebelein (Grand Rapids, Mich.: Zondervan, 1981), 11:175.

We must receive it as those who would be doers. Non-doers are not true believers.

James gives a contrasting example. This is the effectual doer: "one who looks intently at the perfect law, the law of liberty, and abides by it, not having become a forgetful hearer but an effectual doer, this man shall be blessed in what he does" (1:25). The word translated "looks intently" is *parakuptō*, the same word used in John 20:5, 11 to describe how John stooped to peer into Jesus' empty tomb. The word is also used in 1 Peter 1:12 of the angels who long to look into things concerning the gospel. It speaks of a deep and absorbing look, as when someone stoops for a closer examination. Hiebert says the word "pictures the man as bending over the mirror on the table in order to examine more minutely what is revealed therein."[8] Implied is a longing to understand for reasons that go beyond the academic.

This is a description of the true believer. In contrast to the hearer-only, "he bent over the mirror, and, gripped by what he saw, he continued looking and obeying its precepts. This feature marks his crucial difference to the first man."[9] This man is gazing into "the perfect law, the law of liberty" (v. 25). That refers to the gospel in its fullest sense— the whole counsel of God, the implanted word that saves (v. 21). Burdick writes,

> It is not merely the OT law, nor is it the Mosaic law perverted to become a legalistic system for earning salvation by good works. When James calls it the "perfect law," he has in mind the sum total of God's revealed truth—not merely the preliminary portion found in the OT, but also the final revelation made through Christ and his Apostles that was soon to be inscripturated in the NT. Thus it is complete, in contrast to that which is preliminary and preparatory. Furthermore, it is the "law of liberty" (Gr.), by which James means that it does not enslave. It is not forced by external compulsion. Instead, it is freely accepted and fulfilled with glad devotion under the enablements of the Spirit of God (Gal. 5:22-23).[10]

James is not speaking of law in contrast to gospel. "The perfect law of liberty" *is* the implanted Word (v. 21). Those who understand the phrase "the perfect law of liberty" to mean something separate from the

---

[8]D. Edmond Hiebert, *The Epistle of James* (Chicago: Moody, 1979), 135–36.

[9]Ibid.

[10]Burdick, "James," 176.

gospel miss James' point. In describing the man who looks at the Word, continues in it, and is blessed, he is portraying the effect of true conversion.[11]

Does this mean all true believers are doers of the Word? Yes. Do they *always* put the Word into practice? No—or a pastor's task would be relatively simple. Believers do fail, and they sometimes fail in appalling ways. But even when they fail, true believers will not altogether cease having the disposition and motivation of one who is a doer. James, then, offers these words as both a reminder to the true believer (the "effectual doer," v. 25), and a challenge to unbelievers who have identified with the truth but are not obedient to it (the "forgetful hearer[s]").

The unbridled tongue. James further illustrates the deceptive nature of hearing without obeying: "If anyone thinks himself to be religious, and yet does not bridle his tongue but deceives his own heart, this man's religion is worthless. This is pure and undefiled religion in the sight of our God and Father, to visit orphans and widows in their distress, and to keep oneself unstained by the world" (1:26–27).

The word translated "religious" in verse 26 is *thrēskos,* a word often used in reference to ceremonial public worship. It is the word Josephus used, for example, when he described the worship of the Temple. *Thrēskeia* ("religion," vv. 26–27) is the same word Paul used in Acts 26:5 to refer to the tradition of the Pharisees. It emphasizes the externals of ceremony, ritual, liturgy, and so on. James is saying that all such things, when divorced from meaningful obedience, are worthless.

All of us struggle to control our tongues. It was James who wrote, "For we all stumble in many ways. If anyone does not stumble in what he says, he is a perfect man, able to bridle the whole body as well" (3:2). But this man's tongue is like an unbridled horse. He lets it run wild while deceiving his own heart (1:26). He is not battling a transitory lapse in tongue control. He is dominated by a pattern that characterizes his very nature. Though he professes to be religious, his character is out of sync with his claim. While he undoubtedly thinks of himself as righteous, he is misled about the efficacy of his own religion.

Despite this man's external religion, his constantly unbridled and out-of-control tongue demonstrates a deceived and unholy heart, for "the things that proceed out of the mouth come from the heart" (Matt.

---

[11]James' statement that the Word-doer will be blessed parallels Jesus' own words in John 13:17: "If you know these things, you are blessed if you do them," and Luke 11:28: "Blessed are those who hear the word of God, and observe it." The "blessing" these verses speak of is the birthright of all who are redeemed.

15:18). "The good man out of the good treasure of his heart brings forth what is good; and the evil man out of the evil treasure brings forth what is evil; for his mouth speaks from that which fills his heart" (Luke 6:45). Our Lord warned, "By your words you shall be justified, and by your words you shall be condemned" (Matt. 12:37).

Kistemaker notes the significance of the expression "deceiving his own heart":

> This is the third time that James tells his readers not to deceive themselves (1:16, 22, 26). As a pastor he is fully aware of counterfeit religion that is nothing more than external formalism. He knows that many people merely go through the motions of serving God, but their speech gives them away. Their religion has a hollow ring. And although they do not realize it, by their words and by their actions— or lack of them—they deceive themselves. Their heart is not right with God and their fellow man, and their attempt to hide this lack of love only heightens their self-deception. Their religion is worthless.[12]

This worthless religion contrasts sharply with the true religion that is "pure and undefiled . . . in the sight of our God and Father, to visit orphans and widows in their distress, and to keep oneself unstained by the world" (v. 27). James is not here attempting to define religion, but rather to set forth a concrete illustration of the principle he began with: that true religion involves more than mere hearing. True saving faith will inevitably bear the fruit of good works.

Empty Profession

The first thirteen verses of James 2 continue to expand on James' contention that believers are by disposition doers of the Word, not mere hearers. He confronts the problem of favoritism, which evidently had arisen in the church or churches James was writing to. Bearing in mind that this is the context, we move ahead to James 2:14. Here, after warning his readers that they were facing judgment for their unholy and unmerciful behavior (v. 13), James turns to the heart of the matter: their apparent misconception that faith is an inert ingredient in the salvation formula. His challenge could not be clearer:

> What use is it, my brethren, *if a man says he has faith, but he has no works? Can that faith save him?* If a brother or sister is without

---

[12]Simon J. Kistemaker, *Exposition of the Epistle of James* (Grand Rapids, Mich.: Baker, 1986), 64.

clothing and in need of daily food, and one of you says to them, "Go in peace, be warmed and be filled," and yet you do not give them what is necessary for their body, what use is that? Even so *faith, if it has no works, is dead, being by itself.* But someone may well say, "You have faith, and I have works; show me your faith without the works, and I will show you my faith by my works." You believe that God is one. You do well; the demons also believe, and shudder. But are you willing to recognize, you foolish fellow, that *faith without works is useless?* Was not Abraham our father justified by works, when he offered up Isaac his son on the altar? You see that faith was working with his works, and as a result of the works, faith was perfected; and the Scripture was fulfilled which says, "And Abraham believed God, and it was reckoned to him as righteousness," and he was called the friend of God. You see that *a man is justified by works, and not by faith alone.* And in the same way was not Rahab the harlot also justified by works, when she received the messengers and sent them out by another way? For just as the body without the spirit is dead, so also *faith without works is dead.*

James 2:14–26, emphasis added

No less than five times in that passage (vv. 14, 17, 20, 24, 26), James reiterates his thesis: passive faith is not efficacious faith. It is a frontal attack on the empty profession of those whose hope is in a dormant faith.

Reicke writes, "It must be noted that the discussion is about a person who only asserts that he has faith. This person has no real faith, since his faith does not find expression in deeds. The author does not take issue with faith itself, but with a superficial conception of it which permits faith to be only a formal concession. He desires to point out that a Christianity of mere words does not lead to salvation."[13] Cranfield likewise observes, "The clue to the understanding of the section is the fact (very often ignored) that in verse 14 . . . the author has not said, 'if a man have faith,' but 'if a man say he hath faith.' This fact should be allowed to control our interpretation of the whole paragraph. . . . The burden of this section is not (as is often supposed) that we are saved through faith plus works, but that we are saved through genuine, as opposed to counterfeit, faith."[14]

James cannot be teaching that salvation is earned by works. He has already described salvation as a "good thing bestowed" and a "perfect

[13]Bo Reicke, "The Epistles of James, Peter and John" *The Anchor Bible* (Garden City, N.Y.: Doubleday, 1964), 37:32.

[14]C. E. B. Cranfield, "The Message of James," *The Scottish Journal of Theology* 18/3 (September 1965): 338.

gift" given when "in the exercise of His will [God] brought us forth by the word of truth, so that we might be, as it were, the first fruits among His creatures" (1:17–18). Faith is part and parcel of that perfect gift. It is supernaturally bestowed by God, not independently conceived in the mind or will of the individual believer.

As we noted in chapter 3, faith is not a wistful longing, or a blind confidence, or even "*inward conviction.*" It is a supernatural certainty, an understanding of spiritual realities "which eye has not seen and ear has not heard, and which have not entered the heart of man, all that God has prepared for those who love Him. For to us God revealed them through the Spirit; for the Spirit searches all things, even the depths of God" (1 Cor. 2:9–10). Faith is a gift of God, not something conjured up by human effort, so no one can boast—not even about his faith (cf. Eph. 2:8–9).

In the phrase "if a man says he has faith, but he has no works" (v. 14), the verbs are present tense. They describe someone who routinely claims to be a believer yet continuously lacks any external evidence of faith. The question "Can that faith save him?" employs the Greek negative particle *mē,* indicating that a negative reply is assumed. It might literally be rendered, "That faith cannot save him, can it?" James, like the apostle John, challenges the authenticity of a profession of faith that produces no fruit (cf. 1 John 2:4, 5, 9). The context indicates that the "works" he speaks of are not anyone's bid to earn eternal life. These are acts of compassion (v. 15).

Faith in this context is clearly *saving* faith (v. 1). James is speaking of eternal salvation. He has referred to "the word implanted, which is able to save your souls" in 1:21. Here he has the same salvation in view. He is not disputing whether faith saves. Rather, he is opposing the notion that faith can be a passive, fruitless, intellectual exercise and still save. Where there are no works, we must assume no faith exists either. On this matter James merely echoes Jesus, who said, "You will know them by their fruits. Grapes are not gathered from thorn bushes, nor figs from thistles, are they? Even so, every good tree bears good fruit; but the bad tree bears bad fruit. A good tree cannot produce bad fruit, nor can a bad tree produce good fruit" (Matt. 7:16–18). No works, no faith. Real faith *inevitably* produces faith-works.

Here even Charles Ryrie sounds like an advocate of "lordship salvation":

> Can a non-working, dead, spurious faith save a person? James is not saying that we are saved by works, but that a faith that does not produce good works is a dead faith. . . .

Unproductive faith cannot save, because it is not genuine faith. Faith and works are like a two-coupon ticket to heaven. The coupon of works is not good for passage, and the coupon of faith is not valid if detached from works.[15]

James follows with an illustration comparing faith without works to phony compassion, words without action: "If a brother or sister is without clothing and in need of daily food, and one of you says to them, 'Go in peace, be warmed and be filled,' and yet you do not give them what is necessary for their body, what use is that?" (2:15–16). The faith of a false professor is similarly useless: "Even so faith, if it has no works, is dead, being by itself" (v. 17).

James concludes with a challenge to those whose profession is suspect: "But someone may well say, 'You have faith, and I have works; show me your faith without the works, and I will show you my faith by my works'" (v. 18). Commentators disagree on whether "someone" refers to an objector and how much of the discourse that follows is to be attributed to this "someone" as opposed to James himself.[16] However one reads it, the essential point James is making is clear: The only possible evidence of faith is works. How can anyone show faith without works? It cannot be done.

Barnes distills the sense of the passage:

> James was not arguing against real and genuine faith, nor against its importance in justification, but against the supposition that mere faith was all that was necessary to save a man, whether it was accompanied by good works or not. *He* maintains that if there is genuine faith it will always be accompanied by good works, and that it is only *that* faith which can justify and save. If it leads to no practical holiness of life . . . it is of no value whatever.[17]

Demonic Orthodoxy

James continues his assault on passive faith with this shocking statement: "You believe that God is one. You do well; the demons also

---

[15]Charles C. Ryrie, ed., *The Ryrie Study Bible* (Chicago: Moody, 1978), 1859–60.

[16]Hiebert, *The Epistle of James*, 182–85; see also Zane C. Hodges, "Light on James Two," *Bibliotheca Sacra* 120/480 (October-December 1963): 341–50.

[17]Albert Barnes, *Notes on the New Testament* (reprint, Grand Rapids, Mich.: Baker, 1983), 13:50.

believe, and shudder" (v. 19). Orthodox doctrine by itself is no proof of saving faith. Demons affirm the oneness of God and tremble at its implications, but they are not redeemed. Matthew 8:29 tells of a group of demons who recognized Jesus as the Son of God. They even exhibited fear. Demons often acknowledge the existence and authority of Christ (Matt. 8:29–30; Mark 5:7), His deity (Luke 4:41), and even His resurrection (Acts 19:15), but their diabolical nature is not changed by what they know and believe. Their fearful affirmation of orthodox doctrine is not the same as saving faith.

James implies that demonic faith is greater than the fraudulent faith of a false professor, for demonic faith produces fear, whereas unsaved men have "no fear of God before their eyes" (Rom. 3:18). If the demons believe, tremble, and are not saved, what does that say about those who profess to believe and don't even tremble? (cf. Isa. 66:2, 5).[18]

Puritan Thomas Manton perfectly sums up the subtly deceptive nature of the sterile orthodoxy that constitutes demonic faith:

> [It is] a simple and naked assent to such things as are propounded in the word of God, and maketh men more knowing but not better, not more holy or heavenly. They that have it may believe the promises, the doctrines, the precepts as well as the histories . . . but yet, lively saving faith it is not, for he who hath that, findeth his heart engaged to Christ, and doth so believe the promises of the gospel concerning pardon of sins and life eternal that he seeketh after them as his happiness, and doth so believe the mysteries of our redemption by Christ that all his hope and peace and confidence is drawn from thence, and doth so believe the threatenings, whether of temporal plagues or eternal damnation, as that, in comparison with them, all the frightful things of the world are nothing.[19]

---

[18]Lenski writes, "'Thou doest well!' is certainly irony since it is followed by: 'Even the demons believe it and—shudder!' The verb denotes terror which makes one's hair stand on end. This comes like a thunderclap. No more stunning illustration of dead faith has ever been presented. Yes, even the demons have faith. Will this 'someone' tell them that is enough? Will he intimate that the demons are saved by their faith; that the Christian to whom he says: 'Thou hast [professed] faith,' needs no better faith?" R. C. H. Lenski, *The Interpretation of the Epistle to the Hebrews and the Epistle of James* (Minneapolis: Augsburg, 1966), 585.

[19]Thomas Manton, *The Complete Works of Thomas Manton* (London: Nisbet, 1874), 17:113–14.

Dead Faith

James utters his strongest rebuke so far: "Are you willing to recognize, you foolish fellow, that faith without works is useless?" (2:20). He labels the objector "foolish," meaning "empty, defective." The man is hollow, because he lacks a living faith; his claim that he believes is fraudulent; his faith is a sham.

Hiebert writes, "'Wilt thou know' (*theleis gnōnai*), 'are you willing to know,' implies an unwillingness by the objector to face the issue. His unwillingness to agree with the truth set forth is not due to any obscurity of the subject but to his reluctance to acknowledge the truth. The aorist infinitive rendered 'know' also can mean 'recognize' or 'acknowledge' and calls for a definite act of acknowledgment by the objector. His refusal to do so would imply inner perversity of will."[20]

Both "faith" and "works" in verse 20 carry definite articles in the Greek ("the faith without the works"). "Useless" is *argē*, meaning "barren, unproductive." The sense seems to be that it is unproductive for salvation. The King James Version uses the word *dead*. Certainly that is the sense conveyed here (cf. vv. 17, 26). Dead orthodoxy has no power to save. It may in fact even be a hindrance to true and living faith. So James is not contrasting two methods of salvation (faith versus works). His contrast is between two kinds of faith: one that saves and one that doesn't.

James is simply affirming the truth of 1 John 3:7-10: "Little children, let no one deceive you; the one who practices righteousness is righteous, just as He is righteous; the one who practices sin is of the devil; for the devil has sinned from the beginning. The Son of God appeared for this purpose, that He might destroy the works of the devil. By this the children of God and the children of the devil are obvious: anyone who does not practice righteousness is not of God, nor the one who does not love his brother." Righteous behavior is an inevitable result of spiritual life. Faith that fails to produce such behavior is dead.

For brevity's sake, we must forego looking closely at the examples of living faith from the lives of Abraham and Rahab (2:21-25).[21] Nonetheless, here is an abridged statement of the point James is making: Abraham and Rahab, though they came from opposite ends of the

---

[20]Hiebert, *The Epistle of James*, 188.

[21]These verses are covered in detail in John MacArthur, Jr., *True Faith* (Chicago: Moody, 1989), 123-31.

social and religious spectrum, both had an attitude of willingness to sacrifice what mattered most to them because of their faith. That submission was proof their faith was real.

The most serious problem these verses pose is the question of what verse 24 means: "You see that a man is justified by works, and not by faith alone." Some imagine that this contradicts Paul in Romans 3:28: "For we maintain that a man is justified by faith apart from works of the Law." John Calvin explained this apparent difficulty:

> It appears certain that [James] is speaking of the manifestation, not of the imputation of righteousness, as if he had said, Those who are justified by faith prove their justification by obedience and good works, not by a bare and imaginary semblance of faith. In one word, he is not discussing the mode of justification, but requiring that the justification of all believers shall be operative. And as Paul contends that men are justified without the aid of works, so James will not allow any to be regarded as Justified who are destitute of good works. . . . Let them twist the words of James as they may, they will never extract out of them more than two propositions: That an empty phantom of faith does not justify, and that the believer, not contented with such an imagination, manifests his justification by good works.[22]

James is not at odds with Paul. "They are not antagonists facing each other with crossed swords; they stand back to back, confronting different foes of the gospel."[23] As we have seen, in 1:17–18, James affirmed that salvation is a gift bestowed according to the sovereign will of God. Now he is stressing the importance of faith's fruit—the righteous behavior that genuine faith always produces. Paul, too, saw righteous works as the necessary proof of faith.

Those who imagine a discrepancy between James and Paul rarely observe that it was Paul who wrote, "Shall we sin because we are not under law but under grace? May it never be!" (Rom. 6:15); and "Having been freed from sin, you became slaves of righteousness" (v. 18). Thus Paul condemns the same error James is exposing here. Paul never advocated any concept of dormant faith.

---

[22]John Calvin, *Institutes of the Christian Religion,* trans. Henry Beveridge, 3:17:12 (reprint, Grand Rapids, Mich.: Eerdmans, 1966), 2:115.

[23]Alexander Ross, "The Epistles of James and John," *The New International Commentary on the New Testament* (Grand Rapids, Mich.: Eerdmans, 1954), 53.

When Paul writes, "by the works of the Law no flesh will be justified in His sight," (Rom. 3:20), he

> is combatting a Jewish legalism which insisted upon the need for works to be justified; James insists upon the need for works in the lives of those who have been justified by faith. Paul insists that no man can ever win justification through his own efforts. . . . James demands that a man who already claims to stand in right relationship with God through faith must by a life of good works demonstrate that he has become a new creature in Christ. With this Paul thoroughly agreed. Paul was rooting out 'works' that excluded and destroyed saving faith; James was stimulating a sluggish faith that minimized the results of saving faith in daily life.[24]

James and Paul both echo Jesus' preaching. Paul's emphasis resounds with the spirit of Matthew 5:3: "Blessed are the poor in spirit, for theirs is the kingdom of heaven." James' teaching has the ring of Matthew 7:21: "Not everyone who says to Me, 'Lord, Lord,' will enter the kingdom of heaven; but he who does the will of My Father who is in heaven." Paul represents the beginning of the Sermon on the Mount; James the end of it. Paul declares that we are saved by faith *without the deeds of the law.* James declares that we are saved by faith, *which shows itself in works.* Both James and Paul view good works as the proof of faith—not the path to salvation.

James could not be more explicit. He is confronting the concept of a passive, false "faith," which is devoid of the fruits of salvation. He is not arguing for works in addition to or apart from faith. He is showing why and how true, living faith always works. He is fighting against dead orthodoxy and its tendency to abuse grace.

The error James assails closely parallels the teaching of no-lordship salvation. It is faith without works; justification without sanctification; salvation without new life.

Again, James echoes the Master Himself, who insisted on a theology of lordship that involved obedience, not lip-service. Jesus chided the disobedient ones who had attached themselves to Him in name only: "Why do you call Me, 'Lord, Lord,' and do not do what I say?" (Luke 6:46). Verbal allegiance, He said, will get no one to heaven (Matt. 7:21).

---

[24]Hiebert, *The Epistle of James,* 175.

That is in perfect harmony with James: "Prove yourselves doers of the word, and not merely hearers who delude themselves" (1:22); for "faith, if it has no works, is dead, being by itself" (2:17).[25]

---

[25]It is worth noting that Zane Hodges has published a pamphlet on James 2 that challenges more than four centuries of Protestant scholarship. Acknowledging that his views are unusual, he suggests that *all* the conventional interpretations of James 2 are fundamentally in error and proposes in a thirty-two-page tract to straighten them out. Hodges writes, "Not only is there no commonly accepted interpretation of James 2:14–26 in post-Reformation Protestantism, but indeed all of the major ways of reading this text are wrong. *And not simply wrong, but seriously so.* So incorrect are these views, that if James himself had heard them, he would have been both astonished and appalled!" Zane C. Hodges, *Dead Faith: What Is It?* (Dallas: Redención Viva, 1987), 7, emphasis in original. Another professor assesses Hodges' claim with skepticism: "Perhaps one of the most intriguing—and disturbing—features of Zane C. Hodges's book . . . is that to the best of my knowledge not one significant interpreter of Scripture in the entire history of the church has held to Hodges' interpretation of the passages he treats. That does not necessarily mean Hodges is wrong; but it certainly means he is probably wrong, and it probably means he has not reflected seriously enough on the array of fallacies connected with [reading one's own presuppositions into the biblical text]." D. A. Carson, *Exegetical Fallacies* (Grand Rapids, Mich.: Baker, 1984), 137. Because Professor Hodges' voice is so influential among those who are persuaded of the no-lordship position, I mention his booklet. I have responded to it in a journal article: "Faith According to the Apostle James," *Journal of the Evangelical Theological Society* 33/1 (March 1990): 13–34. Much of this chapter was adapted from that article.

10

A Foretaste of Glory

Believers cannot lose the habits, the seeds, the root of grace; yet they may lose assurance, which is the beauty and fragrancy, the crown and glory of grace, 1 John 3. 9; 1 Peter 1. 5. These two lovers, grace and assurance, are not by God so nearly joined together but that they may by sin on our side, and justice on God's, be put asunder. The keeping of these two lovers, grace and assurance, together, will yield the soul two heavens, a heaven of joy and peace here, and a heaven of happiness and blessedness hereafter; but the putting these two lovers asunder will put the soul into a hell here, though it escape a hell hereafter. This Chrysostom knew well, when he professed that the want of the enjoyment of God would be a far greater hell to him than the feeling of any punishment.

Thomas Brooks[1]

*I*s it possible to have full assurance of one's salvation? Can Christians rest in the firm and settled confidence that they are redeemed and bound for eternal heaven?

Scripture categorically answers yes. Not only does the Bible teach that assurance is *possible* for Christians in this life, but the apostle Peter also gave this command: "[Be] diligent to make certain about His calling and choosing you" (2 Pet. 1:10). Assurance is not only a privilege;

---

[1]Thomas Brooks, *Heaven on Earth: A Treatise on Christian Assurance* (reprint, Edinburgh: Banner of Truth, 1982), 49.

it is the birthright and sacred trust of every true child of God. We are commanded to *cultivate* assurance, not take it for granted.

True assurance is a taste of heaven on earth. Fanny Crosby expressed that truth in a well-known hymn:

> Blessed assurance, Jesus is Mine!
> O what a foretaste of glory divine!

Puritan Thomas Brooks observed the same reality and entitled his book on assurance *Heaven on Earth*. To possess genuine assurance is to experience a bit of divine bliss this side of heaven. The greater our sense of assurance, the more we can savor that glory in this earthly life.

Critics often allege that lordship salvation renders personal assurance impossible. That is not true, but the lordship controversy certainly does have serious implications for the matter of assurance. Accordingly, assurance has emerged as one of the principal issues in the discussion. Although I barely touched on the subject in my earlier book,[2] the subsequent dialogue has seemed inevitably to converge on the question of whether and how Christians can be certain they are in the faith.

This is a good direction for the discussion to take, I am convinced. In contemporary Christianity assurance is too often either ignored, or claimed by people who have no right to it. Too many people believe they are saved merely because someone told them so. They do not examine themselves; they do not test their assurance by God's Word; they are taught that doubts about their salvation can only be detrimental to spiritual health and growth. Yet multitudes of these people give no evidence of any spiritual health or growth whatsoever.

---

[2] One editor published a "review" of *The Gospel According to Jesus* that began: "MacArthur's book hits four main issues: assurance, faith, repentance, and the relationship between salvation and discipleship." But there were no such divisions in my book. Assurance certainly was *not* a major issue; I mentioned *false assurance* only incidentally and three or four times at most. Nevertheless, this review continued, "While he never says it in so many words, MacArthur does not believe in assurance." Of course that is nonsense, and it is also a good example of why so many people do not understand what the lordship debate is all about. The review in question was published in the newsletter of an organization that exists to advocate no-lordship theology. The review contained several other gross inaccuracies and outright falsehoods. The editor did not respond to letters asking him to correct his distortions.

Assurance in the Reformation

Once again, the modern lordship controversy touches an issue that was at the heart of the Protestant Reformation. The Roman Catholic Church denied—and denies to this day—that anyone on earth can have assurance of salvation. Because Catholic theology sees salvation as a joint effort between God and the sinner, the outcome must be in doubt right up to the end. If a person fails spiritually before salvation is complete, that person forfeits eternal life. Since no one can know with certainty whether he or she will have the strength to endure to the end, no one can really be certain of heaven.[3]

The Reformers, by contrast, taught that believers can and should be fully assured of their salvation. The early Reformers went so far as to define faith in a way that included assurance. Calvin's definition of faith is often quoted: "It is a firm and sure knowledge of the divine favour toward us, founded on the truth of a free promise in Christ, and revealed to our minds, and sealed on our hearts, by the Holy Spirit."[4] Calvin emphasized faith as *knowledge,* in contrast to the Catholic Scholastics' idea that faith is a naive trust antithetical to knowledge. He thus built assurance into his definition of faith.

In other words, Calvin taught that *assurance is of the essence of faith.* That means the moment someone trusts Christ for salvation, that person will have *some* sense of assurance. As we noted in chapter 3, Hebrews 11:1 says, "Faith is the assurance of things hoped for, the conviction of things not seen." Thus it seems clear from Scripture that a measure of assurance *is* inherent in believing.

Often, however, the assurance of faith is darkened by doubt. Calvin also recognized that self-doubt can coexist with true belief. He wrote, "When we say that faith must be certain and secure, we certainly speak not of an assurance which is never affected by doubt, nor a security which anxiety never assails, we rather maintain that believers have a perpetual struggle with their own distrust, and are thus far from thinking that their consciences possess a placid quiet, uninterrupted by perturbation [distress]."[5]

---

[3]Obviously, a similar problem exists in Wesleyan and Arminian theology, and any other system of belief that makes room for Christians to fall away and lose their salvation.

[4]John Calvin, *Institutes of the Christian Religion,* trans. Henry Beveridge, 3:2:7 (reprint, Grand Rapids, Mich.: Eerdmans, 1966), 1:475.

[5]Ibid., 1:484.

Scripture is clearly on Calvin's side here. Some assurance belongs to the essence of faith, but believing does not necessarily bring *full* assurance. "I do believe; help my unbelief" (Mark 9:24) is a sincere expression of every new believer's heart. Even the apostles pleaded with Jesus, "Increase our faith!" (Luke 17:5).

Later Reformed theologians, recognizing that genuine Christians often lack assurance, denied that *any* assurance is implicit in believing. On this issue they were in disagreement with Calvin. Calvin, arguing against Rome, was eager to emphasize the possibility of immediate assurance. The later Reformers, battling antinomian tendencies in their movement, wanted to emphasize the importance of practical evidences in the lives of believers.

The Westminster Confession of Faith, drawn up in 1646, distinguished faith from assurance. The Confession included this:

> [CHAPTER 18] SECTION III.—This infallible assurance *doth not so belong to the essence of faith, but that a true believer may wait long, and conflict with many difficulties before he be partaker of it:* yet, being enabled by the Spirit to know the things which are freely given him of God, he may, without extraordinary revelation, in the right use of ordinary means, attain thereunto. And therefore it is the duty of every one to give all diligence to make his calling and election sure (emphasis added).

In other words, the Confession taught that assurance is something distinct from faith. A person can thus become a genuine believer yet remain unsure of salvation. To the Westminster divines, assurance was possible—even highly desirable—but not automatic. They believed some Christians need to "wait long" and wrestle with God before He grants them assurance. Most of the *Puritans* (seventeenth-century English Reformers) shared this view on assurance.

So on the one hand, Calvin tended to make the grounds for assurance wholly *objective,* urging believers to look to the promises of Scripture to gain a sense of personal assurance. On the other hand the Puritans tended to emphasize *subjective* means of establishing assurance, counseling people to examine their lives and behavior for evidences of their election.[6]

---

[6]Zane Hodges sees great significance in this divergence between Calvin and those who came after him. Hodges even tries to enlist Calvin in support of the no-lordship position! (*AF* 207–9, 214–15). Hodges, however, goes miles beyond Calvin on this issue, making assurance the sum and substance of saving faith (*AF* 50–51) and denying any

In fact, some of the Puritans carried their teaching on assurance to implausible extremes. They tended to become mystical on the issue, implying that assurance was something God grants supernaturally in His time and in special measures for select saints—almost like a heavenly vision one could be zapped with, or an added work of grace. Most of the Puritans taught that believers could not expect assurance until long after conversion, and only after a life of extended faithfulness.[7] They tended to make assurance dependent on the believer's ability to live at an almost unattainable level of personal holiness. I have profited greatly from reading their works, but I often wonder how many of them were able to live up to their own standards.

As we might expect, the Puritans' demanding preaching led to a widespread *lack* of assurance among their flocks. Christians became obsessed with whether they were truly elect, and many lapsed into morbid introspection and utter despair. That explains why so much of the Puritan literature is written for people struggling with the question of assurance.

By contrast, today assurance is rarely made an issue. Few professing Christians seem to lack assurance because evangelistic preaching is usually devoid of any call to holy living. Evangelists and counselors normally seek to dispel doubts about salvation by pronouncing them groundless, or by teaching converts to view all doubt as an attack by the enemy. Preachers are so fearful of shattering anyone's confidence that they seem to forget *false* assurance is a more serious problem than *no* assurance (cf. Matt. 7:21–23).

---

need for self-examination in the matter of assurance (*AF* 174–75). According to Hodges assurance *is* faith and vice versa. No other evidence of regeneration is necessary. He assumes the great Reformer taught the same thing.

But whatever Calvin's views on faith and assurance, it is clear that he would have been no supporter of Hodges' brand of no-lordship soteriology. Calvin wrote: "We must take care not to separate what the Lord perpetually conjoins. What then? Let men be taught that it is impossible they can be regarded as righteous by the merit of Christ, without being renewed by his Spirit unto a holy life . . . *God receives none into favour who are not also made truly righteous.*" Henry Beveridge and Jules Bonnet, eds., *Selected Works of John Calvin*, 7 vols. (reprint, Grand Rapids, Mich.: Baker, 1983), 3:246 (emphasis added).

Calvin added, "[Faith] is not a bare knowledge which flutters in the mind, [but] it carries along with it a lively affection, which has its seat in the heart." Ibid., 250.

[7]John Owen's writings on assurance are a refreshing exception to this rule. Cf. Sinclair B. Ferguson, *John Owen on the Christian Life* (Edinburgh: Banner of Truth, 1987), 99–124.

Surely there is a middle ground. Scripture encourages *true believers* with the promise of full assurance, while making *false professors* uncomfortable by seeking to destroy their false sense of security. A true believer's sense of assurance should not rise and fall with the emotions; assurance is meant to be an anchor even in the midst of life's difficulties. But a false professor has no right to assurance. Aren't those the twin emphases our preaching should reflect? Can we recover a biblical understanding of assurance?

We must. This is where the lordship debate touches almost every Christian at the most practical level. If we confuse the issue of assurance, we will have multitudes, on the one hand, whose spiritual lives are crippled by doubt, and multitudes, on the other, who expect to be ushered into heaven but will one day be devastated to hear the Lord say, "I never knew you; depart from Me" (Matt. 7:23).

Is Assurance Objective or Subjective?

The difference between Calvin and the Puritans raises a question that goes to the heart of the lordship debate: Should Christians seek assurance through clinging only to the *objective* promises of Scripture, or through *subjective* self-examination? If we opt for the objective promises only, those who profess faith in Christ while denying Him by their deeds (cf. Titus 1:16) can claim an assurance they have no entitlement to. But if we say assurance is available only through subjective self-examination we render full assurance practically impossible and make assurance a wholly mystical affair.

Those who argue for a subjective approach will point out that Scripture clearly calls for self-examination. We are commanded to examine ourselves regularly—at least as often as we participate in the Lord's Supper (1 Cor. 11:28). Paul also issued this challenge to the church at Corinth: "Test yourselves to see if you are in the faith; examine yourselves! Or do you not recognize this about yourselves, that Jesus Christ is in you—unless indeed you fail the test?" (2 Cor. 13:5). Clearly Paul was dealing here with the matter of assurance. The Corinthians were to test themselves *to see if they were "in the faith."*

But what kind of self-examination was Paul calling for? What was the "test" the Corinthians needed to pass? Was the apostle counseling them to look within themselves and anchor their assurance on their own goodness? Was he challenging them to think back and remember some moment of faith on which they could fix their hopes? Or was he suggesting that they should look to their works and place confidence in their spiritual accomplishments?

None of those suggestions answers the matter adequately. Works alone can no more guarantee genuine assurance than they can be the basis for our eternal salvation. After all, external works can be performed even by non-Christians. On the other hand, as we have seen, even the most spiritual Christians discover sin when they look within. So no one's works measure up to God's standard of perfection. In this regard, no-lordship teachers are correct: Those who only look within themselves to establish their assurance merely set themselves up for a life of frustration. Settled assurance cannot be found in any amount of works. If we must base our assurance solely on something in ourselves or our experience, our confidence will be resting on an inadequate foundation.[8] That approach to assurance is *too subjective.*

But no-lordship teaching offers this alternative:

> The promises of God are sufficient for assurance. While one's works can have a confirmatory value, they are not essential for assurance. Any believer can have 100% certainty of his salvation if he but looks to the promises in God's Word to the believer.
>
> One can have firm assurance of salvation and yet walk in sin. Sin, while a grievous thing, does not necessarily weaken assurance. Only if sin results in a person taking his eyes off God's promises can sin weaken assurance.[9]

So according to no-lordship teaching, as long as a person clings to the *objective promises* of God's Word, no amount of sin can trouble that person's assurance. Someone who chooses to "walk in sin" can do so with full assurance of faith.[10]

---

[8]"Faith totters if it pays attention to works, since no one, even the most holy, will find there anything on which to rely." John Calvin, *Institutes of the Christian Religion,* trans. Ford Lewis Battles (Philadelphia: Westminster, 1960), 3:11:11.

[9]Bob Wilkin, "Putting the Gospel Debate in Sharper Focus," *The Grace Evangelical Society News* (May 1991): 1.

[10]Assurance apart from sanctification is the essence of antinomianism. And antinomianism is often the result of an extreme emphasis on assurance as the essence of faith. Even in the early 1800s Charles Hodge noted that tendency: "Those who make assurance the essence of faith, generally reduce faith to a mere intellectual assent. They are often censorious, refusing to recognize as brethren those who do not agree with them; and sometimes they are antinomian." Charles Hodge, *Systematic Theology* (reprint, Grand Rapids, Mich.: Eerdmans, 1989), 3:106–7.

Berkhof, while recognizing the danger of antinomianism, nevertheless saw that one can hold the position that assurance is of the essence of faith yet keep that view in balance. He wrote, "Over against Rome the position must be maintained that this sure knowledge belongs to the essence of faith; and in opposition to [antinomian]

But that extreme cannot be supported practically *or* biblically. Hebrews 10:22 specifically says that to possess "full assurance of faith" we must have "our hearts sprinkled clean from an evil conscience." Second Peter 1:5–10 lists several spiritual virtues that are essential to salvation: faith, moral excellence, knowledge, self-control, perseverance, godliness, brotherly kindness, and love. The person who lacks these virtues will also lack assurance according to Peter: "He who lacks these qualities is blind or short-sighted, *having forgotten his purification from his former sins*" (v. 9, emphasis added).

Those who "walk in sin" may be convinced in their *minds* that their salvation is secure, but unless their heart and conscience are utterly seared, they will have to admit that sin ruins their assurance. The no-lordship approach to assurance is *too objective.*

What Are Biblical Grounds for Assurance?

The Bible suggests that a well-grounded assurance has both objective and subjective support.[11] The objective ground is *the finished work of Christ on our behalf,* including the promises of Scripture, which have their yea and amen in Him (2 Cor. 1:20). The subjective ground is *the ongoing work of the Holy Spirit in our lives,* including His convicting and sanctifying ministries. Romans 15:4 mentions both aspects of assurance: "Whatever was written in earlier times was written for our instruction, that through *perseverance* [subjective] *and the encouragement of the Scriptures* [objective] we might have hope."

Both the objective and subjective grounds for our assurance are applied to us by the Holy Spirit, who "bears witness with our spirit that we are children of God" (Rom. 8:16).

The objective basis for our assurance includes the truth of justification by faith, the promise that Christ will never leave us or forsake us (Heb. 13:5), the guarantee of our security in Christ (Rom. 8:38–39),

---

theologians such as Sandeman, Wardlaw, Alexander, Chalmers, and others, that a mere intellectual acceptance of truth is not the whole of faith." Louis Berkhof, *Systematic Theology* (Grand Rapids, Mich.: Eerdmans, 1939), 503.

[11]"In its NT context, the word [*assurance*] has both objective and subjective references. As objective, it denotes the ground of the believer's confidence and certainty. . . . As subjective, assurance has reference to the experience of the believer. . . . Inward assurance must be checked by moral and spiritual tests (cf. e.g., 1 Cor. 6:9; Eph. 4:17; 1 John 2:3–5, etc) by which we know we are of the truth and that our hearts are assured before God (1 John 3:19)." H. D. McDonald, "Assurance," *The New International Dictionary of the Christian Church* (Grand Rapids, Mich.: Zondervan, 1978), 79.

and all the objective truths of God's Word on which our faith is founded. The objective question asks, "Do you believe?" If you *truly* believe, you can be sure you are saved (John 3:16; Acts 16:31).

The subjective question asks, "Is your faith real?" That is the question Paul was asking in 2 Corinthians 13:5.

Here we return to a question we raised earlier but have not yet answered: What *kind* of self-examination was Paul calling for in that verse? We know that he was not suggesting Christians may find assurance in themselves or in their works. What then is the test we must pass?

Paul had hinted at the answer several chapters earlier in the same epistle. In 2 Corinthians 3:18 he wrote, "We all, with unveiled face beholding as in a mirror the glory of the Lord, are being transformed into the same image from glory to glory, just as from the Lord, the Spirit." As true Christians look into the mirror of God's Word (cf. James 1:23), they should see the glory of the Lord reflected back. To be sure, it is a dim reflection. "Now we see in a mirror dimly, but then face to face; now I know in part, but then I shall know fully just as I also have been fully known" (1 Cor. 13:12). But it is that dim reflection of *His* glory—not anything inherent in us—that is the subjective basis for our assurance.

Even Calvin recognized a subjective ground for assurance, though it was not a major emphasis in his teaching. While emphasizing that all works are nonmeritorious, Calvin said believers' good works are "divine gifts, in which [believers] recognise [God's] goodness and signs of calling, in which they discern their election."[12] They are *God's* work in us, not our own accomplishments. In this same context Calvin quotes a prayer of Augustine: "'I commend not the works of my hands, for I fear that when thou examinest them thou wilt find more faults than merits. This only I say, this ask, this desire, Despise not the works of thy hands. See in me thy work, not mine. If thou seest mine, thou condemnest; if thou seest thine own, thou crownest. Whatever good works I have are of thee' (August. in Ps. cxxxvii)."[13]

God's glory—albeit a dim reflection of that glory—is what we will see in the mirror if we are true believers. This is the test Paul laid before the Corinthians: Can you see Christ's glory reflected in you—even dimly? "Test yourselves to see if you are in the faith; examine yourselves! Or *do you not recognize this about yourselves, that Jesus Christ is in you—*

---

[12]Calvin, *Institutes of the Christian Religion* [Beveridge], 3:14:20, 2:87.

[13]Ibid., 88.

unless indeed you fail the test?" (2 Cor. 13:5). The image of Christ in us thus provides the subjective ground of our assurance. In other words, Christ in you is the hope of glory (cf. Col. 1:27).

In Order That You May Know

The New Testament epistles are filled with enough material on assurance to fill volumes of commentary. It is not possible in a book of this nature to give a full overview of the New Testament doctrine of assurance. Even the little epistle of 1 John, written to deal with precisely the issue of assurance, is so rich with material that we cannot do full justice to it in these few pages. But I do want to underscore some of the highlights of this treasured epistle and its clear teaching on this subject. Surely no other passage of Scripture confronts no-lordship theology with more force than this brief but potent letter.

John's purpose statement is explicit in 1 John 5:13: "These things I have written to you who believe in the name of the Son of God, *in order that you may know that you have eternal life*" (emphasis added). There the apostle spells out his intention. He is not trying to make believers *doubt;* he wants them to have full assurance. What he has to say will not shake genuine believers; though it should certainly alarm those with a false sense of assurance.

Note that the apostle presupposes faith in Christ as the bedrock of all assurance: "I have written to you who believe . . ." There is no place for self-examination outside of faith in Christ. So everything John says about assurance is predicated on faith in Christ and the promises of Scripture.[14]

Throughout this epistle the apostle John maintains a careful balance between the objective and subjective grounds of assurance. The objective evidence constitutes a *doctrinal* test. The subjective evidence is not a works test, but a *moral* test. John moves in and out between the two kinds of tests. Here are the proofs he says will be evident in every genuine believer:

True believers walk in the light. "If we say that we have fellowship with Him and yet walk in the darkness, we lie and do not practice the truth; but if we walk in the light as He Himself is in the light, we

---

[14]"The grounds of assurance are more objective than subjective; they are not so much within us as without us. Hence the basis of assurance must rest on sufficient objective evidence." Robert F. Boyd, "Assurance," *Baker's Dictionary of Theology* (Grand Rapids, Mich.: Baker, 1960), 70.

have fellowship with one another, and the blood of Jesus His Son cleanses us from all sin" (1 John 1:6–7). Throughout Scripture, light is used as a metaphor for truth—both intellectual and moral truth.

Psalm 119:105 says, "Thy word is a lamp to my feet, and a light to my path." Verse 130 adds, "The unfolding of Thy words gives light; it gives understanding to the simple." Proverbs 6:23 says, "For the commandment is a lamp, and the teaching is light." Those verses all speak of truth as something that may be *known* and *obeyed*. It is both doctrinal and moral. The light of all truth is embodied in Christ, who said, "I am the light of the world; he who follows Me shall not walk in the darkness, but shall have the light of life" (John 8:12).

Walking in darkness is the antithesis of following Christ. All unsaved people walk in darkness; Christians have been delivered into the light: "You were formerly darkness, but now you are light in the Lord; walk as children of light" (Eph. 5:8). "You, brethren, are not in darkness" (1 Thess. 5:4). To "walk in the light" means to live in the realm of truth. So all true believers are walking in the light—even when we sin. When we sin, "The blood of Jesus . . . cleanses us" (1 John 1:7). The verb tense there indicates that Christ's blood *continually* cleanses us. When we sin, we are already being cleansed, so that no darkness ever clouds the light in which we dwell (cf. 1 Pet. 2:9).

"Walk[ing] in the light" describes both positional and practical reality for the believer. To trust Jesus Christ is to walk in the light. To walk in the light is to heed the light and live accordingly. So in this first test the apostle points us to both the *objective* and *subjective* grounds of assurance. To determine if we walk in the light we must answer the objective question, "Do I believe?" as well as the subjective question, "Is my faith real?"

True believers confess their sin. "If we say that we have no sin, we are deceiving ourselves, and the truth is not in us. If we confess our sins, He is faithful and righteous to forgive us our sins and to cleanse us from all unrighteousness. If we say that we have not sinned, we make Him a liar, and His word is not in us. My little children, I am writing these things to you that you may not sin. If anyone sins, we have an Advocate with the Father, Jesus Christ the righteous" (1 John 1:8–2:1).

The word for "confess" (Gk., *homologeō*) means "to say the same thing." To "confess our sins" means to agree with God about them. This is a characteristic of all true Christians. They agree with God about their sin. That means they hate their sin; they don't love it. They acknowledge that they are sinful, and yet they know they are forgiven and that they have an Advocate with the Father (2:1).

Here it seems the apostle is suggesting an *objective* test of assurance: "Do you believe?" Specifically, "Do you agree with what God has said about your sin?"

True assurance of salvation always goes hand in hand with an awareness of our own sinfulness. In fact, the more certain we are of salvation, the deeper our awareness of our sin becomes. John Owen wrote, "A man, then, may have a deep sense of sin all his days, walk under the sense of it continually, abhor himself for his ingratitude, unbelief, and rebellion against God, without any impeachment of his assurance."[15] That may sound paradoxical, but it is the very thing that keeps Christians from falling into utter despair. We *know* we are sinners. We agree with God about that. We're not surprised to discover sin in our lives, but nevertheless we hate it. We know we are forgiven and cleansed and that Christ is our Advocate. Far from using that knowledge to justify our sin, however, we see it as a motivation to mortify sin all the more: "I am writing these things to you *that you may not sin*" (2:1, emphasis added).

True believers keep His commandments. "And by this we know that we have come to know Him, if we keep His commandments. The one who says, 'I have come to know Him,' and does not keep His commandments, is a liar, and the truth is not in him" (2:3–4). "By this we know that we love the children of God, when we love God and observe His commandments. For this is the love of God, that we keep His commandments; and His commandments are not burdensome" (5:2–3).

Here the apostle focuses on the *subjective* ground for assurance. He is prodding us to ask the question, "Is my faith real?" Here's how we can be sure if we have come to know Him: We keep His commandments. This is a test of obedience. The Greek word translated "keep" in 2:3–4 conveys the idea of a watchful, observant obedience. It is not an obedience that is only the result of external pressure. It is the eager obedience of one who "keeps" the divine commandments as if they were something precious to guard.

In other words, this speaks of an obedience motivated by love. Verse 5 spells it out: "Whoever keeps His word, in him the love of God has truly been perfected. By this we know that we are in Him."

Those who claim to know God yet despise His commandments are liars (v. 4). "They profess to know God, but by their deeds they deny Him, being detestable and disobedient, and worthless for any good deed" (Titus 1:16).

---

[15]John Owen, *The Works of John Owen,* 16 vols. (reprint, London: Banner of Truth, 1966), 6:549.

True believers love the brethren. This test and the previous one are closely related: "By this the children of God and the children of the devil are obvious: anyone who does not practice righteousness is not of God, nor the one who does not love his brother" (1 John 3:10). "The one who says he is in the light and yet hates his brother is in the darkness until now. The one who loves his brother abides in the light and there is no cause for stumbling in him. But the one who hates his brother is in the darkness and walks in the darkness, and does not know where he is going because the darkness has blinded his eyes" (2:9–11). "We know that we have passed out of death into life, because we love the brethren. He who does not love abides in death. Everyone who hates his brother is a murderer; and you know that no murderer has eternal life abiding in him" (3:14–15). "By this we know that we love the children of God, when we love God and observe His commandments" (5:2).

The reason these two tests are so closely related is that love perfectly fulfills the law. "He who loves his neighbor has fulfilled the law" (Rom. 13:8). To love God and to love one's neighbor fulfills the whole moral law. Jesus said, "'You shall love the Lord your God with all your heart, and with all your soul, and with all your mind.' This is the great and foremost commandment. The second is like it, 'You shall love your neighbor as yourself.' On these two commandments depend the whole Law and the Prophets" (Matt. 22:37–40).

Love for fellow believers is a particularly important evidence of genuine faith. The point is not that love is intrinsic to us, or something that rises out of our own goodness. "Beloved, let us love one another, for *love is from God;* and everyone who loves is born of God and knows God" (1 John 4:7, emphasis added). The love that is evidence of true faith is *God's* love, which is being perfected in us: "If we love one another, God abides in us, and His love is perfected in us" (4:12). Once again, it is that dim reflection of divine glory in us that provides the subjective ground of our assurance.

True believers affirm sound doctrine. Here we return to the objective ground: "You have an anointing from the Holy One, and you all know. I have not written to you because you do not know the truth, but because you do know it, and because no lie is of the truth. Who is the liar but the one who denies that Jesus is the Christ? This is the antichrist, the one who denies the Father and the Son" (2:20–23). "Whoever denies the Son does not have the Father; the one who confesses the Son has the Father also. By this you know the Spirit of God: every spirit that confesses that Jesus Christ has come in the flesh is from

God. . . . We are from God; he who knows God listens to us; he who is not from God does not listen to us. By this we know the spirit of truth and the spirit of error" (4:2, 6).

John was writing in opposition to an early form of the gnostic heresy, which denied that Jesus Christ is fully God and fully man. He is saying that no one who truly is saved can fall into serious, Christ-denying error or heresy. Why? Because "you have an anointing from the Holy One, [and] the anointing which you received from Him abides in you, and you have no need for anyone to teach you; but as His anointing teaches you about all things, and is true and is not a lie, and just as it has taught you, you abide in Him" (2:20, 27). Again, it is the divine work in us, not our own skill or achievements, that provide a sound basis for our assurance.

What about those who depart completely from sound doctrine? John answers that question explicitly: "They went out from us, but they were not really of us; for if they had been of us, they would have remained with us; but they went out, in order that it might be shown that they all are not of us" (2:19). No-lordship teaching at this point rather blatantly contradicts Scripture (cf. *SGS* 141, *AF* 111). Those who fall away and deny Christ only prove that their faith was never genuine to begin with. We shall examine this idea closely in chapter 11.

True believers follow after holiness. "If you know that He is righteous, you know that everyone also who practices righteousness is born of Him" (2:29). "And everyone who has this hope fixed on Him purifies himself, just as He is pure. Everyone who practices sin also practices lawlessness; and sin is lawlessness" (3:3–4). "No one who abides in Him sins; no one who sins has seen Him or knows Him. Little children, let no one deceive you; the one who practices righteousness is righteous, just as He is righteous; the one who practices sin is of the devil; for the devil has sinned from the beginning. The Son of God appeared for this purpose, that He might destroy the works of the devil. No one who is born of God practices sin, because His seed abides in him; and he cannot sin, because he is born of God" (3:6–9).

Those verses have tripped many people up. The key to their meaning is the definition of sin in 3:4: "Sin is lawlessness." The Greek word for "lawlessness" is *anomia*. It literally means, "without law," and it describes those who live immoral, ungodly, unrighteous lives as a matter of continuous practice. They hate God's righteousness and perpetually live as if they were sovereign over God's law. This cannot be true of a genuine Christian.

The apostle is clearly *not* making sinless perfection a test of salvation. After all, he began his epistle by saying, "If we say that we have no sin, we are deceiving ourselves, and the truth is not in us" (1:8).

Nor is he making an issue about the frequency, duration, or magnitude of one's sins. As we noted in chapter 8, all Christians sin, and true believers are capable even of prolonged and heinous sin. The issue John is raising here has to do with our attitude toward sin and righteousness, our heart's response when we *do* sin, and the overall direction of our walk.

The test is this: What is the object of your affections—sin or righteousness? If your chief love is sin, then you are "of the devil" (3:8, 10). If you love righteousness and practice righteousness, you are born of God (2:29). What is the direction of your affection? As John Owen aptly wrote, "Your state is not at all to be measured by the opposition that sin makes to you, but by the opposition you make to it."[16]

Those who cling to the *promise* of eternal life but care nothing for Christ's holiness have nothing to be assured of. Such people do not really believe. Either their professed "faith" in Christ is an utter sham, or they are simply deluded. If they did truly have their hope fixed on Christ, they would purify themselves, just as He is pure (3:3).

True believers have the Holy Spirit. This is the overarching test that sums up all the others: Does the Holy Spirit reside in you?[17] John writes, "By this we know that we abide in Him and He in us, because He has given us of His Spirit" (4:13). "The one who believes in the Son of God has the witness in himself; the one who does not believe God has made Him a liar, because he has not believed in the witness that God has borne concerning His Son. And the witness is this, that God has given us eternal life, and this life is in His Son" (5:10–11).

There is an echo of Pauline theology in these verses. Paul wrote, "The Spirit Himself bears witness with our spirit that we are children of God" (Rom. 8:16). Scripture says, "On the evidence of two or three witnesses a matter shall be confirmed" (Deut. 19:15; cf. Matt. 18:16; 2 Cor. 13:1). Romans 8:16 is saying that the Holy Spirit adds His testimony to the witness of our spirit, thereby confirming our assurance.

This utterly dispels the notion that self-examination is tantamount to placing one's faith in one's own works. The evidence we

---

[16]Ibid., 6:605.

[17]The test John is suggesting here is virtually identical to the self-examination Paul was calling for in 2 Corinthians 13:5: Does Jesus Christ live in you?

seek through self-examination is nothing other than the fruit of the Spirit (Gal. 5:22–23), the proof that He resides within. It is on that testimony that our assurance is confirmed.

The Danger of False Assurance

Before we move on to another chapter, we must deal briefly with the issue of false assurance. Throughout 1 John the apostle attacks the false profession of those who have no right to assurance: "The one who says, 'I have come to know Him,' and does not keep His commandments, is a liar, and the truth is not in him" (2:4). "The one who hates his brother is in the darkness and walks in the darkness, and does not know where he is going because the darkness has blinded his eyes" (2:11). "Whoever denies the Son does not have the Father" (2:23). "The one who practices sin is of the devil" (3:8). "Everyone who hates his brother is a murderer; and you know that no murderer has eternal life abiding in him" (3:15). "The one who does not love does not know God" (4:8). "If someone says, 'I love God,' and hates his brother, he is a liar; for the one who does not love his brother whom he has seen, cannot love God whom he has not seen" (4:20).

One of the dangers of radical no-lordship teaching is that it ignores the danger of false assurance. How? First of all, this view sees assurance and saving faith as virtually synonymous: "Simply put, [the gospel] message brings with it the assurance of salvation. . . . When a person believes, that person has assurance of life eternal. How could it be otherwise? . . . To doubt the guarantee of eternal life is to doubt the message itself. In short, if I do not believe that I am saved, I do not believe the offer that God has made to me. . . . A person who has *never been sure* of eternal life has *never believed* the saving message of God" (*AF* 50–51).

In effect, then, according to this view, a conviction of assurance in one's mind is the best evidence of salvation. "People know whether they believe something or not, and that is the real issue where God is concerned" (*AF* 31). Obviously, there is no room in such a view for *false* assurance. Everyone who professes to trust Christ is encouraged to claim "100 percent assurance." Everyone who professes assurance is accepted as a genuine believer, even if that person's lifestyle opposes everything Christ stands for.

The conscience screams against such a doctrine! It promises an "assurance" that the heart will never affirm. It offers no real peace to the soul. Instead it makes assurance a wholly intellectual property.

No-lordship doctrine is therefore forced to deny the subjective ground of assurance, because self-examination would immediately reveal the emptiness of every false professor's ungrounded hope. Laying half a foundation, no-lordship doctrine declares the building complete. The objective test is all they can endure. If the mind is convinced, there is no need to involve the conscience. That is the epitome of false assurance.

John Owen called false assurance a "notional apprehension of the pardon of sin."[18] The effect of such assurance, Owen believed, is that "it rather secretly insinuates into the soul encouragements unto a continuance in [sin]." "There are none in the world that deal worse with God than those who have an ungrounded persuasion of forgiveness. . . . Carnal boldness, formality, and despising of God, are the common issues of such a notion and persuasion."[19] "Where conscience accuses, [false assurance] must supply the defect."[20] Owen was not afraid to point out that those who turn the grace of our God into licentiousness are, after all, ungodly (Jude 4). "Let them profess what they will," Owen wrote, "they are ungodly men."[21]

No-lordship theology tells obstinately ungodly people that they can rest secure in the hope of heaven. That is not genuine assurance. Real assurance springs from faith that works, allowing us to look in the mirror and see beyond our sinful selves a reflection of *God's* glory that is dim but growing brighter in ever-increasing waves: "We all, with unveiled face beholding as in a mirror the glory of the Lord, are being transformed into the same image from glory to glory, just as from the Lord, the Spirit" (2 Cor. 3:18).[22]

---

[18]Owen, *The Works of John Owen*, 6:397.

[19]Ibid., 6:396.

[20]Ibid., 6:398.

[21]Ibid., 6:397

[22]For a fuller discussion about assurance, see John MacArthur, *Saved Without a Doubt* (Wheaton, Ill.: Victor, 1992).

11

Kept by the Power of God

> In order to place the doctrine of perseverance in proper light we need to know what it is not. It does not mean that every one who professes faith in Christ and who is accepted as a believer in the fellowship of the saints is secure for eternity and may entertain the assurance of eternal salvation. Our Lord himself warned his followers in the days of his flesh when he said to those Jews who believed on him, "If ye continue in my word, then are ye truly my disciples, and ye shall know the truth, and the truth shall make you free" (John 8:31, 32). He set up a criterion by which true disciples might be distinguished, and that criterion is continuance in Jesus' Word.
>
> John Murray[1]

*I*f any New Testament character was ever prone to failure, it was Simon Peter. Judging from the biblical record, none of our Lord's disciples—excluding Judas the betrayer—stumbled more often or more miserably than he. Peter was the disciple with the foot-shaped mouth. He seemed to have a knack for saying the worst possible thing at the most inappropriate time. He was impetuous, erratic, vacillating—sometimes cowardly, sometimes weak, sometimes hotheaded. On several occasions he merited strong rebukes from the Lord, none more severe than that recorded in Matthew 16:23: "Get behind Me, Satan! You are a stumbling

---

[1]John Murray, *Redemption Accomplished and Applied* (Grand Rapids, Mich.: Eerdmans, 1955), 151–52.

block to Me; for you are not setting your mind on God's interests, but man's." *That* occurred almost immediately after the high point in Peter's experience with Christ, when Peter confessed, "Thou art the Christ, the Son of the living God" (Matt. 16:16).

Peter's life is proof that a true believer's spiritual experience is often filled with ups and downs.

But Peter illustrates another, more significant, biblical truth: the keeping power of God. On the night Jesus was betrayed, He gave Peter an insight into the behind-the-scenes spiritual battle over Peter's soul: "Simon, Simon, behold, Satan has demanded permission to sift you like wheat; but *I have prayed for you,* that your faith may not fail" (Luke 22:31–32, emphasis added).

Peter was confident of his willingness to stand with Jesus whatever the cost. He told the Lord, "Lord, with You I am ready to go both to prison and to death!" (v. 33).

But Jesus knew the truth and sadly told Peter, "The cock will not crow today until you have denied three times that you know Me" (v. 34).

Did Peter fail? Miserably. Was his faith overthrown? Never. Jesus Himself was interceding on Peter's behalf, and His prayers did not go unanswered.

Did you know that our Lord intercedes like that for all genuine believers? We get a glimpse of how He prays in John 17:11: "I am no more in the world; and yet they themselves are in the world, and I come to Thee. Holy Father, *keep them in Thy name,* the name which Thou hast given Me, that they may be one, even as We are" (emphasis added).

He continues:

> I do not ask Thee to take them out of the world, but to *keep them from the evil one.* They are not of the world, even as I am not of the world. *Sanctify them in the truth;* Thy word is truth. As Thou didst send Me into the world, I also have sent them into the world. And *for their sakes I sanctify Myself, that they themselves also may be sanctified in truth.* I do not ask in behalf of these alone, but for those also who believe in Me through their word; that they may all be one; even as Thou, Father, art in Me, and I in Thee, that they also may be in Us; that the world may believe that Thou didst send Me. And *the glory which Thou hast given Me I have given to them;* that they may be one, just as We are one; I in them, and Thou in Me, *that they may be perfected in unity,* that the world may know that Thou didst send Me, and didst love them, even as Thou didst love Me.
>
> John 17:15–23, emphasis added

Notice what our Lord was praying for: that believers would be kept from the power of evil; that they would be sanctified by the Word; that they would share His sanctification and glory; and that they would be perfected in their union with Christ and one another. He was praying that they would persevere in the faith.

Was our Lord praying for the eleven faithful disciples only? No, He explicitly includes every believer in all succeeding generations: "I do not ask in behalf of these alone, but for those also who believe in Me through their word" (v. 20). That includes all true Christians even in our own day!

Moreover, the Lord Himself is continuing His intercessory ministry for believers even as you read this. "He is able to save forever those who draw near to God through Him, since He always lives to make intercession for them" (Heb. 7:25). The King James Version translates that verse like this: "He is able also to *save them to the uttermost* that come unto God by him, seeing he ever liveth to make intercession for them" (emphasis added).

Saved to the Uttermost

All true believers will be saved to the uttermost. Christ's high priestly ministry guarantees it. We have been justified, we are being sanctified, and we shall be glorified. No true believer will miss out on any stage of the process, though in this life we all find ourselves at different points along the way. This truth has been known historically as *the perseverance of the saints.*

No doctrine has been more savaged by no-lordship theology. That is to be expected, because the doctrine of perseverance is antithetical to the entire no-lordship system. In fact, what they have pejoratively labeled "lordship salvation" is nothing but this very doctrine!

Perseverance means that "those who have true faith can lose that faith neither totally nor finally."[2] It echoes God's promise through Jeremiah: "I will make an everlasting covenant with them that I will not turn away from them, to do them good; *and I will put the fear of Me in their hearts so that they will not turn away from Me*" (32:40, emphasis added).

That flatly contradicts the no-lordship notion of faith that can evaporate, leaving "believers" who no longer believe (cf. *SGS* 141). It stands in opposition to the radical no-lordship teaching that genuine

[2]Anthony A. Hoekema, *Saved by Grace* (Grand Rapids, Mich.: Eerdmans, 1989), 234.

Christians can choose to "drop out" of the spiritual growth process (*AF* 79–88) and "cease to confess Christianity" (*AF* 111). It is the polar opposite of the brand of theology that makes faith a "historical moment," a one-time "act" that secures heaven but offers no guarantee that the "believer's" earthly life will be changed (*AF* 63–64).

Perseverance was defined by the Westminster Confession of Faith this way: "They whom God hath accepted in His Beloved, effectually called and sanctified by his Spirit, can neither totally nor finally fall away from the state of grace; but shall certainly persevere therein to the end, and be eternally saved" (chapter 17, section 1).

This truth does not deny the possibility of miserable failings in one's Christian experience. The Confession also stated:

> Nevertheless [believers] may, through the temptations of Satan and of the world, the prevalency of corruption remaining in them, and the neglect of the means of their preservation, fall into grievous sins; and for a time continue therein; whereby they incur God's displeasure, and grieve his Holy Spirit: come to be deprived of some measure of their graces and comforts; have their hearts hardened, and their consciences wounded; hurt and scandalize others, and bring temporal judgments upon themselves (section 3).

In chapter 8 we dealt with the reality of sin in the believer's experience, so it should be clear that lordship theology does not include the idea of perfectionism. Nevertheless, people steeped in no-lordship teaching often misunderstand the issue with regard to perseverance.

One Christian layman who has embraced no-lordship teaching wrote me a very graciously worded seventeen-page letter explaining why he rejects lordship doctrine. His complaint is that lordship theology "does not seem to allow for anything but highly successful Christian living."

Zane Hodges makes a similar charge:

> The belief that every Christian will live a basically successful life until the end is an illusion. It is not supported by the instruction and warnings of the New Testament. . . . It is not surprising that those who do not perceive this aspect of New Testament revelation have impoverished their ability to motivate both themselves and other believers. Tragically, they often fall back on the technique of questioning the salvation of those whose lives seem not to meet Biblical standards. But in the process they undermine the grounds for a

believer's assurance and take part—however unwittingly—in the siege of the Gospel.[3]

No advocate of lordship salvation I am aware of teaches "that every Christian will live a basically successful life until the end." Professor Hodges is quite right in saying the New Testament does not support such a view.

John Murray, defending the doctrine of perseverance, acknowledged the difficulties it poses: "Experience, observation, biblical history, and certain Scripture passages would appear to provide very strong arguments against the doctrine. . . . Is not the biblical record as well as the history of the church strewn with examples of those who have made shipwreck of the faith?"[4]

Certainly Scripture seems to be filled with warnings to people in the church lest they should fall away (cf. Heb. 6:4–8; 1 Tim. 1:18–19; 2 Tim. 2:16–19). Zane Hodges suggests such warnings prove Christians can fall away: "If anyone supposes that no true Christian could quit, or would quit, they have not been paying attention to the Bible. They need to re-read their New Testament, this time, with their eyes open" (*AF* 83).

But God does not contradict Himself. The warning passages do not negate the many promises that believers will persevere: "Whoever drinks of the water that I shall give him *shall never thirst; but the water that I shall give him shall become in him a well of water springing up to eternal life*" (John 4:14, emphasis added).[5] "I am the bread of life; he who comes to Me shall not hunger, and he who believes in Me shall never thirst" (6:35). "You are not lacking in any gift, awaiting eagerly the revelation of our Lord Jesus Christ, *who shall also confirm you to the end, blameless in the day of our Lord Jesus Christ. God is faithful,* through whom you were called into fellowship with His Son, Jesus Christ our Lord" (1 Cor. 1:7–9, emphasis added). "May the God of peace Himself sanctify you entirely; and *may your spirit and soul and body be preserved complete, without blame* at the coming of our Lord Jesus Christ. Faithful is He who calls you, and *He also will bring it to pass*" (1 Thess. 5:23–24, emphasis added). "They went out from us,

---

[3]Zane Hodges, *The Gospel Under Siege* (Dallas: Redención Viva, 1981), 113.

[4]Murray, *Redemption Accomplished and Applied,* 151.

[5]Ironically, Zane Hodges builds his entire system on Jesus' words to the woman at the well in John 4, but Hodges neglects the truth of perseverance that is included in this promise.

but they were not really of us; for *if they had been of us, they would have remained with us;* but they went out, in order that it might be shown that they all are not of us" (1 John 2:19, emphasis added). "Now unto *him that is able to keep you from falling, and to present you faultless before the presence of his glory with exceeding joy,* to the only wise God our Saviour, be glory and majesty, dominion and power, both now and for ever. Amen" (Jude 24–25 KJV, emphasis added).

Charles Horne observed, "It is noteworthy that when Jude exhorts us to keep ourselves in the love of God (v. 21), he concludes with a doxology for Him who is able to keep us from falling and who will present us without blemish before the presence of His glory (v. 24). The warning passages are *means* which God uses in our life to accomplish His purpose in grace."[6]

And, it might be added, the warning passages like Jude 21 reveal that the writers of Scripture were very keen to alert those whose hope of salvation might be grounded in a spurious faith. Obviously the apostolic authors were not laboring under the illusion that every person in the churches they were writing to was genuinely converted (cf. *AF* 98).

Once Saved, Always Saved?

It is crucial that we understand what the biblical doctrine of perseverance does *not* mean. It does not mean that people who "accept Christ" can then live any way they please without fear of hell. The expression "eternal security" is often used in this sense, as is "once saved, always saved." R. T. Kendall, arguing for the latter phrase, defines its meaning thus: *"Whoever once truly believes that Jesus was raised from the dead, and confesses that Jesus is Lord, will go to heaven when he dies.* But I will not stop there. *Such a person will go to heaven when he dies no matter what work (or lack of work) may accompany such faith."*[7] Kendall states, "I hope no one will take this as an attack on the Westminster Confession. It is not that."[8] But it is *precisely* that! Kendall is expressly

---

[6]Charles Horne, *Salvation* (Chicago: Moody, 1971), 95.

[7]R. T. Kendall, *Once Saved, Always Saved* (Chicago: Moody, 1983), 19 (emphasis in original). Kendall later expands that: "I therefore state categorically that the person who is saved—who confesses that Jesus is Lord and believes in his heart that God raised Him from the dead—*will go to heaven when he dies no matter what work (or lack of work) may accompany such faith.* In other words, no matter what sin (or absence of Christian obedience) may accompany such faith." Ibid., 52–53.

[8]Ibid., 22.

arguing against Westminster's assertion that faith cannot fail. Kendall believes faith is best characterized as a single look: "One need only *see* the Sin Bearer once to be saved."[9] This is a full-scale assault against the doctrine of perseverance affirmed in the Westminster Confession. Worse, it subverts Scripture itself. Unfortunately, it is a view that has come to be widely believed by Christians today.

John Murray, noting this trend nearly forty years ago, defended the expression "Perseverance of the saints":

> It is not in the best interests of the doctrine involved to substitute the designation, "The Security of the Believer," not because the latter is wrong in itself but because the other formula is much more carefully and inclusively framed. . . . It is not true that the believer is secure however much he may fall into sin and unfaithfulness. Why is this not true? It is not true because it sets up an impossible combination. It is true that a believer sins; he may fall into grievous sin and backslide for lengthy periods. But it is also true that a believer cannot abandon himself to sin; he cannot come under the dominion of sin; he cannot be guilty of certain kinds of unfaithfulness. And therefore it is utterly wrong to say that a believer is secure quite irrespective of his subsequent life of sin and unfaithfulness. The truth is that the faith of Jesus Christ is *always respective* of the life of holiness and fidelity. And so it is never proper to think of a believer irrespective of the fruits in faith and holiness. To say that a believer is secure whatever may be the extent of his addiction to sin in his subsequent life is to abstract faith in Christ from its very definition and it ministers to that abuse which turns the grace of God into lasciviousness. The doctrine of perseverance is the doctrine that believers *persevere.* . . . It is not at all that they will be saved irrespective of their perseverance or their continuance, but that they will assuredly persevere. Consequently the security that is theirs is inseparable from their perseverance. Is this not what Jesus said? "He that endureth to the end, the same shall be saved."
>
> Let us not then take refuge in our sloth or encouragement in our lust from the abused doctrine of the security of the believer. But let us appreciate the doctrine of the perseverance of the saints and recognize that we may entertain the faith of our security in Christ only as we persevere in faith and holiness to the end.[10]

---

[9]Ibid., 23. Hodges' similar rhetoric on this same issue is patently offensive: "People are not saved by staring at Christ. They are saved by looking at Him in faith" (*AF* 107).

[10]Murray, *Redemption Accomplished and Applied,* 154–55.

Any doctrine of eternal security that leaves out perseverance distorts the doctrine of salvation itself. Heaven without holiness ignores the whole purpose for which God chose and redeemed us:

> God elected us for this very purpose. "He chose us in him [Christ] before the creation of the world to be holy and blameless in his sight" (Eph. 1:4). We were predestinated to be conformed to the image of Christ in all His spotless purity (*Rom. 8.29*). This divine choice makes it certain that we shall be like Him when He appears (*I John 3:2*). From this fact, John deduces that everyone who has this hope in him purifies himself just as Christ is pure (*I John 3:3*). His use of the word "everyone" makes it quite certain that those who do not purify themselves will not see Christ, nor be like Him. By their lack of holiness they prove that they were not so predestinated. The apostle thus deals a crushing blow to Antinomianism.[11]

God's own holiness thus *requires* that we persevere. "God's grace insures our persevering—but this does not make it any less *our* persevering."[12] We cannot acquire "the prize of the upward call of God in Christ Jesus" unless we "press on toward the goal" (Phil. 3:14). But as we "work out [our] salvation with fear and trembling" (Phil. 2:12), we find that "it is God who is at work in [us], both to will and to work for His good pleasure" (v. 23).

The Outcome of Your Faith

Perhaps no apostle understood better than Peter the keeping power of God in the life of an inconsistent believer. God had preserved him and matured him through every kind of faux pas and failure, including severe sin and compromise—even repeated denials of the Lord accompanied by cursing and swearing! (Matt. 26:69–75). Yet Peter was kept in faith by the power of God despite his own failures. It is therefore appropriate that he was the instrument the Holy Spirit used to pen this glorious promise:

> Blessed be the God and Father of our Lord Jesus Christ, who according to His great mercy has caused us to be born again to a living

---

[11]Richard Alderson, *No Holiness, No Heaven!* (Edinburgh: Banner of Truth, 1986), 88.
[12]Horne, *Salvation*, 95.

hope through the resurrection of Jesus Christ from the dead, to obtain an inheritance which is imperishable and undefiled and will not fade away, reserved in heaven for you, who are protected by the power of God through faith for a salvation ready to be revealed in the last time. In this you greatly rejoice, even though now for a little while, if necessary, you have been distressed by various trials, that the proof of your faith, being more precious than gold which is perishable, even though tested by fire, may be found to result in praise and glory and honor at the revelation of Jesus Christ; and though you have not seen Him, you love Him, and though you do not see Him now, but believe in Him, you greatly rejoice with joy inexpressible and full of glory, obtaining as the outcome of your faith the salvation of your souls.

1 Peter 1:3–9

Peter was writing to scattered believers living in Asia Minor. They were facing a horrible persecution that had begun at Rome and was spreading through the Roman Empire. After the city of Rome burned, Nero blamed Christians for the disaster. Suddenly, believers everywhere had become targets of tremendous persecution. These people feared for their lives, and they feared they would fail if their faith were put to the test.

Peter wrote this epistle to encourage them. He reminded them that they were aliens in this world, citizens of heaven, a royal aristocracy, children of God, residents of an unearthly kingdom, living stones, a holy priesthood, and a people for God's own possession. Peter told them they were not to fear the threats, they were not to be intimidated, they were not to be troubled by the world's animosity, and they were not to be afraid when they suffered.

Why? Because Christians are "protected by the power of God through faith." Instead of giving them doses of sympathy and commiseration, Peter pointed them to their absolute security as believers. He knew they might be losing all their earthly possessions and even their lives, but he wanted them to know they would never lose what they had in Christ. Their heavenly inheritance was guaranteed. They were being kept by divine power. Their faith would endure through anything. They would persevere through their trials and be found worthy at the end. Their love for Christ would remain intact. Even now, in the midst of their difficulties, God would provide the spiritual deliverance they needed, according to His eternal plan. Those six means of perseverance sum up how God sustains every Christian.

We are born again to a living hope. "God . . . has caused us to be born again to a living hope through the resurrection of Jesus Christ from the dead to obtain an inheritance which is imperishable and undefiled and will not fade away, reserved in heaven for you" (vv. 3–4). Every Christian is born again to a *living hope*—that is, a hope that is perpetually alive, a hope that cannot die. Peter seems to be making a contrast to mere human hope, which is always a dying or a dead hope. Human hopes and dreams inevitably fade and ultimately disappoint. That's why Paul told the Corinthians, "If we have hoped in Christ in this life only, we are of all men most to be pitied" (1 Cor. 15:19). This living hope in Christ cannot die. God guarantees that it will finally come to a complete and total, glorious eternal fulfillment. "This hope we have as an anchor of the soul, a hope both sure and steadfast" (Heb. 6:19).

That has clear implications beyond the antinomian concept of eternal security. Again, the point is not only that Christians are saved forever and safe from hell "no matter what." It means more than that: Our *hope* doesn't die. Our *faith* won't fail. That is the heart of the doctrine of perseverance.

But this passage *does* teach eternal security as well. We are guaranteed "an inheritance which is imperishable and undefiled and will not fade away, reserved in heaven" (v. 4). Unlike everything in this life, which may be corrupted, decay, grow old, rust, corrode, be stolen, or lose its value, our heavenly inheritance is reserved for us where it remains incorruptible, undefiled, and unfading. Our full inheritance will one day be the culmination of our living hope. It is "reserved in heaven"—"not like a hotel reservation which may be unexpectedly cancelled, but permanently and unchangeably."[13]

Did you realize that we have already received part of that inheritance? Ephesians 1:13–14 says, "[Having] believed, you were sealed in Him with the Holy Spirit of promise, who is given as a pledge of our inheritance, with a view to the redemption of God's own possession, to the praise of His glory" (cf. 2 Cor. 1:22; 5:5). "Pledge" in verse 14 comes from the Greek word *arrabōn,* which means "down payment." When a person first believes, the Holy Spirit Himself moves into that person's heart. He is the security deposit on our eternal salvation. He is an advance on the Christian's inheritance. He is the guarantee that God will finish the work He has started. "And do not grieve the Holy Spirit

---

[13]Hoekema, *Saved by Grace,* 244.

of God, by whom you were *sealed for the day of redemption*" (Eph. 4:30, emphasis added).

We are kept by God's own power. "[We are] protected by the power of God through faith for a salvation ready to be revealed in the last time" (v. 5). That is a rich statement, guaranteeing the consummation of every believer's eternal salvation. The phrase, "a salvation ready to be revealed in the last time," speaks of our full, final salvation—from the curse of the law, the power and presence of sin, all decay, every stain of iniquity, all temptation, all grief, all pain, all death, all punishment, all judgment, and all wrath. God has begun this work in us already, and He will thoroughly complete it (cf. Phil 1:6).

Working our way carefully through that sentence, we note this phrase: "you . . . are protected by the power of God through faith." We are *protected* by the power of a supreme, omnipotent, sovereign, omniscient, almighty God. The verb tense speaks of continuous action. Even now we are *being protected*. "Neither death, nor life, nor angels, nor principalities, nor things present, nor things to come, nor powers, nor height, nor depth, nor any other created thing, shall be able to separate us from the love of God, which is in Christ Jesus our Lord" (Rom. 8:38–39). "If God be for us, who can be against us?" (Rom. 8:31 KJV). "[He] is able to keep you from stumbling, and to make you stand in the presence of His glory blameless with great joy" (Jude 24).

Furthermore, we are protected *through faith*. Our continued faith in Christ is the instrument of God's sustaining work. God didn't save us apart from faith, and He doesn't keep us apart from faith. Our faith is God's gift, and through His protecting power He preserves it and nurtures it. The maintenance of our faith is as much His work as every other aspect of salvation. Our faith is kindled and driven and maintained and fortified by God's grace.

But to say that faith is God's gracious gift, which He maintains, is not to say that faith operates apart from the human will. It is *our* faith. We believe. We remain steadfast. We are not passive in the process. The means by which God maintains our faith involves our full participation. We cannot persevere apart from faith; only *through* faith.

We are strengthened by the testing of our faith. "In this you greatly rejoice, even though now for a little while, if necessary, you have been distressed by various trials, that the proof of your faith, being more precious than gold which is perishable, even though tested by fire, may be found to result in praise and glory and honor at the revelation of

Jesus Christ" (1 Peter 1:5–6). Here we discover the chief means by which God maintains our faith: He subjects it to trials.

The little phrase "you greatly rejoice" may catch the unsuspecting reader off guard. Remember, the recipients of this epistle were facing life-threatening persecutions. They were fearful of the future. Yet Peter says, "you greatly rejoice." How could they be rejoicing?

Trials produce joy because the testing strengthens our faith. James said exactly the same thing: "Consider it all joy, my brethren, when you encounter various trials, knowing that the testing of your faith produces endurance" (James 1:2–3). Temptations (same word in the Greek) and tests don't weaken or shatter real faith—just the opposite. They strengthen it. People who lose their faith in a trial only show that they never had real faith to begin with. Real faith emerges from trials stronger than ever.

Trials themselves are anything but joyful, and Peter recognizes this: "though now for a little while, if necessary, you have been distressed by various trials" (v. 6). They come like fire to burn the dross off metal. But that's the point. The faith that emerges is that much more glorious. When the fire has done its burning, what is left is purer, brighter, stronger faith.

For whom does God test our faith? For His own sake? Is He wanting to find out whether our faith is real? Of course not. He knows. He tests us for our own benefit, so we will know if our faith is genuine. He tests our faith in order to refine it, strengthen it, bring it to maturity. What emerges from the crucible is "more precious than gold" (v. 7). Unlike gold, proven faith has eternal value. Mere gold may survive the refiner's fire, but it does not pass the test of eternity.

Peter wasn't giving these Christians empty platitudes. He had tasted the joy that accrues from a trial of persecution. Acts 5:41 says the apostles "went on their way from the presence of the [Sanhedrin] Council, *rejoicing that they had been considered worthy to suffer shame for His name*" (emphasis added). May I add that they must have gone on their way with a stronger faith, too? They had suffered, but their faith had passed the test. The great confidence of the believer is to know that his faith is real. Thus trials produce that mature faith by which God preserves us.

We are preserved by God for ultimate glory. "The proof of your faith . . . may be found to result in praise and glory and honor at the revelation of Jesus Christ" (v. 7). Here is an astonishing promise. The ultimate result of our proven faith will be praise, glory, and honor at Christ's appearing. The direction of this praise is from God to the believer, not vice versa! Peter is not talking about our praising, glorifying and honoring God, but His approval directed to us.

First Peter 2:20 says, "If when you do what is right and suffer for it you patiently endure it, this finds favor with God." Like the master of the faithful servant, God will say, "Well done, good and faithful slave . . . enter into the joy of your master" (Matt. 25:21, 23). Romans 2:29 says, "He is a Jew who is one inwardly; and circumcision is that which is of the heart, by the Spirit, not by the letter; *and his praise is not from men, but from God*" (emphasis added). True faith, tested and proved, receives praise from God.

Notice 1 Peter 1:13. Peter writes, "Therefore, gird your minds for action, keep sober in spirit, fix your hope completely on the grace to be brought to you at the revelation of Jesus Christ." What is that grace? "Praise and glory and honor." In 4:13 he says, "To the degree that you share the sufferings of Christ, keep on rejoicing; so that also at the revelation of His glory, you may rejoice with exultation." Paul says, "I consider that the sufferings of this present time are not worthy to be compared with the glory that is to be revealed to us" (Rom. 8:18).

Some people misunderstand 1 Peter 1:7 and think it is saying that our faith has to wait for the Second Coming to be found genuine. "That the proof of your faith . . . may be found [worthy] *at the revelation of Jesus Christ*"—as if the outcome were uncertain until that day. But the verse actually says that our faith, already tested and proved genuine, is awaiting its eternal reward. There's no insecurity in this. In fact, the opposite is true. We can be certain of the final outcome, because God Himself is preserving us through faith until that day.

We are motivated by love for the Savior. "Though you have not seen Him, you love Him, and though you do not see Him now, but believe in Him, you greatly rejoice with joy inexpressible and full of glory" (v. 8). That is a profound statement about the character of genuine faith. I am convinced beyond equivocation that the two key factors that guarantee our perseverance from the human side are love for and trust in the Savior. Peter knew this better than anyone.

After he denied Christ, Peter had to face Jesus Christ and have his love questioned. Jesus asked him three times, "Do you love Me?" and Peter was deeply grieved (John 21:17). Of course he *did* love Christ, and that is why he returned to Him and was restored. Peter's own faith was purified by that trial. I see here in 1 Peter a beautiful humility. Peter commends these suffering believers and says to them, "You've never seen Him and you love Him and you don't see Him now but you believe in Him." He might have been remembering that when he denied Christ he was standing close enough for their eyes to meet (Luke 22:60–61). Surely the pain of his own failure was still very real in his heart, even after many years.

A normal relationship involves love and trust for someone you can know face-to-face. But Christians love Someone they cannot see, hear, or touch. It is a supernatural, God-given love. "We love him, because he first loved us" (1 John 4:19 KJV).

There is no such thing as a Christian who lacks this love. Peter is saying categorically that the essence of what it means to be a Christian is to love Jesus Christ. In fact, there may be no better way to describe the essential expression of the new nature than to say it is *continual love for Christ*. The King James Version translates 1 Peter 2:7 like this: "Unto you therefore which believe he is precious." Note what Paul said in the very last verse of Ephesians: "Grace be with all those who love our Lord Jesus Christ with a love incorruptible" (6:24). Romans 8:28, one of the most familiar passages in all of Scripture, refers to believers as "those who love God." But Paul makes his strongest statement on this matter in 1 Corinthians 16:22: "If anyone does not love the Lord, let him be accursed."

No-lordship theology ignores this vital truth. Consequently, many people today who utterly lack any love for the Lord Jesus Christ are being given a false hope of heaven. True Christians love Christ. His love for us, producing our love for Him (1 John 4:19), is one of the guarantees that we will persevere to the end (Rom. 8:33–39). Jesus said, "If you love Me, you will keep My commandments." "He who has My commandments and keeps them, he it is who loves Me" (v. 21). Conversely, "He who does not love Me does not keep My words" (v. 24).

Those who are devoted to Christ long to promote His glory. They long to serve Him with heart and soul and mind and strength. They delight in His beauty. They love to talk about Him, read about Him, fellowship with Him. They desire to know Him better and to know Him deeper. They are compelled in their hearts to want to be like Him. Like Peter, they may stumble frequently and fail in pathetic ways as sinful flesh assaults holy longings. But like Peter, all true believers *will* persevere until the goal is ultimately reached.[14] "Beloved, now we are

---

[14]This is not to suggest that all believers will experience the same degree of spiritual success, only that none of them will turn away from Christ by giving in to settled unbelief.

children of God, and it has not appeared as yet what we shall be. We know that, when He appears, we shall be like Him, because we shall see Him just as He is" (1 John 3:2).

Robert Leighton, writing in 1853 in a wonderful commentary on 1 Peter, said this:

> *Believe, and you shall love; believe much, and you shall love much;* labour for strong and deep persuasions of the glorious things which are spoken of Christ, and this will command love. Certainly, did men indeed believe his worth, they would accordingly love him; for the reasonable creature cannot but affect that most which it firmly believes to be worthiest of affection. Oh! this mischievous unbelief is that which makes the heart cold and dead towards God. Seek then to believe Christ's excellency in himself, and his love to us, and our interest in him, and this will kindle such a fire in the heart, as will make it ascend in a sacrifice of love to him.[15]

So our love for Christ is another of the means God uses to assure our perseverance. That love and the faith that accompanies it are a source of inexpressible joy, full of glory (1 Peter 1:8).

We are saved through a working faith. ". . . obtaining as the outcome of your faith the salvation of your souls" (1:9). Here Peter is speaking of a present deliverance. "Obtaining" is a present-tense verb, middle voice. The word could be literally translated, "Presently receiving for yourselves . . ." This present salvation is "the outcome" of our faith—a working faith. In practical terms, it means a present-tense deliverance from sin, guilt, condemnation, wrath, ignorance, distress, confusion, hopelessness—everything that defiles. This is not speaking of the perfect consummation of salvation Peter mentioned in verse 5.

The salvation in view here in verse 9 is a constant, present-tense salvation. Sin no longer has dominion over us (Rom. 6:14). There is no way we can fail to persevere. We will certainly falter at times. We won't always be successful. In fact, some people may seem to experience more failure than success. But no true believer can fall into settled unbelief or permanent reprobation. To allow for such a possibility is a disastrous misunderstanding of God's keeping power in the lives of His chosen ones.

Thus Peter opens his first epistle. At the end of this same epistle he returns again to the theme of perseverance. There he writes, "After you have suffered for a little while, the God of all grace, who called you to

---

[15]Robert Leighton, *Commentary on First Peter* (reprint, Grand Rapids, Mich.: Kregel, 1972), 55.

His eternal glory in Christ, will Himself perfect, confirm, strengthen and establish you" (5:10).

Can you grasp the magnitude of that promise? *God Himself* perfects, confirms, strengthens, and establishes His children. Though His purposes for the future involve some pain in the present, He will nevertheless give us grace to endure and persevere. Even while we are being personally attacked by the enemy, we are being personally perfected by God. He Himself is doing it. He will accomplish His purposes in us, bringing us to wholeness, setting us on solid ground, making us strong, and establishing us on a firm foundation. All those terms speak of strength, resoluteness.

The Problem of Quantification

Inevitably, the question is raised, "How faithfully must one persevere?" Charles Ryrie wrote,

> So we read a statement like this: "A moment of failure does not invalidate a disciple's credentials." My immediate reaction to such a statement is to want to ask if two moments would? Or a week of defection, or a month, or a year? Or two? How serious a failure and for how long before we must conclude that such a person was in fact not saved? Lordship teaching recognizes that "no one will obey perfectly," but the crucial question is simply how imperfectly can one obey and yet be sure that he "believed"? . . .
>
> . . . A moment of defection, we have been told, is not an invalidation. Or "the true disciple will never turn away completely." Could he turn away almost completely? Or ninety percent? Or fifty percent and still be sure he was saved? . . .
>
> *Frankly, all this relativity would leave me in confusion and uncertainty. Every defection, especially if it continued, would make me unsure of my salvation.* Any serious sin or unwillingness would do the same. If I come to a fork in the road of my Christian experience and choose the wrong branch and continue on it, does that mean I was never on the Christian road to begin with? For how long can I be fruitless without having a lordship advocate conclude that I was never really saved? (*SGS* 48–49, emphasis added).

Ryrie suggests that if we cannot state precisely *how much* failure is possible for a Christian, true assurance becomes impossible. He wants the terms to be quantified: "Could he turn away almost completely? Or ninety percent? Or fifty percent?" To put it another way, Ryrie is suggesting that the doctrines of perseverance and assurance are incompatible. Astonishingly, he wants a doctrine of assurance that allows those who have defected from Christ to be confident of their salvation.

There are no quantifiable answers to the questions Ryrie raises. Indeed, some Christians persist in sin for extended periods of time. But those who do, forfeit their right to genuine assurance. "Serious sin or unwillingness" certainly *should* cause someone to contemplate carefully the question of whether he or she really loves the Lord. Those who turn away completely (not *almost* completely, or 90 percent, or 50 percent) demonstrate that they never had true faith.

Quantification poses a dilemma for no-lordship teaching, too. Zane Hodges speaks of faith as a "historical moment." How brief may that moment be? Someone listening to a debate between a Christian and an atheist might believe for an instant while the Christian is speaking, but immediately be led back into doubt or agnosticism by the atheist's arguments. Would we classify such a person as a believer? One suspects some no-lordship advocates would answer yes, although that view goes against everything God's word teaches about faith.

Jesus never quantified the terms of His demands; He always made them *absolute*. "So therefore, no one of you can be My disciple who does not give up all his own possessions" (Luke 14:33); "He who loves father or mother more than Me is not worthy of Me; and he who loves son or daughter more than Me is not worthy of Me" (Matt. 10:37); "He who loves his life loses it; and he who hates his life in this world shall keep it to life eternal" (John 12:25). Those conditions are *impossible* in human terms (Matt. 19:26).[16] That does not alter or mitigate the truth of the gospel. It certainly is no excuse for going to the other extreme and doing away with any necessity for commitment to Christ.

Ryrie's comments raise another issue that is worth considering. It is the question of whether lordship teaching is inherently judgmental: "How long can I be fruitless without having a lordship advocate conclude that I was never really saved?" Zane Hodges has made similar comments: "Lordship teaching reserves to itself the right to strip professing Christians of their claims to faith and to consign such people to the ranks of the lost" (*AF* 19).

Certainly no individual can judge another's heart. It is one thing to challenge people to examine themselves (2 Cor. 13:5); it is entirely another matter to set oneself up as another Christian's judge (Rom. 14:4, 13; James 4:11).

---

[16]Even those who want to make these statements of Christ apply to a postconversion step of discipleship don't solve the dilemma of their absoluteness.

But while individual Christians must never be judgmental, the church body as a whole very definitely has a responsibility to maintain purity by exposing and excommunicating those who live in continual sin or defection from the faith. Our Lord gave very explicit instructions on how to handle a fellow believer who falls into such sin. We are to go to the brother (or sister) privately first (Matt. 18:15). If he or she refuses to hear, we are to go again with one or two more people (v. 16). Then if he or she refuses to hear, we are to "tell it to the church" (v. 17). If the sinning one still fails to repent, "let him be to you as a Gentile and a tax-gatherer" (v. 17). In other words, pursue that person for Christ evangelistically as if he or she were utterly unsaved.

This process of discipline is how Christ mediates His rule in the church. He went on to say, "Truly I say to you, whatever you shall bind on earth shall be bound in heaven; and whatever you loose on earth shall be loosed in heaven. Again I say to you, that if two of you agree on earth about anything that they may ask, it shall be done for them by My Father who is in heaven" (Matt. 18:18–19). The context shows this is not talking about "binding Satan" or about praying in general. Our Lord was dealing with the matter of sin and forgiveness among Christians (cf. v. 21ff). The verb tenses in verse 18 literally mean, "Whatever you bind on earth shall have been bound in heaven; and whatever you loose on earth shall have been loosed in heaven." Our Lord is saying that He Himself works personally in the discipline process: "For where two or three have gathered together in My name, there I am in their midst" (v. 20).

Thus the process of church discipline, properly followed, answers all of Dr. Ryrie's questions. How long can a person continue in sin before we "conclude that [he or she] was never really saved?" All the way through the discipline process. Once the matter has been told to the church, if the person still refuses to repent, we have instructions from the Lord Himself to regard the sinning one "as a Gentile and a tax-gatherer."

The church discipline process our Lord outlined in Matthew 18 is predicated on the doctrine of perseverance. Those who remain hardened in sin only demonstrate their lack of true faith. Those who respond to the rebuke and return to the Lord give the best possible evidence that their salvation is genuine. They can be sure that if their faith is real it will endure to the end—because God Himself guarantees it.

"I am confident of this very thing, that He who began a good work in you will perfect it until the day of Christ Jesus (Phil. 1:6). "I know whom I have believed and I am convinced that He is able to guard what I have entrusted to Him until that day" (2 Tim. 1:12).

12

What Must I Do
to Be Saved?

If one were to suggest that the time would come when a group of evangelical Christians would be arguing for a salvation without repentance, without a change of behavior or lifestyle, without a real avowal of the lordship and authority of Christ, without perseverance, without discipleship, and a salvation which does not necessarily result in obedience and works, and with a regeneration which does not necessarily change one's life, most believers of several decades ago would have felt such would be an absolute impossibility. But believe it or not, the hour has come.

Richard P. Belcher[1]

What is the gospel? Here we get practical. The real question we are asking is, "How should I evangelize my friends, family, and neighbors?" For parents an even more important question is, "How should I present the gospel to my children?"

Twentieth-century Christianity has tended to take a minimalist approach to the gospel. Unfortunately, the legitimate desire to express the heart of the gospel clearly has given way to a less wholesome endeavor. It is a campaign to distill the essentials of the message to the barest possible terms. The glorious gospel of Christ—which Paul called "the power of God for salvation to everyone who believes" (Rom. 1:16)—

---

[1]Richard P. Belcher, *A Layman's Guide to the Lordship Controversy* (Southbridge, Mass.: Crowne, 1990), 71.

includes *all* the truth about Christ. But American evangelicalism tends to regard the gospel as a "plan of salvation." We have reduced the message to a list of facts stated in the fewest possible words—and getting fewer all the time. You've probably seen these prepackaged "plans of salvation": "Six Steps to Peace with God"; "Five Things God Wants You to Know"; "Four Spiritual Laws"; "Three Truths You Can't Live Without"; "Two Issues You Must Settle"; or "One Way to Heaven."

Christians today are often cautioned not to say *too much* to the lost. Certain spiritual issues are labeled taboo when speaking to the unconverted: God's law, Christ's lordship, turning from sin, surrender, obedience, judgment, and hell. Such things are not to be mentioned, lest we "add something to the offer of God's free gift." Proponents of no-lordship evangelism take the reductionist trend to its furthest extreme. Wrongly applying the Reformed doctrine of *sola fide* ("faith alone"), they make faith the only permissible topic when speaking to non-Christians about their duty before God. Then they render faith utterly meaningless by stripping it of everything but its notional aspects.

This, some believe, preserves the purity of the gospel.

What it actually has done is emasculate the message of salvation. It has also populated the church with "converts" whose faith is counterfeit and whose hope hangs on a bogus promise. Numbly saying they "accept Christ as Savior," they brazenly reject His rightful claim as Lord. Paying Him glib lip service, they utterly scorn Him with their hearts (Mark 7:6). Casually affirming Him with their mouths, they deliberately deny Him with their deeds (Titus 1:16). Addressing Him superficially as "Lord, Lord," they stubbornly decline to do His bidding (Luke 6:46). Such people fit the tragic description of the "many" in Matthew 7 who will one day be stunned to hear Him say, "I never knew you; depart from Me, *you who practice lawlessness*" (v. 23, emphasis added).

The gospel is not primarily news about a "plan," but a call to trust in a *Person*. It is not a formula that must be prescribed to sinners in a series of steps. It does not call for a mere decision of the mind, but a surrender of the heart, mind, and will—the whole person—to Christ. It is not a message that can be capsulized, abridged, and shrink-wrapped, then offered as a generic remedy for every kind of sinner. *Ignorant* sinners need to be instructed about who He is and why He has the right to demand their obedience. *Self-righteous* sinners need to have their sin exposed by the demands of God's law. *Careless* sinners need to be confronted with the reality of God's impending judgment. *Fearful* sinners need to hear that God in His mercy has provided a way of deliverance. *All* sinners must understand how utterly holy God is.

They must comprehend the basic truths of Christ's sacrificial death and the triumph of His resurrection. They need to be confronted with God's demand that they turn from their sin to embrace Christ as Lord and Savior.

The *form* of the message will vary in each case. But the *content* must always drive home the reality of God's holiness and the sinner's helpless condition. *Then* it points sinners to Christ as a sovereign but merciful Lord who has purchased full atonement for all who will turn to Him in faith.

Twentieth-century evangelicalism seems obsessed with the idea that unsaved people should never be told they have any duty other than believing. Lewis Sperry Chafer, for example, suggested that "in all gospel preaching every reference to the life to be lived beyond regeneration should be avoided as far as possible."[2] He claimed it was faulty evangelism to tell sinners they must "repent and believe," "believe and confess Christ," "believe and be baptized," "believe and surrender to God," or "believe and confess sin."[3] Yet Scripture employs *all* those expressions! Jesus Himself preached, "*Repent and believe* in the gospel" (Mark 1:15). Paul wrote, "If you *confess* with your mouth Jesus as Lord, *and believe* in your heart that God raised Him from the dead, you shall be saved" (Rom. 10:9). At Pentecost, Peter preached, "*Repent, and let each of you be baptized* in the name of Jesus Christ for the forgiveness of your sins; and you shall receive the gift of the Holy Spirit" (Acts 2:38). John wrote, "He who does not *obey* the Son shall not see life, but the wrath of God abides on him" (John 3:36). The writer to the Hebrews said that Christ "became to all those who *obey* Him the source of eternal salvation" (Heb. 5:9). James wrote, "*Submit* therefore to God. Resist the devil and he will flee from you. Draw near to God and He will draw near to you. *Cleanse your hands, you sinners;* and *purify your hearts, you double-minded*" (James 4:7, emphasis added). Jesus responded by preaching law and lordship to a man who asked Him how he might obtain eternal life! (Matt. 19:16–22).

Are we to believe that the inspired Scripture constitutes poorly worded theology?

I agree that terminology is important, and we dare not confuse the gospel message or add anything to the biblical terms for salvation. But it should be obvious that Jesus and the apostles certainly did not fuss

---

[2]Lewis Sperry Chafer, *Systematic Theology*, 8 vols. (Dallas: Seminary Press, 1948), 3:387.

[3]Ibid., 3:371–93.

about the phraseology of evangelistic invitations the way many Christians today do. Nor did they avoid mentioning God's law. On the contrary, the law is where they began! (cf. Rom. 1:16–3:20). The law reveals our sin (Rom. 3:20) and is a tutor to lead us to Christ (Gal. 3:24). It is the means God uses to make sinners see their own helplessness. Clearly, Paul saw a key place for the law in evangelistic contexts. Yet many today believe the law, with its inflexible demand for holiness and obedience, is contrary to and incompatible with the gospel.

Why should we make such distinctions where Scripture does not? If *Scripture* cautioned against preaching repentance, obedience, righteousness, or judgment to unbelievers, that would be one thing. But Scripture contains no such warnings. The opposite is true. If we want to follow a biblical model, we cannot ignore those issues. "Sin, righteousness, and judgment" are the very matters about which the Holy Spirit convicts the unsaved (John 16:8). Can we omit them from the message and still call it the gospel? Apostolic evangelism inevitably culminated in a call for repentance (Acts 2:38; 3:19; 17:30; 26:20). Can we tell sinners they *don't* have to turn from their sin, and then call that evangelism? Paul ministered to unbelievers by "declaring . . . that they should repent and turn to God, performing deeds appropriate to repentance" (Acts 26:20). Can we reduce the message to simply, "accept Christ" and still believe we are ministering biblically?

Furthermore, in all the instances where Jesus and the apostles evangelized—whether they were ministering to individuals or crowds—there are no two incidents where they presented the message in precisely the same terminology. They knew that salvation is a sovereign work of God. Their role was to preach truth; God Himself would apply it individually to the hearts of His elect.

The new birth is a sovereign work of the Holy Spirit. "That which is born of the flesh is flesh, and that which is born of the Spirit is spirit" (John 3:6). The Spirit sovereignly chooses where, how, and on whom He will work: "The wind blows where it wishes and you hear the sound of it, but do not know where it comes from and where it is going; so is everyone who is born of the Spirit" (John 3:8).

Clear proclamation of truth is the means through which the Spirit works—not inventive methodology or human charm (1 Cor. 1:21; 2:1–5).

Decisionism and Easy-Believism

Two fallacies—*decisionism* and *easy-believism*—taint much of what is labeled evangelism in contemporary Christianity. Decisionism is the idea that eternal salvation may be secured by the sinner's own movement toward Christ. A "decision for Christ" is usually signified by some physical or verbal act—raising a hand, walking an aisle, repeating a prayer, signing a card, reciting a pledge, or something similar. If the sinner performs the prescribed activity, he or she is usually pronounced saved and told to claim assurance. The "moment of decision" becomes the ground of the person's assurance.

Decisionism is often employed in evangelizing children. Youngsters in large groups are asked to raise a hand, stand, come forward, ask Jesus into their hearts, or make some similar gesture. Those things are supposed to indicate a positive response to the gospel. But because children are so susceptible to suggestion, so sensitive to peer pressure, and so desirous of gaining their leaders' approval, it is very easy to get large groups of children to profess faith in Christ through such means, even if they are utterly oblivious to the message. Unfortunately, many people go through life caring nothing for Christ but believing they are Christians only because they responded with a childhood "decision." Their hope of heaven hangs solely on the memory of that event. I'm afraid that in many cases it is a vain and damning hope.

Here is a familiar technique for counseling people who are unsure of their salvation: "Decide for Christ here and now, note the date, then drive a stake in your backyard and write the date on it. Whenever you doubt your salvation, go out and look at the stake. It will be a reminder of the decision you have made." But that is tantamount to telling people they should have faith in their own decision. Dr. Chafer even went so far as to give this advice to people struggling with a lack of assurance:

> The only cure for this uncertainty is to end it with certainty. Let such an one face his own utter sinfulness and meritlessness with the revelations of the cross and discover, as he must, no hope in himself, and then and there, once for all, appropriate the provisions of divine grace for every need of a sin-cursed soul. If need be, note the very day and hour of such a decision and *then believe in the decision itself* enough to thank God for His saving grace and faithfulness, and in every thought, act and word thereafter treat the decision as final and real.[4]

Ironically, Chafer simultaneously denounced trends in mass evangelism that were based on the same decisionist presuppositions reflected in that paragraph. In another book, he criticized the evangelists of his day for requiring converts to "come forward" publicly as an outward act of

---

[4]Lewis Sperry Chafer, *Salvation* (Philadelphia: Sunday School Times, 1917), 80 (emphasis added).

receiving Christ: "Such acts, if urged at all, should be so presented that they could not be thought of by any individual as forming a part of the one condition of salvation."[5] He believed that such methods could lead to false assurance: "If questioned carefully, the basis of assurance with all such converts will be found to be no more than a consciousness that they have acted out the program prescribed for them."[6] That is precisely the problem with decisionism. It offers a false hope based on a wrong premise. Salvation cannot be obtained by following any prescribed course of outward action. "For by grace you have been saved through faith; and that not of yourselves, it is the gift of God; not as a result of works, that no one should boast" (Eph. 2:8–9).

Decisionism and no-lordship doctrine do not always go hand in hand. In fact, the most aggressive advocates of modern no-lordship teaching nearly all recognize the fallacy of overt decisionism. They would affirm with us that no one is saved because of raising a hand, walking an aisle, praying a prayer, or any other physical act.

Most nevertheless believe saving faith hinges on human initiative. In their system, faith begins with a human response, not the work of God in the believer. Therefore they must scale back the definition of faith to make believing something depraved sinners are capable of. This is *easy-believism*.

Even those who are willing to grant that faith is a gift of God sometimes fall into easy-believism. Dr. Chafer, for example, seemed confused at this point. On the one hand, he roundly condemned those who tell sinners they must "believe and surrender." That places an undue demand on sinners, he argued. If unbelievers are dead in trespasses and sins, how can they surrender to God? "To impose a need to surrender the life to God as an added condition of salvation is most unreasonable," he wrote.[7]

On the other hand, Chafer evidently realized that if unsaved people are dead in trespasses and sins, they cannot even *believe* apart from God's initiative. Oddly, Chafer made this observation in the very same paragraph as the sentence I just quoted: "Saving faith is not a possession of all men but is imparted specifically to those who do believe (Eph. 2:8)."[8] Chafer rightly saw that only God can provoke faith in an unbelieving heart. But for some reason Chafer could not accept the idea that the

[5]Lewis Sperry Chafer, *True Evangelism* (Grand Rapids, Mich.: Zondervan, 1919), 13.
[6]Ibid., 15.
[7]Chafer, *Systematic Theology*, 3:385.
[8]Ibid.

faith God imparts comes with a built-in attitude of surrender and self-abandonment. So he defined faith in terms that posed no challenge to human depravity.

At its heart, easy-believism is a misunderstanding of the depth of human sinfulness. If ungodly, depraved, spiritually dead sinners are capable of believing solely on their own initiative, then faith must be something that makes no moral or spiritual demands. That is precisely why no-lordship theology has unsanctified the act of believing and made faith a nonmoral exercise. That is easy-believism.

The rationale of easy-believism is expressed most clearly in a newspaper clipping I received from a radio listener. A pastor had published a column criticizing me for my stand against easy-believism. He wrote, "I think God intended for the act of salvation to be easy. . . . *God made it easy for us to receive him because he knew in our sinful state that easy was the only way we would be saved.*"[9]

But that is faulty and unbiblical theology. Believing isn't *easy*.[10] It isn't even *hard*.[11] It is *impossible* in human terms. Jesus Himself acknowledged this (Matt. 19:26). No one can come to Christ unless it has been granted by the Father (John 6:65). The unregenerate do not accept the things of the Spirit of God; spiritual things are foolishness to them. They cannot even begin to understand them, much less believe (1 Cor. 2:14). Only God can open the heart and initiate faith (cf. Acts 13:48; 16:14; 18:27).

The faith God grants trembles before Him (Luke 18:13). It is a faith that provokes obedience from the heart and makes the sinner a slave to righteousness (Rom. 6:17–18). It is a faith that works though love (Gal. 5:6). It has nothing to do with the sterile faith of easy-believism.

How Should We Call People to Faith?

There are many helpful books on how to witness offering practical advice and how-tos.[12] In this brief chapter, I want to focus on some crucial

---

[9]Stephen Kern, "It Is Easy to Receive Salvation from God," *The Idaho Statesman,* 29 June 1991, 3D (emphasis added).

[10]Hodges seems to be arguing that, after all, believing is supposed to be easy. Responding to the phrase "easy-believism," he writes: "Presumably the opposite would be 'hard believism.' And if any system of thought teaches 'hard believism,' lordship salvation certainly does. . . . But salvation really *is* simple and, in that sense, it is easy! After all, what could be simpler than to 'take of the water of life freely'?" (*AF* 30).

[11]Ryrie includes a chapter titled, "It's Not Easy to Believe" (*SGS* 117–23).

issues relating to the *content* of the message we are called to share with un-believers. Specifically, if we want to articulate the gospel as precisely as pos-sible, what are the points we need to make clear?

Teach them about God's holiness. "The fear of the Lord is the beginning of wisdom" (Ps. 111:10, cf. Job 28:28; Prov. 1:7; 9:10; 15:33; Mic. 6:9). No-lordship theology misses this point entirely. In fact, much of contemporary evangelism aims to arouse anything *but* fear of God. "God loves you and has a wonderful plan for your life," is the opening line of the typical evangelistic appeal today. No-lordship theol-ogy takes it a step further: God loves you and will save you from hell no matter *whose* plan you choose for your life.

The remedy for such thinking is the biblical truth of God's holi-ness. *God is utterly holy, and His law therefore demands perfect holiness:* "I am the Lord your God. Consecrate yourselves therefore, and be holy; for I am holy. . . . You shall be holy for I am holy" (Lev. 11:44–45). "You will not be able to serve the Lord, for He is a holy God. He is a jealous God; He will not forgive your transgression or your sins" (Josh. 24:19). "There is no one holy like the Lord, indeed, there is no one besides Thee, Nor is there any rock like our God" (1 Sam. 2:2). "Who is able to stand before the Lord, this holy God?" (6:20).

Even the gospel requires this holiness: "You shall be holy, for I am holy" (1 Pet. 1:16). "Without [holiness] no one will see the Lord" (Heb. 12:14).

Because He is holy, God hates sin: "I, the Lord your God, am a jeal-ous God, visiting the iniquity of the fathers on the children, on the third and the fourth generations of those who hate Me" (Exod. 20:5). *Sinners cannot stand before Him:* "The wicked will not stand in the judgment, nor sinners in the assembly of the righteous" (Ps. 1:5).

Show them their sin. Gospel means "good news." What makes it truly good news is not just that heaven is free, but that sin has been conquered by God's Son. Sadly, it has become stylish to present the gospel as something other than a remedy for sin. "Salvation" is offered as an escape from punishment, God's plan for a wonderful life, a means of fulfillment, an answer to life's problems, and a promise of

[12]One particularly helpful resource is by Will Metzger, *Tell the Truth,* 2d ed. (Downers Grove, Ill.: InterVarsity, 1984). Along with very practical information, Metzger also decries the reductionist trend in evangelism I have described, and he includes a very insightful section contrasting God-centered evangelism with man-centered evangelism. A helpful tract is "Who Do You Think I Am?" (Valencia, Calif.: Grace to You, 1991).

free forgiveness. All those things are true, but they are byproducts of redemption, not the main issue. When sin is left unaddressed, such promises of divine blessings cheapen the message.

Some no-lordship teachers go so far as to say that sin is not an issue in the gospel invitation. Sin, they believe, is a postsalvation concern. Others believe it is optional whether we confront unbelievers with their sin. One man who edits a no-lordship newsletter replied to a reader's question: "No, I do not believe that one *must* recognize that he is a sinner to be saved. The key word is *must*. It is conceivable that a person could be ignorant of the fact that he is a sinner and yet know that he was bound for hell and could only be saved by trusting in Christ alone. Some small children might fall into this category."[13]

He did not attempt to explain why people with no understanding of their own sinfulness would believe they are headed for hell. But one wonders what sort of salvation is available to those who don't even recognize their sin. Didn't Jesus say, "It is not those who are healthy who need a physician, but those who are sick; I did not come to call the righteous, but sinners" (Mark 2:17)? To offer salvation to someone who doesn't even understand the gravity of sin is to fulfill Jeremiah 6:14: "They have healed the brokenness of My people superficially, Saying, 'Peace, peace,' But there is no peace."

Sin is what makes true peace impossible for unbelievers: "The wicked are like the tossing sea, for it cannot be quiet, and its waters toss up refuse and mud. 'There is no peace,' says my God, 'for the wicked'" (Isa. 57:20–21).

All have sinned:

> There is none righteous, not even one; there is none who understands, there is none who seeks for God; all have turned aside, together they have become useless; there is none who does good, there is not even one. Their throat is an open grave, with their tongues they keep deceiving, the poison of asps is under their lips; whose mouth is full of cursing and bitterness; their feet are swift to shed blood, destruction and misery are in their paths, and the path of peace have they not known. There is no fear of God before their eyes (Rom. 3:10–18).

Sin makes the sinner worthy of death: "When sin is accomplished, it brings forth death" (James 1:15). "For the wages of sin is death" (Rom. 6:23).

---

[13]Bob Wilkin, "Letters to the Editor," *The Grace Evangelical Society News* (August 1990): 3.

Sinners can do nothing to earn salvation: "For all of us have become like one who is unclean, and all our righteous deeds are like a filthy garment; and all of us wither like a leaf, and our iniquities, like the wind, take us away" (Isa. 64:6). "By the works of the Law no flesh will be justified in His sight" (Rom. 3:20). "A man is not justified by the works of the Law . . . by the works of the Law shall no flesh be justified" (Gal. 2:16).

Sinners are therefore in a helpless state: "It is appointed for men to die once and after this comes judgment" (Heb. 9:27). "There is nothing covered up that will not be revealed, and hidden that will not be known" (Luke 12:2). "God will judge the secrets of men through Christ Jesus" (Rom. 2:16). "The cowardly and unbelieving and abominable and murderers and immoral persons and sorcerers and idolaters and all liars, their part will be in the lake that burns with fire and brimstone, which is the second death" (Rev. 21:8).

Instruct them about Christ and what He has done. The gospel is good news about who Christ is and what He has done for sinners. No-lordship doctrine tends to emphasize His *work* and de-emphasize His *Person,* particularly the aspect of His divine authority. But Scripture never presents Jesus as something less than Lord in salvation. The notion that His Lordship is an addendum to the gospel is utterly foreign to Scripture.

He is eternally God: "In the beginning was the Word, and the Word was with God, and the Word was God. He was in the beginning with God. All things came into being by Him, and apart from Him nothing came into being that has come into being. . . . And the Word became flesh, and dwelt among us, and we beheld His glory, glory as of the only begotten from the Father, full of grace and truth" (John 1:1–3, 14). "In Him all the fulness of Deity dwells in bodily form" (Col. 2:9).

He is Lord of all: "He is Lord of lords and King of kings, and those who are with Him are the called and chosen and faithful" (Rev. 17:14). "God highly exalted Him, and bestowed on Him the name which is above every name, that at the name of Jesus every knee should bow, of those who are in heaven, and on earth, and under the earth, and that every tongue should confess that Jesus Christ is Lord, to the glory of God the Father" (Phil. 2:9–11). "He is Lord of all" (Acts 10:36).

He became man: "Although He existed in the form of God, [He] did not regard equality with God a thing to be grasped, but emptied Himself, taking the form of a bond-servant, and being made in the likeness of men" (Phil. 2:6–7).

He is utterly pure and sinless: "[He was] tempted in all things as we are, yet without sin" (Heb. 4:15). He "committed no sin, nor was any deceit found in His mouth; and while being reviled, He did not revile in return; while suffering, He uttered no threats, but kept entrusting Himself to Him who judges righteously" (1 Pet. 2:22–23). "He appeared in order to take away sins; and in Him there is no sin" (1 John 3:5).

The sinless one became a sacrifice for our sin: "He made Him who knew no sin to be sin on our behalf, that we might become the righteousness of God in Him" (2 Cor. 5:21). He "gave Himself for us, that He might redeem us from every lawless deed and purify for Himself a people for His own possession, zealous for good deeds" (Titus 2:14). *He shed His own blood as an atonement for sin:* "In Him we have redemption through His blood, the forgiveness of our trespasses, according to the riches of His grace which He lavished upon us" (Eph. 1:7–8). "[He] loves us, and released us from our sins by His blood" (Rev. 1:5). *He died on the cross to provide a way of salvation for sinners:* "He Himself bore our sins in His body on the cross, that we might die to sin and live to righteousness; for by His wounds you were healed" (1 Pet. 2:24). "Through Him to reconcile all things to Himself, having made peace through the blood of His cross" (Col. 1:20).

He rose triumphantly from the dead: Christ "was declared the Son of God with power by the resurrection from the dead" (Rom. 1:4). "[He] was delivered up because of our transgressions, and was raised because of our justification" (4:25). "I delivered to you as of first importance what I also received, that Christ died for our sins according to the Scriptures, and that He was buried, and that He was raised on the third day according to the Scriptures" (1 Cor. 15:3–4).

Tell them what God demands of them. Repentant faith is the requirement. It is not merely a "decision" to trust Christ for eternal life, but a wholesale forsaking of everything else we trust, and a turning to Jesus Christ as Lord and Savior.

Repent: "Repent and turn away from all your transgressions" (Ezek. 18:30). "'I have no pleasure in the death of anyone who dies,' declares the Lord GOD. 'Therefore, repent and live'" (v. 32). "God is now declaring to men that all everywhere should repent" (Acts 17:30). "Repent and turn to God, performing deeds appropriate to repentance" (Acts 26:20).

Turn your heart from all that you know dishonors God: "[Turn] to God from idols to serve a living and true God" (1 Thess. 1:9). *Follow Jesus:* "If anyone wishes to come after Me, let him deny himself, and take up his cross daily, and follow Me" (Luke 9:23). "No one, after putting his hand to the plow and looking back, is fit for the kingdom of God" (v. 62). "If anyone serves Me, let him follow Me; and where I am, there shall My servant also be; if anyone serves Me, the Father will honor him" (John 12:26).

Trust Him as Lord and Savior: "Believe in the Lord Jesus, and you shall be saved" (Acts 16:31). "If you confess with your mouth Jesus as Lord, and believe in your heart that God raised Him from the dead, you shall be saved" (Rom. 10:9).

Advise them to count the cost thoughtfully. Salvation *is* absolutely free. So is joining the army. You don't have to buy your way in. Everything you will need is provided. But there is a sense in which following Christ—like joining the army—will cost you dearly. It can cost freedom, family, friends, autonomy, and possibly even your life. The job of the evangelist—like that of the army recruiter—is to tell potential inductees the full story. That is exactly why Jesus' message was often so full of hard demands:

> If anyone comes to Me, and does not hate his own father and mother and wife and children and brothers and sisters, yes, and even his own life, he cannot be My disciple. Whoever does not carry his own cross and come after Me cannot be My disciple. For which one of you, when he wants to build a tower, does not first sit down and calculate the cost, to see if he has enough to complete it? Otherwise, when he has laid a foundation, and is not able to finish, all who observe it begin to ridicule him, saying, "This man began to build and was not able to finish." Or what king, when he sets out to meet another king in battle, will not first sit down and take counsel whether he is strong enough with ten thousand men to encounter the one coming against him with twenty thousand? Or else, while the other is still far away, he sends a delegation and asks terms of peace. So therefore, no one of you can be My disciple who does not give up all his own possessions.
>
> Luke 14:26–33

> Do not think that I came to bring peace on the earth; I did not come to bring peace, but a sword. For I came to set a man against his father, and a daughter against her mother, and a daughter-in-law against her mother-in-law; and a man's enemies will be the members of his household. He who loves father or mother more than Me is not worthy of Me; and he who loves son or daughter more than Me is not worthy of Me. And he who does not take his cross and follow after Me is not worthy of Me.
>
> Matthew 10:34–38

The free-costly, death-life enigma is expressed in the clearest possible terms by John 12:24–25: "Truly, truly, I say to you, unless a grain of wheat falls into the earth and dies, it remains by itself alone; but if it dies, it bears much fruit. He who loves his life loses it; and he who hates his life in this world shall keep it to life eternal."

The cross is central to the gospel precisely because of its graphic message, including the awfulness of sin, the profundity of God's wrath against sin, and the efficacy of Jesus' work in crucifying the old man (Rom. 6:6). A. W. Tozer wrote,

> The cross is the most revolutionary thing ever to appear among men.
>
> The cross of Roman times knew no compromise; it never made concessions. It won all its arguments by killing its opponent and silencing him for good. It spared not Christ, but slew Him the same as the rest. He was alive when they hung Him on that cross and completely dead when they took Him down six hours later. That was the cross the first time it appeared in Christian history. . . .
>
> The cross effects its ends by destroying one established pattern, the victim's, and creating another pattern, its own. Thus it always has its way. It wins by defeating its opponent and imposing its will upon him. It always dominates. It never compromises, never dickers nor confers, never surrenders a point for the sake of peace. It cares not for peace; it cares only to end its opposition as fast as possible.
>
> With perfect knowledge of all this, Christ said, "If any man will come after me, let him deny himself, and take up his cross, and follow me." So the cross not only brings Christ's life to an end, it ends also the first life, the old life, of every one of His true followers. It destroys the old pattern, the Adam pattern, in the believer's life, and brings it to an end. Then the God who raised Christ from the dead raises the believer and a new life begins.
>
> This, and nothing less, is true Christianity. . . .
>
> We must do something about the cross, and one of two things only we can do—flee it or die upon it.[14]

"For whoever wishes to save his life shall lose it; but whoever loses his life for My sake and the gospel's shall save it. For what does it profit a man to gain the whole world, and forfeit his soul? For what shall a man give in exchange for his soul?" (Mark 8:35–37).

---

[14]A. W. Tozer, *The Root of the Righteous* (Harrisburg, Pa.: Christian Publications, 1955), 61–63.

Urge them to trust Christ. "Knowing the fear of the Lord, we persuade men" (2 Cor. 5:11). "[God] reconciled us to Himself through Christ, and gave us the ministry of reconciliation, namely, that God was in Christ reconciling the world to Himself, not counting their trespasses against them, and He has committed to us the word of reconciliation. Therefore, we are ambassadors for Christ, as though God were entreating through us; we beg you on behalf of Christ, be reconciled to God" (2 Cor. 5:20).

"Seek the Lord while He may be found; Call upon Him while He is near. Let the wicked forsake his way, and the unrighteous man his thoughts; and let him return to the Lord, and He will have compassion on him; and to our God, for He will abundantly pardon" (Isa. 55:7). "If you confess with your mouth Jesus as Lord, and believe in your heart that God raised Him from the dead, you shall be saved; for with the heart man believes, resulting in righteousness, and with the mouth he confesses, resulting in salvation" (Rom. 10:9–10).

Where Do Good Works Fit?

Nowhere in either the Old or New Testaments do we find an invitation for sinners to believe now, obey later. The call to trust and obey is a single summons. The word *obey* is sometimes even used to describe the conversion experience: "He became to all those who obey Him the source of eternal salvation" (Heb. 5:9).

Does anyone really suppose it is possible to *believe,* to really fathom everything that Jesus did in suffering and dying for sin, to accept the offer of forgiveness from His hand—and then turn away, not exalt Him with one's life, and even grow to despise and reject and disbelieve Him exactly like those who put Him to death? That kind of theology is grotesque.

The truth is, our surrender to Christ is never purer than at the moment we are born again. In that sacred moment we are wholly under the sovereign control of the Holy Spirit, united to Christ, and recipients of a new heart. Then more than ever, obedience is not negotiable, nor would any genuine convert desire it to be (cf. Rom. 6:17).

The apostle Paul's conversion furnishes the archetypical illustration. In Paul's conversion, the issue was clearly Jesus' lordship. What were Paul's first words as a believer? "What shall I do, Lord?" (Acts 22:10). Years later Paul wrote about all that he gave up on the road to Damascus:

> Though I might also have confidence in the flesh. If any other man thinketh that he hath whereof he might trust in the flesh, I

more: Circumcised the eighth day, of the stock of Israel, of the tribe of Benjamin, an Hebrew of the Hebrews; as touching the law, a Pharisee; concerning zeal, persecuting the church; touching the righteousness which is in the law, blameless. *But what things were gain to me, those I counted loss for Christ. Yea doubtless, and I count all things but loss for the excellency of the knowledge of Christ Jesus my Lord: for whom I have suffered the loss of all things, and do count them but dung,* that I may win Christ, and be found in him, not having mine own righteousness, which is of the law, but that which is through the faith of Christ, the righteousness which is of God by faith.

Philippians 3:4–9 KJV, emphasis added

Can we honestly look at Paul's conversion, life, and ministry, and believe that he ever espoused a gospel that taught people they could be saved without surrender to Christ's authority?

Lordship salvation is often caricatured as teaching people that they must change their lives in order to be saved.[15] But no advocate of lordship theology I know of has ever taught such a thing. There is not a legitimate teacher of the lordship doctrine anywhere who would ever tell any unbeliever he needs to "'prove' he qualifies for salvation."[16] As we have seen time and time again in our study, meritorious works have no place in salvation.

But *faith works* have everything to do with *why* we are saved. God's whole purpose in choosing us is "that He might redeem us from every lawless deed and purify for Himself a people for His own possession, *zealous for good deeds*" (Titus 2:14, emphasis added). This is God's purpose from eternity past: "We are His workmanship, created in Christ Jesus for *good works, which God prepared beforehand, that we should walk in them*" (Eph. 2:10, emphasis added).

The first command for every Christian is baptism. I mentioned earlier that the apostles sometimes included baptism in the call to faith (Acts 2:38; cf. Mark 16:16). Baptism is not a condition of salvation but an initial step of obedience for the Christian. Conversion is complete before baptism occurs; baptism is only an external sign that testifies to what has occurred in the sinner's heart. Baptism is a ritual, and

---

[15]J. Dwight Pentecost, "A Christian Perspective," *Kindred Spirit* (Winter 1988): 3.

[16]Ibid. This is a prime example of how lordship salvation is often exaggerated, parodied, and made into a caricature easy to debunk. Unfortunately it confuses and prejudices people while failing to address any real issues.

it is precisely the kind of "work" Paul states cannot be meritorious (cf. Rom. 4:10–11).[17]

Nevertheless, one can hardly read the New Testament without noticing the heavy stress the early church placed on baptism. They simply *assumed* that every genuine believer would embark on a life of obedience and discipleship. That was nonnegotiable. Therefore they viewed baptism as the turning point. Only those who were baptized were considered Christians. That is why the Ethiopian eunuch was so eager to be baptized (Acts 8:36–39).

Unfortunately, the church today takes baptism more casually. It is not unusual to meet people who have been professing Christians for years but have never been baptized. That was unheard of in the New Testament church. Unfortunately, we have lost the focus on initial obedience.

Spurgeon wrote, "If the professed convert distinctly and deliberately declares that he knows the Lord's will, but does not mean to attend to it, you are not to pamper his presumptions, but it is your duty to assure him that he is not saved."[18]

How Shall We Witness to Children?

Should we streamline or abbreviate the message when we teach children the gospel? There is no biblical warrant for that. Certainly we need to use terminology they can grasp and be clear and patient in communicating the message. But when Scripture talks about teaching children spiritual truth, the emphasis is on *thoroughness:* "And these words, which I am commanding you today, shall be on your heart; and you shall teach them diligently to your sons and shall talk of them when you sit in your house and when you walk by the way and when you lie down and when you rise up" (Deut. 6:6–7). Oversimplification is a greater danger, it seems, than giving too much detail.

Children cannot be saved before they are old enough to understand the gospel clearly and can embrace it with genuine faith. They must therefore be mature enough to understand good and evil, sin and punishment, and repentance and faith. Certainly they need to be old

---

[17]If baptism were necessary for salvation, Paul certainly would not have written, "I thank God that I baptized none of you except Crispus and Gaius . . . for Christ did not send me to baptize, but to preach the gospel" (1 Cor. 1:14, 17).

[18]Charles Haddon Spurgeon, *The Soul Winner* (reprint, Grand Rapids, Mich.: Eerdmans, 1963), 38.

enough to understand the gravity of sin and the nature of God's holiness. What is that age? Surely it varies from child to child. Children mature at different times. Part of our task in teaching them is to help them come to a developed understanding of these very issues.

Don't soften the parts of the message that sound unpleasant. Christ's blood, the cross, and atonement for sins are at the heart of the message. If we bypass such topics, we're not giving the full gospel. Don't tone down the demand for surrender. Christ's lordship is not too difficult for children to understand. Any child who is old enough to understand the basic gospel is also able by God's grace to trust Him completely and respond with the purest, most sincere kind of surrender. Jesus "called a child to Himself and set him before them, and said, 'Truly I say to you, unless you are converted and become like children, you shall not enter the kingdom of heaven. Whoever then humbles himself as this child, he is the greatest in the kingdom of heaven'" (Matt. 18:2–4).

Remember that the primary factor in any person's coming to Christ is not *how much doctrine* he or she knows. The real issue is the extent of God's work in the heart. Even the most mature believer does not comprehend all of God's truth. We can only begin to fathom the riches of God's Word in this present life. Full understanding of every aspect of the gospel certainly is not required for salvation. After all, the thief on the cross next to Jesus knew only that he himself was guilty and that Jesus, who was Lord and the true Messiah, had done nothing wrong (Luke 23:40–42). How did he know that much? As Jesus said to Peter, "Flesh and blood did not reveal this . . . but My Father who is in heaven" (Matt. 16:17). The thief's appeal was simple: "Jesus, remember me when You come in Your kingdom!" (v. 42). But despite the meager amount of doctrine he knew, our Lord assured him, "Truly I say to you, today you shall be with Me in Paradise" (v. 43).

It is the Holy Spirit's task, not ours, to offer assurance (Rom. 8:14–16). So don't overemphasize objective assurance with children. As I noted earlier, too many people whose hearts are utterly cold to the things of the Lord believe they are going to heaven simply because they responded positively as children to an evangelistic invitation. Having "asked Jesus to come into their hearts," they were then taught never to examine themselves and never to entertain any doubt about their salvation.

Certainly we cannot assume that every profession of faith reflects a genuine work of God in the heart, and this is particularly true of children. Children often respond positively to gospel invitations for a host of reasons. Many of these reasons are unrelated to any awareness of sin and are apart from any real understanding of spiritual truth. If we prod children to "faith" by external pressure, their "conversion" will prove to be spurious. Only those who understand and are prompted to believe by the Spirit are truly born again (John 3:6).

Remember, an early childhood response does not necessarily guarantee that the question of eternal salvation is settled forever. While many people *do* make a genuine commitment to Christ when young, many others—perhaps most—don't come to an adequate realization of the meaning of the gospel until their teenage years. Others who profess Christ in childhood turn away. That is exactly why we must eschew the quick, easy response and teach our children patiently, consistently, faithfully over all their developing years. Encourage every step of faith as they grow.

We must take extreme care lest we inoculate children against any real commitment to Christ when they do come to an age of full spiritual understanding. Teach children the gospel—all of it—but understand that you may be planting the seeds for a harvest that may not be mature for many years. If you mow a field as soon as it sprouts you will never be able to reap a full harvest.

A Final Word

The first creed of the early church was "Jesus is Lord" (cf. Rom. 10:9–10; 1 Cor. 12:3). The lordship of Christ permeated apostolic preaching, and it permeates the New Testament. In the very first apostolic sermon, Peter's message at Pentecost, this was the pinnacle:

> This Jesus God raised up again, to which we are all witnesses. Therefore having been exalted to the right hand of God, and having received from the Father the promise of the Holy Spirit, He has poured forth this which you both see and hear. For it was not David who ascended into heaven, but he himself says: "The Lord said to my Lord, 'Sit at My right hand, until I make Thine enemies a footstool for Thy feet.'" Therefore let all the house of Israel know for certain that *God has made Him both Lord and Christ*—this Jesus whom you crucified."
>
> Acts 2:32–36, emphasis added

The context leaves no doubt about Peter's meaning. This was a message about Christ's absolute authority as the blessed and only Sovereign, the King of kings and Lord of lords (cf. 1 Tim. 6:15–16).

Throughout the Book of Acts Jesus' absolute lordship is a recurring theme. When Peter opened the gospel ministry to Gentiles at the house of Cornelius, he again declared, "He is Lord of all" (Acts 10:36). In the Book of Acts alone, the title "Lord" is used of Jesus fifty times as often as "Savior." The truth of His lordship was the key to apostolic preaching. Christ's lordship *is* the gospel according to the apostles.

T. Alan Chrisope, in his wonderful book, *Jesus Is Lord,* writes, "There is no element of apostolic preaching more prominent than the resurrection, exaltation and lordship of Jesus."[19] He adds,

> The confession "Jesus is Lord" is the single most predominant Christian confession in the New Testament. Not only does it occur in several passages which emphasize its singular character as *the* Christian confession (e. g., Phil. 2:9–11; Rom. 10:9; 1 Cor. 12:3; 8:5–6; cf. Eph. 4:5), but it also occurs numerous times in a variant form in the phrase "our Lord," a designation of Jesus which was so widely used that it became the distinctive and universally recognized Christian confession, known and acknowledged by all believers.[20]

"All the basic facts of the gospel story are implicit in the single brief confession, 'Jesus is Lord.'"[21]

The apostle Paul said, "We do not preach ourselves but Christ Jesus as Lord" (2 Cor. 4:5). Jesus' lordship *is* the apostolic message.

I closed my earlier book on the gospel with these words, which make a fitting conclusion for this work as well:

> [Jesus] is Lord, and those who refuse Him as Lord cannot use Him as Savior. Everyone who receives Him must surrender to His authority, for to say we receive Christ when in fact we reject His right to reign over us is utter absurdity. It is a futile attempt to hold onto sin with one hand and take Jesus with the other. What kind of salvation is it if we are left in bondage to sin?
>
> This, then is the gospel we are to proclaim: That Jesus Christ, who is God incarnate, humbled Himself to die on our behalf. Thus He became the sinless sacrifice to pay the penalty of our guilt. He rose from the dead to declare with power that He is Lord over all,

---

[19]T. Alan Chrisope, *Jesus Is Lord* (Hertfordshire, England: Evangelical Press, 1982), 57.

[20]Ibid., 61.

[21]Ibid., 63.

and He offers eternal life freely to sinners who will surrender to Him
in humble, repentant faith. This gospel promises nothing to the
haughty rebel, but for broken, penitent sinners, it graciously offers
everything that pertains to life and godliness (2 Peter 1:3).[22]

[22]John MacArthur, Jr., *The Gospel According to Jesus* (Grand Rapids, Mich.: Zondervan,
1988), 210.

Appendix 1

A Comparison of Three Views

The chart on the following pages is a side-by-side comparison of positions on the major issues of the lordship controversy. Refer to chapter 2 (pages 23-29) for documentation.

Readers interested in a further analysis of the key issues in the lordship controversy will benefit much from Robert Lescelius's superb book *Lordship Salvation: Some Crucial Questions and Answers* (Asheville, N.C.: Revival Literature, 1992). Another very helpful resource is Richard P. Belcher's *A Layman's Guide to the Lordship Controversy* (Southbridge, Mass.: Crowne Publications, 1990).

	Lordship	No-lordship	Radical No-lordship
The cross	Christ's death on the cross paid the full penalty for our sins and purchased eternal salvation. His atoning sacrifice enables God to justify sinners freely without compromising the perfection of divine righteousness. His resurrection from the dead declares His victory over sin and death.	Agree.	Agree.
Justification by faith	Salvation is by grace through faith in the Lord Jesus Christ alone—plus and minus nothing.	Agree.	Agree.
Good works	Sinners cannot earn salvation or favor with God.	Agree.	Agree.
Prerequisites for salvation	God requires of those who are saved no preparatory works or prerequisite self-improvement.	Agree.	Agree.
Eternal life	Eternal life is a gift of God.	Agree.	Agree.
Immediate justification	Believers are saved and fully justified before their faith ever produces a single righteous work.	Agree.	Agree.
Believers and sin	Christians can and do sin. Even the strongest Christians wage a constant and intense struggle against sin in the flesh. Genuine believers sometimes commit heinous sins.	Agree.	Agree.

	Lordship	No-lordship	Radical No-lordship
Repentance	The gospel calls sinners to faith joined in oneness with repentance. Repentance is turning from sin. It is not a work but a divinely bestowed grace. Repentance is a change of heart, but genuine repentance will effect a change of behavior as well.	Repentance is a change of mind about Christ. In the context of the gospel invitation, *repentance* is just a synonym for *faith*. No turning from sin is required for salvation.	Repentance is not essential to the gospel message. In no sense is repentance related to saving faith.
Faith	Salvation is all God's work. Those who believe are saved utterly apart from any effort on their own. Even faith is a gift of God, not a work of man. Real faith therefore cannot be defective or short-lived but endures forever.	The whole of salvation, including faith, is a gift of God. But faith might not last. A true Christian can completely cease believing.	Faith is a human act, not a gift from God. It occurs in a decisive moment but does not necessarily continue. True faith can be subverted, be overthrown, collapse, or even turn to unbelief.
Faith's object	The object of faith is Christ Himself, not only a creed or a promise. Faith therefore involves personal commitment to Christ. In other words, all true believers follow Jesus.	Saving faith is simply being convinced or giving credence to the truth of the gospel. It is confidence that Christ can remove guilt and give eternal life, not a personal commitment to *Him*.	To "believe" unto salvation is to believe the *facts* of the gospel. "Trusting Jesus" means believing the "saving facts" about Him, and to believe those facts is to appropriate the gift of eternal life. Those who add any suggestion of commitment have departed from the New Testament idea of salvation.
Faith's effects	Real faith inevitably produces a changed life. Salvation includes a transformation of the inner person. The nature of the Christian is different, new. The unbroken pattern of sin and enmity with God will not continue when a person is born again.	*Some* spiritual fruit is inevitable in every Christian's experience. The fruit, however, might not be visible to others. Christians can even lapse into a state of permanent spiritual barrenness.	Spiritual fruit is not guaranteed in the Christian life. Some Christians spend their lives in a barren wasteland of defeat, confusion, and every kind of evil.

	Lordship	No-lordship	Radical No-lordship
Salvation's extent	The "gift of God," eternal life, includes all that pertains to life and godliness, not just a ticket to heaven.	Only the *judicial* aspects of salvation—such as justification, adoption, imputed righteousness, and positional sanctification—are guaranteed for believers in this life. *Practical* sanctification and growth in grace require a postconversion act of dedication.	Heaven is guaranteed to believers but Christian victory is not. One could even say "the saved" still need salvation. Christ offers a whole range of postconversion deliverance experiences to supply what Christians lack. But these other "salvations" all require the addition of human works, such as obedience, submission, and confession of Jesus as Lord. Thus God is dependent to some degree on human effort in achieving deliverance from sin in this life.
Christ's lordship	Jesus is Lord of all, and the faith He demands involves unconditional surrender. He does not bestow eternal life on those whose hearts remain set against Him.	Submission to Christ's supreme authority as Lord is not germane to the saving transaction. Neither dedication nor *willingness* to be dedicated to Christ are issues in salvation. The news that Christ died for our sins and rose from the dead is the *complete* gospel. Nothing else must be believed for salvation.	Submission is not in any sense a condition for eternal life. "Calling on the Lord" means *appealing* to Him, not *submitting* to Him.
Holy desires	Those who truly believe will love Christ. They will therefore long to obey Him.	Christians may fall into a state of lifelong carnality. A whole category of "carnal Christians"—born-again people who continuously live like the unsaved—exists in the church.	Nothing guarantees that a true Christian will love God. Salvation does not necessarily even place the sinner in a right relationship of harmonious fellowship with God.

	Lordship	No-lordship	Radical No-lordship
Assurance	Behavior is an important test of faith. Obedience is evidence that one's faith is real. On the other hand, the person who remains utterly unwilling to obey Christ does not evidence true faith.	Disobedience and prolonged sin are no reason to doubt the reality of one's faith.	If people are sure they believe, their faith *must* be genuine. *All* who claim Christ by faith as Savior—even those involved in serious or prolonged sin—should be assured that they belong to God come what may. It is dangerous and destructive to question the salvation of professing Christians. The New Testament writers *never* questioned the reality of their readers' faith.
Perseverance	Genuine believers may stumble and fall, but they *will* persevere in the faith. Those who later turn completely away from the Lord show that they were never truly born again.	A believer may utterly forsake Christ and come to the point of not believing. God has guaranteed that He will not disown those who thus abandon the faith. Those who have once believed are secure forever, even if they turn away.	It is possible to experience a moment of faith that guarantees heaven for eternity, then to turn away permanently and live a life that is utterly barren of any spiritual fruit. Genuine believers might even cease to name the name of Christ or confess Christianity.

Appendix 2

What Is Dispensationalism and What Does It Have to Do with Lordship Salvation?

*O*ne of the most confusing elements of the entire lordship controversy involves dispensationalism. Some have supposed that my attack on no-lordship theology is an all-out assault against dispensationalism. That is not the case. It may surprise some readers to know that the issue of dispensationalism is one area where Charles Ryrie, Zane Hodges, and I share some common ground. We are all dispensationalists.

Many people are understandably confused by the term *dispensationalism*. I've met seminary graduates and many in Christian leadership who haven't the slightest idea how to define dispensationalism. How does it differ from covenant theology? What does it have to do with lordship salvation? Perhaps we can answer those questions simply and without a lot of theological jargon.

Dispensationalism is a system of biblical interpretation that sees a distinction between God's program for Israel and His dealings with the church. It's really as simple as that.

A *dispensation* is the plan of God by which He administers His rule within a given era in His eternal program. Dispensations are not periods of *time,* but different *administrations* in the eternal outworking of God's purpose. It is especially crucial to note that the way of salvation—by grace through faith—is the same in every dispensation. God's redemptive plan remains unchanged, but the way He administers it will vary from one dispensation to another. Dispensationalists note that Israel was the focus of God's redemptive plan in one dispensation. The church, consisting of redeemed people including Jews and Gentiles, is the focus in another. All dispensationalists believe at least one dispensation is still future—during the thousand-year reign of Christ on earth, known as the millennium, in which Israel will once again play a pivotal role.

Dispensationalism teaches that all God's remaining covenant promises to Israel will be literally fulfilled—including the promises of earthly blessings and an earthly messianic kingdom. God promised Israel, for example, that they would possess the promised land forever (Gen. 13:14–17; Exod. 32:13). Scripture declares that Messiah will rule over the kingdoms of the earth from Jerusalem (Zech. 14:9–11). Old Testament prophecy says that all Israel will one day be restored to the promised land (Amos 9:14–15); the temple will be rebuilt (Ezek. 37:26–28); and the people of Israel will be redeemed (Jer. 23:6; Rom. 11:26–27). Dispensationalists believe all those promised blessings will come to pass as literally as did the promised curses.

Covenant theology, on the other hand, usually views such prophecies as *already* fulfilled allegorically or symbolically. Covenant theologians believe that the church, not literal Israel, is the recipient of the covenant promises. They believe the church has superseded Israel in God's eternal program. God's promises to Israel are therefore fulfilled in spiritual blessings realized by Christians.[1] Since their system does not allow for literal fulfillment of promised blessings to the Jewish nation, covenant theologians allegorize or spiritualize those prophetic passages of God's Word.

I am a dispensationalist because dispensationalism generally understands and applies Scripture—particularly prophetic Scripture—in a way that is more consistent with the normal, literal approach I believe is God's design for interpreting Scripture.[2] For example, dispensationalists can take at face value Zechariah 12–14, Romans 11:25–29, and Revelation 20:1–6. The covenant theologian, on the other hand, cannot.

So I am convinced that the dispensationalist distinction between the church and Israel is an accurate understanding of God's eternal plan

---

[1]Here is the main inconsistency I see in the covenant approach: We all acknowledge that the promises of *judgment* on Israel were fulfilled literally. But covenant theology makes the church the recipient of the promised *blessings*, which then must be spiritualized to apply to the church. It seems to me that consistency would require that if the promises of judgment were fulfilled literally, the blessings should have a literal fulfillment as well.

[2]See the chapter "How Should We Interpret the Bible?" in my book *Charismatic Chaos* (Grand Rapids, Mich.: Zondervan, 1992), 85–105.

as revealed in Scripture. I have not abandoned dispensationalism, nor do I intend to.

Note, by the way, that Dr. Ryrie's description of dispensationalism and his reasons for embracing the system are very similar to what I have written here. Some years ago he wrote, "The essence of dispensationalism, then, is the distinction between Israel and the church. This grows out of the dispensationalist's consistent employment of normal or plain interpretation."[3] On these matters, it seems, Dr. Ryrie and I are in fundamental agreement. It is in the practical outworking of our dispensationalism that we differ. Dr. Ryrie's system turns out to be somewhat more complex than his own definition might suggest.

The lordship debate has had a devastating effect on dispensationalism. Because no-lordship theology is so closely associated with dispensationalism, many have imagined a cause-and-effect relationship between the two. In *The Gospel According to Jesus,* I made the point that some early dispensationalists had laid the foundation for no-lordship teaching. I disagreed with dispensational extremists who relegate whole sections of Scripture—including the Sermon on the Mount and the Lord's Prayer—to a yet-future kingdom era. I was critical of the way some dispensationalists have handled the preaching and teaching of Jesus in a way that erases the evangelistic intent from some of His most important invitations. I decried the methodology of dispensationalists who want to isolate salvation from repentance, justification from sanctification, faith from works, and Christ's lordship from His role as Savior, in a way that breaks asunder what God has joined together.

Several outspoken anti-dispensationalists hailed the book as a major blow to dispensationalism. They wanted to declare the system dead and hold a celebratory funeral.

Frankly, some mongrel species of dispensationalism ought to die, and I will be happy to join the cortege. But it is wrong to write off dispensationalism as altogether invalid. My purpose is not to attack the roots of dispensationalism, but rather to plead for a purer, more biblical application of the literal, historical, grammatical principle of interpretation. The hermeneutic method that underlies dispensationalism is fundamentally sound and must not be abandoned. That is *not* the point of the lordship debate.

Who are dispensationalists? Virtually all dispensationalists are theologically conservative evangelicals. Our view of Scripture is typically very high; our method of interpretation is consistently literal; and our zeal for

---

[3]Charles C. Ryrie, *Dispensationalism Today* (Chicago: Moody, 1965), 47.

spiritual things is inflamed by our conviction that we are living in the last days.

How does dispensationalism influence our overall theological perspective? Obviously, the central issue in any dispensationalist system is *eschatology,* or the study of prophecy. All dispensationalists are *premillennialists.* That is, they believe in a future earthly thousand-year reign of Christ. That's what a literal approach to prophecy mandates (cf. Rev. 20:1–10). Dispensationalists may disagree on the timing of the rapture, the number of dispensations, or other details, but their position on the earthly millennial kingdom is settled by their mode of biblical interpretation.

Dispensationalism also carries implications for *ecclesiology,* or the doctrine of the church, because of the differentiation between the church and Israel. Many dispensationalists, myself included, agree that there is some continuity between the Old and New Testament people of God in that we share a common salvation purchased by Jesus Christ and appropriated by grace through faith. But dispensationalists do not accept covenant theology's teaching that the church is spiritual Israel. Covenant theology sees continuity between Jewish ritual and the New Testament sacraments, for example. In their system, baptism and circumcision have similar significance. In fact, many covenant theologians use the analogy of circumcision to argue for infant baptism. Dispensationalists, on the other hand, tend to view baptism as a sacrament for believers only, distinct from the Jewish rite.

So dispensationalism shapes one's *eschatology* and *ecclesiology.* That is the extent of it. Pure dispensationalism has no ramifications for the doctrines of God, man, sin, or sanctification. More significantly, true dispensationalism makes no relevant contribution to *soteriology,* or the doctrine of salvation. In other words, nothing in a legitimate dispensational approach to Scripture mandates that we define the gospel in any unique or different way. In fact, if the same zealous concern for literal hermeneutics that yields a distinction between Israel and the church were followed consistently in the salvation issue, there would be no such thing as no-lordship soteriology.

What Is the Connection Between Dispensationalism and No-lordship Doctrine?

Yet the fact remains that virtually all the champions of no-lordship doctrine are dispensationalists. No covenant theologian defends the no-lordship gospel. Why?

Understand, first of all, that dispensationalism has not always been well represented by its most enthusiastic advocates. As I have noted, the uniqueness of dispensationalism is that we see a distinction in Scripture between Israel and the church. That singular perspective, common to all dispensationalists, sets us apart from nondispensationalists. It is, by the way, the only element of traditional dispensationalist teaching that is yielded as a result of literal interpretation of biblical texts. It also is the only tenet virtually all dispensationalists hold in common. That is why I have singled it out as the characteristic that defines dispensationalism. When I speak of "pure" dispensationalism, I'm referring to this one common denominator—the Israel-church distinction.

Admittedly, however, most dispensationalists carry far more baggage in their systems than that one feature. Early dispensationalists often packaged their doctrine in complex and esoteric systems illustrated by intricate diagrams. They loaded their repertoire with extraneous ideas and novel teachings, some of which endure today in various strains of dispensationalism. Dispensationalism's earliest influential spokesmen included J. N. Darby, founder of the Plymouth Brethren and considered by many the father of modern dispensationalism; Cyrus I. Scofield, author of the *Scofield Reference Bible;* Clarence Larkin, whose book of dispensational charts has been in print and selling briskly since 1918; and Ethelbert W. Bullinger, an Anglican clergyman who took dispensationalism to an unprecedented extreme usually called *ultradispensationalism.*[4] Many of these men were self-taught in theology and were professionals in secular occupations. Darby and Scofield, for example, were attorneys, and Larkin was a mechanical draftsman. They were laymen whose teachings gained enormous popularity largely through grass-roots enthusiasm.

Unfortunately some of these early framers of dispensationalism were not as precise or discriminating as they might have been had they had the benefit of a more complete theological education. C. I. Scofield, for example, included a note in his reference Bible that contrasted "legal obedience as the condition of [Old Testament] salvation" with "acceptance . . . of Christ" as the condition of salvation in the current dispensation.[5] Nondispensationalist critics have often attacked dispensationalism for teaching that the conditions for salvation differ from dispensation to dispensation. Here, at least, Scofield left himself open to

---

[4] Ultradispensationalism is disowned by most dispensationalists (cf. ibid., 192–205).

[5] *The Scofield Reference Bible* (New York: Oxford, 1917), 1115.

that criticism, though he seemed to acknowledge in other contexts that the law was never a means of salvation for Old Testament saints.[6]

The maturing of dispensationalism, then, has mainly been a process of refining, distilling, clarifying, paring down, and cutting away what is extraneous or erroneous. Later dispensationalists, including Donald Grey Barnhouse, Wilbur Smith, Allan MacRae, and H. A. Ironside, were increasingly wary of the fallacies that peppered much early dispensationalist teaching. Ironside's written works show his determination to confront error within the movement. He attacked Bullinger's ultradispensationalism.[7] He criticized teaching that relegated repentance to some other era.[8] He condemned the "carnal Christian" theology that helped pave the way for today's radical no-lordship teaching.[9] Ironside's writings are replete with warnings against antinomianism.[10]

Nondispensationalists have tended to caricature dispensationalism by emphasizing its excesses, and frankly the movement has produced more than its share of abominable teaching. Dispensationalists have often been forced to acknowledge that some of their critics' points have been valid.[11] The biblical distinction between Israel and the church remains unassailed, however, as the essence of pure dispensationalism.

In recent years, dispensationalism has been hit with a blistering onslaught of criticism, mostly focusing on dispensationalism's love affair with the no-lordship gospel. Evidence of this may be seen in John Gerstner's *Wrongly Dividing the Word of Truth: A Critique of Dispensationalism.*[12] Gerstner rightly attacks elements of antinomianism and

---

[6]In a note at Exodus 19:3, where Moses was being given the law, Scofield wrote, "The law is not proposed as a means of life, but as a means by which Israel might become 'a peculiar treasure' and a 'kingdom of priests'" (ibid., 93).

[7]*Wrongly Dividing the Word of Truth* (New York: Loizeaux, n.d.)

[8]*Except Ye Repent* (Grand Rapids, Mich.: Zondervan, 1937).

[9]*Eternal Security of Believers* (New York: Loizeaux, 1934).

[10]See, for example, *Full Assurance* (Chicago: Moody, 1937), 64, 77–87; also *Holiness: The False and the True* (Neptune, N.J.: Loizeaux, 1912), 121–26.

[11]Ryrie, for example, conceded in *Dispensationalism Today* that Scofield had made "unguarded statements" about dispensationalist soteriology and that dispensationalists often give a wrong impression about the role of grace during the Old Testament era (112, 117).

[12]Brentwood, Tenn.: Wolgemuth & Hyatt, 1991. Cf. Richard L. Mayhue, "Who Is Wrong? A Review of John Gerstner's *Wrongly Dividing the Word of Truth*," *Master's Seminary Journal* 3:1 (Spring 1992): 73–94.

no-lordship soteriology in some dispensationalists' teaching. He wrongly assumes, however, that those things are inherent in all dispensationalism. He dismisses the movement altogether because of the shoddy theology he finds in the teaching of several prominent dispensationalists.

It is a gross misunderstanding to assume that antinomianism is at the heart of dispensationalist doctrine. Moreover, it is unfair to portray all dispensationalists as unsophisticated or careless theologians. Many skilled and discerning students of Scripture have embraced dispensationalism and managed to avoid antinomianism, extremism, and other errors. The men who taught me in seminary were all dispensationalists. Yet none of them would have defended no-lordship teaching.[13]

Nevertheless, no one can deny that dispensationalism and antinomianism have often been advocated by the same people. All the recent arguments that have been put forth in defense of no-lordship theology are rooted in ideas made popular by dispensationalists. The leading proponents of contemporary no-lordship theology are all dispensationalists. The lordship controversy is merely a bubbling to the surface of tensions that have always existed in and around the dispensationalist community. That point is essential to a clear understanding of the whole controversy.

Thus to appreciate some of the key tenets of the no-lordship gospel, we must comprehend their relationship to the dispensationalist tradition.

Tritely Dividing the Word?

For some dispensationalists, the Israel-church distinction is only a starting point. Their theology is laden with similar contrasts: church and kingdom, believers and disciples, old and new natures, faith and repentance. Obviously, there are many important and legitimate distinctions found in Scripture and sound theology: Old and New Covenants, law and grace, faith and works, justification and sanctification. But dispensationalists often tend to take even the legitimate contrasts too far. Most dispensationalists who have bought into no-lordship doctrine imagine, for example, that law and grace are mutually exclusive opposites, or that faith and works are somehow incompatible.

---

[13]Moreover, everyone on The Master's Seminary faculty is a dispensationalist. None of us holds any of the antinomian views Dr. Gerstner claims are common to all dispensationalists.

Some dispensationalists apply 2 Timothy 2:15 ("Study to show thyself approved unto God, a workman that needeth not to be ashamed, *rightly dividing the word of truth*"—KJV, emphasis added) as if the key word were *dividing* rather than *rightly*. The dispensationalist tendency to divide and contrast has led to some rather inventive exegesis. Some dispensationalists teach, for example, that "the kingdom of heaven" and "the kingdom of God" speak of different domains.[14] The terms are clearly synonymous in Scripture, however, as a comparison of Matthew and Luke shows (Matt. 5:3 // Luke 6:20; Matt. 10:7 // Luke 10:9; Matt. 11:11 // Luke 7:28; Matt. 11:12 // Luke 16:16; Matt. 13:11 // Luke 8:10; Matt. 13:31–33 // Luke 13:18–21; Matt. 18:4 // Luke 18:17; Matt. 19:23 // Luke 18:24). Matthew is the only book in the entire Bible that ever uses the expression "kingdom of heaven." Matthew, writing to a mostly Jewish audience, understood their sensitivity to the use of God's name. He simply employed the common euphemism *heaven*. Thus the kingdom of heaven *is* the kingdom of God.

This tendency to set parallel truths against each other is at the heart of no-lordship theology. Jesus' lordship and His role as Savior are isolated from one another, making it possible to claim Him as Savior while refusing Him as Lord. Justification is severed from sanctification, legitimizing the notion of salvation without transformation. Mere believers are segregated from disciples, making two classes of Christians, carnal and spiritual. Faith is pitted against obedience, nullifying the moral aspect of believing. Grace becomes the antithesis of law, providing the basis for a system that is inherently antinomian.

The grace-law dichotomy is worth a closer look. Many early dispensationalist systems were unclear on the role of grace in the Mosaic economy and the place of law in the current dispensation. As I noted, Scofield left the unfortunate impression that Old Testament saints were saved by keeping the law. Scofield's best-known student was Lewis Sperry Chafer, co-founder of Dallas Theological Seminary. Chafer, a prolific author, wrote dispensationalism's first unabridged systematic theology. Chafer's system became the standard for several generations of dispensationalists trained at Dallas. Yet Chafer repeated Scofield's error. In his summary on *justification*, he wrote,

> According to the Old Testament men were just because they were true and faithful in keeping the Mosaic Law. Micah defines such a life after this manner: "He hath shewed thee, O man, what is good;

---

[14]Scofield, *The Scofield Reference Bible*, 1003.

and what doth the LORD require of thee, but to do justly, and to love mercy, and to walk humbly with thy God?" (6:8). *Men were therefore just because of their own works for God, whereas New Testament justification is God's work for man in answer to faith* (Rom. 5:1).[15]

Though Chafer elsewhere denied that he taught multiple ways of salvation, it is clear that he fixed a great gulf between grace and law. He believed the Old Testament law imposed "an obligation to gain merit" with God.[16] On the other hand, Chafer believed grace delivers the child of God "from every aspect of the law—as a rule of life, as an obligation to make himself acceptable to God, and as a dependence on impotent flesh."[17] "Grace teachings are not *laws;* they are *suggestions.* They are not *demands;* they are *beseechings,*" he wrote.[18]

In Chafer's system, God seems to fluctuate between dispensations of law and dispensations of grace. Grace was the rule of life from Adam to Moses. "Pure law" took over when a new dispensation began at Sinai. In the current dispensation, "pure grace" is the rule. The millennial kingdom will be another dispensation of "pure law." Chafer evidently believed grace and law could not coexist side by side, and so he seemed to eliminate one or the other from every dispensation. He wrote,

> Both the age before the cross and the age following the return of Christ represent the exercise of pure law; while the period between the two ages represents the exercise of pure grace. *It is imperative, therefore, that there shall be no careless co-mingling of these great age-characterizing elements,* else the preservation of the most important distinctions in the various relationships between God and man are lost, and the recognition of the true force of the death of Christ and His coming again is obscured.[19]

No one denies that Scripture clearly contrasts law and grace. John 1:17 says, "The Law was given through Moses; grace and truth were realized through Jesus Christ." Romans 6:4 says, "You are not under

---

[15]Lewis Sperry Chafer, *Systematic Theology,* 8 vols. (Dallas: Seminary Press, 1948), 7:219 (emphasis added).

[16]Ibid., 7:179.

[17]Lewis Sperry Chafer, *Grace* (Wheaton, Ill.: Van Kampen, 1922), 344.

[18]Ibid.

[19]Ibid., 124 (emphasis added).

law, but under grace." So the distinction between law and grace is obvious in Scripture.

But grace *and* law operate in every dispensation. Grace is and always has been the only means of eternal salvation. The whole point of Romans 4 is that Abraham, David, and all other Old Testament saints were justified by grace through faith, not because they kept the law.[20] Did the apostle Paul believe we can nullify the law in this age of pure grace? Paul's reply to that question was unequivocal: "May it never be! On the contrary, we establish the Law" (Rom. 3:31).

In fairness, it is important to note that when pressed on the issue, Chafer acknowledged that God's grace and Christ's blood were the only ground on which sinners in any age could be saved.[21] It must be stressed, however, that Chafer, Scofield, and others who have followed their lead have made too much of the differences between Old and New Testament dispensations. Wanting to avoid what he thought was "careless comingling" of law and grace, Chafer ended up with an "age of law" that is legalistic and an "age of grace" that smacks of antinomianism.

Chafer himself was a godly man, committed to holiness and high standards of Christian living. In practice, he would never have condoned carnality. But his dispensationalist system—with the hard dichotomies it introduced; its "grace teachings" that were "suggestions," not demands; and its concept of "pure" grace that stood in opposition to law of any kind—paved the way for a brand of Christianity that has legitimized careless and carnal behavior.

Chafer could rightly be called the father of twentieth-century no-lordship theology. He listed repentance and surrender as two of "the more common features of human responsibility which are too often erroneously added to the one requirement of *faith* or *belief*."[22] He wrote, "to impose a need to surrender the life to God as an added condition of salvation is most unreasonable. God's call to the unsaved is never said to be unto the Lordship of Christ; it is unto His saving grace."[23] "Next to

---

[20]Galatians 3 also makes clear that it was never God's intent that righteousness should come through the law or that salvation could be earned through obedience (see especially vv. 7, 11). The law acted as a tutor, to bring people to Christ (v. 24). Thus even in the Old Testament, people were saved because of faith, not because of obedience to the law (cf. Romans 3:19–20).

[21]Lewis Sperry Chafer, "Dispensational Distinctions Denounced," *Bibliotheca Sacra* (July 1944): 259.

[22]Chafer, *Systematic Theology*, 3:372.

[23]Ibid., 3:385.

sound doctrine itself, no more important obligation rests on the preacher than that of preaching the Lordship of Christ to Christians exclusively, and the Saviorhood of Christ to those who are unsaved."[24]

It is important to note that when Chafer wrote those things, he was arguing against the Oxford Movement, a popular but dangerous heresy that was steering Protestants back into the legalism and works-righteousness of Roman Catholicism. Chafer wrote,

> The error of imposing Christ's Lordship upon the unsaved is disastrous. . . . A destructive heresy is abroad under the name The Oxford Movement, which specializes in this blasting error, except that the promoters of the Movement omit altogether the idea of believing on Christ for salvation and promote exclusively the obligation to surrender to God. They substitute consecration for conversion, faithfulness for faith, and beauty of daily life for believing unto eternal life. As is easily seen, the plan of this movement is to ignore the need of Christ's death as the ground of regeneration and forgiveness, and to promote the wretched heresy that it matters nothing what one believes respecting the Saviorhood of Christ if only the daily life is dedicated to God's service. . . . The tragedy is that out of such a delusion those who embrace it are likely never to be delivered by a true faith in Christ as Savior. No more complete example could be found today of "the blind leading the blind" than what this Movement presents.[25]

But Chafer prescribed the wrong remedy for the false teachings of the Oxford Movement. To answer a movement that "omit[s] altogether the idea of believing on Christ for salvation and promote[s] exclusively the obligation to surrender to God," he devised a notion of faith that strips believing of any suggestion of surrender. Although the movement he opposed was indeed an insidious error, Chafer unfortunately laid the foundation for the opposite error, with equally devastating results.

The notion of faith with no repentance and no surrender fit well with Chafer's concept of an age of "pure grace," so it was absorbed and expanded by those who developed their theology after his model. It endures today as the basis of all no-lordship teaching.

One other particularly unfortunate outgrowth of Chafer's rigid partitioning of "the age of law" and "the age of grace" is its effect on Chafer's view of Scripture. Chafer believed that "The teachings of the

---

[24]Ibid., 3:387.

[25]Ibid., 3:385–86.

law, the teachings of grace, and the teachings of the kingdom are separate and complete systems of divine rule."[26] Accordingly, he consigned the Sermon on the Mount and the Lord's Prayer to the yet-future kingdom age, and concluded that the only Scriptures directly applicable to this age of grace are "portions of the Gospels, portions of the Book of Acts, and the Epistles of the New Testament"[27]—the "grace teachings." How does one know *which* portions of the Gospels and Acts are "grace teachings" meant for this age? Chafer was vague:

> The grace teachings are not, for convenience, isolated in the Sacred Text. The three economies appear in the four Gospels. The grace teachings are rather to be identified by their intrinsic character wherever they are found. Large portions of the New Testament are wholly revelatory of the doctrine of grace. The student, like Timothy, is enjoined to study to be one approved of God in the matter of rightly dividing the Scriptures.[28]

In other words, there is a lot of law and kingdom teaching mixed into the New Testament. It is not explicitly identified for us, but we can fall into error if we wrongly try to apply it to the present age. Scripture is therefore like a puzzle. We must discern and categorize which portions apply to this age and categorize them accordingly. We can do this only by "their intrinsic character."

Chafer was certain about one thing: much if not most of Christ's earthly teaching is *not* applicable to the Christian in this age:

> There is a dangerous and entirely baseless sentiment abroad which assumes that every teaching of Christ must be binding during this age simply because Christ said it. The fact is forgotten that Christ, while living under, keeping, and applying the Law of Moses, also taught the principles of His future kingdom, and, at the end of His ministry and in relation to His cross, He also anticipated the teachings of grace. If this threefold division of the teachings of Christ is not recognized, there can be nothing but confusion of mind and consequent contradiction of truth.[29]

---

[26]Ibid., 4:225.

[27]Ibid., 4:206.

[28]Ibid., 4:185.

[29]Ibid., 4:224.

Dispensationalists who follow Chafer at this point *wrongly* divide the Word of truth, assigning whole sections of the New Testament to some other dispensation, nullifying the force of major segments of the Gospels and our Lord's teaching for today.[30]

Which Gospel Should We Preach Today?

Not long ago I received a paper that has been circulated widely by a well-known dispensationalist. He wrote, "Dr. MacArthur was quite correct in titling his book *The Gospel According to Jesus.* The Gospel that Jesus taught in His pre-Cross humiliation, as Israel's Messiah and to covenant people under the law was, for all intents and purposes, Lordship salvation." But, he added, "Lordship salvation is based upon the Gospel according to Jesus, John the Baptist, and the early disciples. This Gospel is directed to the covenant nation of Israel. . . . The Lord Jesus' Kingdom Gospel had nothing whatsoever to do with Christians, or the Church."

The paper quotes heavily from Dr. Chafer's writings, attempting to demonstrate that Jesus' gospel "was on the level of the law and the earthly kingdom" and has nothing to do with grace or the current dispensation. The paper's author notes that I wrote, "On a disturbing number of fronts, the message being proclaimed today is not the gospel according to Jesus." To that he replies, "How blessedly true! Today we are to minister Paul's 'by grace are ye saved through faith' Gospel . . . not the Lord Jesus' Gospel relating to the law-oriented theocratic kingdom."

He continues, "The convert via the Gospel according to Jesus became a child of the kingdom [not a Christian]. And divine authority will ever be the driving force in his heart—the indwelling Spirit writing the law upon his heart to enable him to surrender to the theocratic kingdom law, under his King. . . . [But the Christian] is not under authority, he is not seeking to obey—unless he is under law as described in Romans Seven. For him to live is Christ, and that life is not under authority. . . . Paul was offering an altogether different salvation."

---

[30]Ultradispensationalists take Chafer's methodology even a step further. Noting that the apostle Paul called the church a mystery "which in other generations was not made known to the sons of men, as it has now been revealed to His holy apostles and prophets in the Spirit" (Eph. 3:5), they conclude that the church age did not begin until this point in Paul's ministry. Thus they abrogate all the New Testament except for Paul's prison epistles.

There, as clearly as can be stated, are all the follies that have ever defiled dispensationalism, synthesized into a single system. Blatant antinomianism: "the Christian . . . is not under authority, he is not seeking to obey"; multiple ways of salvation: "Paul was offering an altogether different salvation"; a fragmented approach to Scripture: "the Lord Jesus' Kingdom Gospel had nothing whatsoever to do with Christians, or the Church"; and the tendency to divide and disconnect related ideas: "Today we are to minister Paul's [Gospel] . . . not the Lord Jesus' Gospel."

Note carefully: This man acknowledges that Jesus' gospel demanded surrender to His lordship. His point is that Jesus' message has no relevance to this present age. He believes Christians today ought to proclaim a different gospel than the one Jesus preached. He imagines that Jesus' invitation to sinners was of a different nature than the message the church is called to proclaim. He believes we should be preaching a different gospel.

None of those ideas is new or unusual within the dispensationalist community. All of them can be traced to one or more of dispensationalism's early spokesmen. But it is about time all of them were abandoned.

In fairness, we should note that the paper I have quoted expresses some rather extreme views. Most of the principal defenders of no-lordship evangelism would probably not agree with that man's brand of dispensationalism. But the no-lordship doctrine they defend is the product of precisely that kind of teaching. It is not enough to abandon the rigid forms of extreme dispensationalism; we must abandon the antinomian tendencies as well.

The careful discipline that has marked so much of our post-Reformation theological tradition must be carefully guarded. Defenders of no-lordship salvation lean too heavily on the assumptions of a predetermined theological system. They often draw their support from presupposed dispensationalist distinctions (salvation/discipleship, carnal/spiritual believers, gospel of the kingdom/gospel of grace, faith/repentance). They become entangled in "what-ifs" and illustrations. They tend to fall back on rational, rather than biblical, analysis. When they deal with Scripture, they are too willing to allow their theological system to dictate their understanding of the text. As a result, they regularly adopt novel interpretations of Scripture in order to make it conform to their theology.

A reminder is in order: Our theology must be biblical before it can be systematic. We must start with a proper interpretation of Scripture and build our theology from there, not read into God's Word unwarranted presuppositions. Scripture is the only appropriate gauge by which we may ultimately measure the correctness of our doctrine.

Dispensationalism is at a crossroads. The lordship controversy represents a signpost where the road forks. One arrow marks the road of biblical orthodoxy. The other arrow, labeled "no-lordship," points the way to a sub-Christian antinomianism. Dispensationalists who are considering that path would do well to pause and check the map again.

The only reliable map is Scripture, not someone's dispensational diagrams. Dispensationalism as a movement must arrive at a consensus based solely on God's Word. We cannot go on preaching different gospels to an already-confused world.

Appendix 3

Voices from the Past

Zane Hodges claims lordship salvation is propelling the church backward into the dark ages. He makes this allegation:

> It may even be said that lordship salvation throws a veil of obscurity over the entire New Testament revelation. In the process, the marvelous truth of justification by faith, apart from works, recedes into shadows not unlike those which darkened the days before the Reformation. What replaces this doctrine is a kind of faith/works synthesis which differs only insignificantly from official Roman Catholic dogma (*AF* 19–20).

Elsewhere Hodges writes, "Let it be said clearly: *lordship salvation holds a doctrine of saving faith that is in conflict with that of Luther and Calvin and, most importantly, in conflict with God's Word*" (*AF* 209, emphasis in original).

No-lordship teachers often claim that they are the true heirs of the Reformation. Many have echoed the tired charge that lordship salvation "is paving the road back to Rome." They selectively quote from the great Reformers on the issues of faith and assurance, then make the preposterous suggestion that no-lordship theology is "comfortably aligned with both Calvin and Luther and many of their successors."[1]

---

[1]Thomas G. Llewellen, "Has Lordship Salvation Been Taught throughout Church History? *Bibliotheca Sacra* (January-March 1990): 59.

It is extremely difficult to understand how anyone at all familiar with the literature of the Reformation could ever make such a claim. The writings of Luther and Calvin are filled with material that argues explicitly against many of the same errors no-lordship theology has embraced. Nowhere in their writings do we find any support for the idea that someone who is justified can remain unsanctified. That is a topic about which the Reformers had much to say.

Why not let them speak for themselves?

Luther on Justification by Faith

Martin Luther's discovery of the biblical truth about justification by faith launched the Reformation. Note how Luther contends against the notion that true faith might coexist with an unbroken pattern of unholy living:

> True faith, of which we speak, cannot be manufactured by our own thoughts, for it is solely a work of God in us, without any assistance on our part. As Paul says to the Romans, it is God's gift and grace, obtained by one man, Christ. *Therefore, faith is something very powerful, active, restless, effective, which at once renews a person and again regenerates him, and leads him altogether into a new manner and character of life, so that it is impossible not to do good without ceasing.*
>
> For just as natural as it is for the tree to produce fruit, so natural is it for faith to produce good works. And just as it is quite unnecessary to command the tree to bear fruit, so there is no command given to the believer, as Paul says [1 Thess. 4:9], nor is urging necessary for him to do good, for he does it of himself, freely and unconstrained; just as he of himself without command sleeps, eats, drinks, puts on his clothes, hears, speaks, goes and comes.
>
> Whoever has not this faith talks but vainly about faith and works, and does not himself know what he says or whither it tends. He has not received it. He juggles with lies and applies the Scriptures where they speak of faith and works to his own dreams and false thoughts, which is purely a human work, whereas the Scriptures attribute both faith and good works not to ourselves, but to God alone.
>
> Is not this a perverted and blind people? They teach we cannot do a good deed of ourselves, and then in their presumption go to work and arrogate to themselves the highest of all the works of God, namely faith, to manufacture it themselves out of their own perverted thoughts. Wherefore I have said that we should despair of ourselves and pray to God for faith as the apostles did in Luke

17:5. When we have faith, we need nothing more; for it brings with it the Holy Spirit, who then teaches us not only all things, but also establishes us firmly in it, and leads us through death and hell to heaven.

Now observe, we have given these answers, that the Scriptures have such passages concerning works, on account of such dreamers and self-invented faith; *not that man should become good by works, but that man should thereby prove and see the difference between false and true faith. For wherever faith is right it does good. If it does no good, it is then certainly a dream and a false idea of faith.* So, just as the fruit on the tree does not make the tree good, but nevertheless outwardly proves and testifies that the tree is good, as Christ says, "By their fruits ye shall know them." Thus we should also learn to know faith by its fruits.

From this you see, there is a great difference between being good, and to be known as good; or to become good and to prove and show that you are good. *Faith makes good, but works prove the faith and goodness to be right.* Thus the Scriptures speak plainly, which prevails among the common people, as when a father says unto his son, "Go and be merciful, good and friendly to this or to that poor person." He does not command him to be merciful, good and friendly, but because he is already good and merciful, he requires that he should also show and prove it outwardly toward the poor by his act, in order that the goodness which he has in himself may also be known to others and be helpful to them.

You should explain all passages of Scripture referring to works, that God thereby desires to let the goodness received in faith express and prove itself, and become a benefit to others, so that false faith may become known and rooted out of the heart. *God gives no one His grace that it may remain inactive and accomplish nothing good, but in order that it may bear interest, and by being publicly known and proved externally, draw every one to God,* as Christ says: "Let your light so shine before men, that they may see your good works, and glorify your Father which is in heaven" (Matthew 5:16). Otherwise it would be but a buried treasure and a hidden light. But what profit is there in either? Yea, goodness does not only thereby become known to others, but we ourselves also become certain that we are honest, as Peter says: "Wherefore, brethren, give the more diligence to make your calling and election sure" (2 Peter 1:10). *Where works do not follow, a man cannot know whether his faith is right; yea, he may be certain that his faith is a dream, and not right as it should be.* Thus Abraham became certain of his faith, and that he feared God, when he offered up his son. As God by the angel said to Abraham: "Now I know, that is, it is manifest, that thou fearest

God, seeing thou hast not withheld thy son, thine only son, from me" (Genesis 22:12).

Then abide by the truth, that man is internally, in spirit before God, justified by faith alone without works, but externally and publicly before men and himself, he is justified by works, that he is at heart an honest believer and pious. The one you may call a public or outward justification, the other an inner justification, yet in the sense that the public or external justification is only the fruit, the result and proof of the justification in the heart, that a man does not become just thereby before God, but must previously be just before Him. So you may call the fruit of the tree the public or outward good of the tree, which is only the result and proof of its inner and natural goodness.

This is what James means when he says in his Epistle: "Faith without works is dead" (2:26). *That is, as the works do not follow, it is a sure sign that there is no faith there; but only an empty thought and dream, which they falsely call faith. . . .*

. . . Inasmuch as works naturally follow faith, as I said, it is not necessary to command them, for it is impossible for faith not to do them without being commanded, in order that we may learn to distinguish the false from the true faith.[2]

Calvin on the Nature of Faith

John Calvin defended himself vigorously against those who would "throw odium" on the doctrine of justification by faith by saying those who teach it "destroy good works, and give encouragement to sin."[3] He wrote, "We acknowledge that faith and works are necessarily connected."[4] Calvin debated a Catholic cardinal on this very issue:

If you would duly understand how inseparable faith and works are, look to Christ. . . . Where zeal for integrity and holiness is not vigor, there neither is the Spirit of Christ nor Christ Himself; and wherever Christ is not, there is no righteousness, nay, there is no faith; for faith cannot apprehend Christ for righteousness without the Spirit of sanctification.[5]

---

[2]Martin Luther, "Justification by Faith," in *Classic Sermons on Faith and Doubt,* ed. Warren W. Wiersbe (Grand Rapids, Mich.: Kregel, 1985), 78–83 (emphasis added).

[3]John Calvin, *Institutes of the Christian Religion,* trans. Henry Beveridge, 3:16:1 (reprint, Grand Rapids, Mich.: Eerdmans, 1966), 2:98.

[4]Ibid.

[5]John C. Olin, ed., *A Reformation Debate* (Grand Rapids, Mich.: Baker, 1966), 68.

Calvin attacked the Scholastic movement of the Roman Catholic Church over their definition of faith. The Scholastics taught that there is a kind of "faith" that has no transforming effect on the affections or behavior of those who "believe." This "faith," they taught, exists in people who have no desire for holiness and no love for God. Calvin was clearly offended by this suggestion. Listen to his diatribe against this error:

> I must refute the nugatory distinction of the Schoolmen as to formed and unformed faith. For *they imagine that persons who have no fear of God, and no sense of piety, may believe all that is necessary to be known for salvation;* as if the Holy Spirit were not the witness of our adoption by enlightening our hearts unto faith. Still, however, though the whole Scripture is against them, *they dogmatically give the name of faith to a persuasion devoid of the fear of God.* It is unnecessary to go farther in refuting their definition, than simply to state the nature of faith as declared in the word of God. From this it will clearly appear how unskillfully and absurdly they babble, rather than discourse, on this subject. I have already done this in part, and will afterwards add the remainder in its proper place. At present, I say that nothing can be imagined more absurd than their fiction. *They insist that faith is an assent with which any despiser of God may receive what is delivered by Scripture.* But we must first see whether any one can by his own strength acquire faith, or whether the Holy Spirit, by means of it, becomes the witness of adoption. Hence it is childish trifling in them to inquire whether the faith formed by the supervening quality of love be the same, or a different and new faith. By talking in this style, they show plainly that they have never thought of the special gift of the Spirit; since *one of the first elements of faith is reconciliation implied in man's drawing near to God. Did they duly ponder the saying of Paul, "With the heart man believeth unto righteousness" (Rom. x. 10), they would cease to dream of that frigid quality.* There is one consideration which ought at once to put an end to the debate—viz. that assent itself (as I have already observed, and will afterwards more fully illustrate) is more a matter of the heart than the head, of the affection than the intellect. . . . Assent itself, such at least as the Scripture describes, consists in pious affection. But we are furnished with a still clearer argument. *Since faith embraces Christ as he is offered by the Father, and he is offered not only for justification, for forgiveness of sins and peace, but also for sanctification, as the fountain of living waters, it is certain that no man will ever know him aright without at the same time receiving the sanctification of the Spirit; or, to express the matter more plainly, faith consists*

in the knowledge of Christ; Christ cannot be known without the sanc-
tification of his Spirit: therefore faith cannot possibly be disjoined
from pious affection.

. . . Although, in discoursing of faith, we admit that it has a
variety of forms; yet, when our object is to show what knowledge of
God the wicked possess, *we hold and maintain, in accordance with*
Scripture, that the pious only have faith.

. . . Simon Magus is said to have believed, though he soon
after gave proof of his unbelief (Acts viii, 13–18). In regard to the
faith attributed to him, we do not understand with some, that he
merely pretended a belief which had no existence in his heart: we
rather think that, overcome by the majesty of the Gospel, he
yielded some kind of assent, and so far acknowledged Christ to be
the author of life and salvation, as willingly to assume his name. In
like manner, in the Gospel of Luke, those in whom the seed of the
word is choked before it brings forth fruit, or in whom, from having no depth of earth, it soon withereth away, are said to believe
for a time. Such, we doubt not, eagerly receive the word with a
kind of relish, and have some feeling of its divine power, so as not
only to impose upon men by a false semblance of faith, but even to
impose upon themselves. They imagine that the reverence which
they give to the word is genuine piety, because they have no idea
of any impiety but that which consists in open and avowed contempt. But whatever that assent may be, it by no means penetrates
to the heart, so as to have a fixed seat there. Although it sometimes seems to have planted its roots, these have no life in them.
The human heart has so many recesses for vanity, so many lurking
places for falsehood, is so shrouded by fraud and hypocrisy, that it
often deceives itself. *Let those who glory in such semblances of faith*
know that, in this respect, they are not a whit superior to devils.

. . . Meanwhile, *believers are taught to examine themselves*
carefully and humbly, lest carnal security creep in and take the place
of assurance of faith. We may add, that the reprobate never have any
other than a confused sense of grace laying hold of the shadow
rather than the substance, because the Spirit properly seals the forgiveness of sins in the elect only, applying it by special faith to their
use. Still it is correctly said, that the reprobate believe God to be
propitious to them, inasmuch as they accept the gift of reconciliation, though confusedly and without due discernment; not that they
are partakers of the same faith or regeneration with the children of
God; but because, under a covering of hypocrisy, they seem to have
a principle of faith in common with them. Nor do I even deny that
God illumines their minds to this extent, that they recognise his

grace; *but that conviction he distinguishes from the peculiar testimony which he gives to his elect in this respect, that the reprobate never obtain to the full result or to fruition.* When he shows himself propitious to them, it is not as if he had truly rescued them from death and taken them under his protection. He only gives them a manifestation of his present mercy. *In the elect alone he implants the living root of faith, so that they persevere even to the end.*[6]

The Puritans and Reformation Theology

Zane Hodges believes the English Reformers altered and corrupted the doctrine of justification by faith. They did this, he says, by expanding the early Reformers' definition of faith. He calls Puritan teaching on faith and assurance "a tragic blemish on the history of the Christian church" (*AF* 32). Puritan teaching, he says, is the basis of "lordship salvation": "In the English-speaking world, this radically altered concept of saving faith can with considerable fairness be described as Puritan theology. Lordship salvation, in its best known contemporary form, simply popularizes the Puritanism to which it is heir" (*AF* 33).

In a note at that point, Hodges points out that a catalog of quotations I included as an appendix in *The Gospel According to Jesus* drew heavily from Puritan sources. He repeats his charge that "Puritan theology, especially in the area of faith and assurance, did not at all reflect the doctrine of John Calvin himself and is a distinct departure from Reformation thought" (*AF* 208).

But as I have suggested elsewhere (see chapter 10, footnote 6) Hodges is making far too much of the difference between Calvin and the Puritans. No group of theologians ever defended justification by faith more doggedly than the English Reformers. As the quotations I have cited above prove, no one was more convinced than Luther and Calvin that genuine faith works.

While Luther, Calvin, and the Puritans might have differed somewhat on how to describe faith and how to obtain assurance, they all agreed that sanctification inevitably follows justification. None of them would have tolerated the notion that true believers might fail to persevere in righteousness, or that genuine faith might lapse into inactivity or permanent unbelief. On this point the proponents of modern no-lordship theology are rather seriously deluded.

---

[6]Calvin, *Institutes* [Beveridge], 3:2:8–11, 1:475–79 (emphasis added).

J. C. Ryle on Justification and Sanctification

Bishop J. C. Ryle was an English churchman in the Puritan tradition (though he lived in the nineteenth century). He recognized in his day all the incipient trends that have led to no-lordship theology in our time. His landmark 1879 work, *Holiness,* is his response to those trends. It stands today as an effective answer to the no-lordship error and is in many ways the definitive work on the issue.

Ryle, in harmony with all Puritan and Reformed theology, despised the notion that justification and sanctification could be disjoined or that sanctification might be optional in a true believer's experience. He saw justification and sanctification as distinct but inseparable. He wrote:

In what, then, are justification and sanctification alike?

a. Both proceed originally from the free grace of God. It is of His gift alone that believers are justified or sanctified at all.

b. Both are part of that great work of salvation which Christ, in the eternal covenant, has undertaken on behalf of His people. Christ is the fountain of life, from which pardon and holiness both flow. The root of each is Christ.

c. Both are to be found in the same persons. Those who are justified are always sanctified, and those who are sanctified are always justified. God has joined them together, and they cannot be put asunder.

d. Both begin at the same time. The moment a person begins to be a justified person, he also begins to be a sanctified person. He may not feel it, but it is a fact.

e. Both are alike necessary to salvation. No one ever reached heaven without a renewed heart as well as forgiveness, without the Spirit's grace as well as the blood of Christ, without a meetness for eternal glory as well as a title. The one is just as necessary as the other.

Such are the points on which justification and sanctification agree. Let us now reverse the picture, and see wherein they differ.

a. Justification is the reckoning and counting a man to be righteous for the sake of another, even Jesus Christ the Lord. Sanctification is the actual making a man inwardly righteous, though it may be in a very feeble degree.

b. The righteousness we have by our justification is not our own, but the everlasting perfect righteousness of our great Mediator Christ, imputed to us, and made our own by faith. The righteousness we have by sanctification is our own righteousness, imparted, inherent and wrought in us by the Holy Spirit, but mingled with much infirmity and imperfection.

c. In justification our own works have no place at all and simple faith in Christ is the one thing needful. In sanctification our own works are of vast importance, and God bids us fight and watch and pray and strive and take pains and labour.

d. Justification is a finished and complete work, and a man is perfectly justified the moment he believes. Sanctification is an imperfect work, comparatively, and will never be perfected until we reach heaven.

e. Justification admits of no growth or increase: a man is as much justified the hour he first comes to Christ by faith as he will be to all eternity. Sanctification is eminently a progressive work, and admits of continual growth and enlargement so long as a man lives.

f. Justification has special reference to our persons, our standing in God's sight, and our deliverance from guilt. Sanctification has special reference to our natures, and the moral renewal of our hearts.

g. Justification gives us our title to heaven, and boldness to enter in. Sanctification gives us our meetness for heaven, and prepares us to enjoy it when we dwell there.

h. Justification is the act of God about us, and is not easily discerned by others. Sanctification is the work of God within us, and cannot be hid in its outward manifestation from the eyes of men.

I commend these distinctions to the attention of all my readers, and I ask them to ponder them well. I am persuaded that one great cause of the darkness and uncomfortable feelings of many well-meaning people in the matter of religion is their habit of confounding, and not distinguishing, justification and sanctification. It can never be too strongly impressed on our minds that they are two separate things. No doubt they cannot be divided, and every one that is a partaker of either is a partaker of both. But never, never ought they to be confounded, and never ought the distinction between them to be forgotten.[7]

Charles Spurgeon on Holiness

Charles Spurgeon was an English Baptist in the Puritan tradition. No one preached more powerfully than he against the concept of "accepting Christ as Savior" while spurning His lordship. "Verily I say unto

---

[7]J. C. Ryle, *Holiness* (reprint, Durham, England: Evangelical Press, 1979), 29–30.

you, you cannot have Christ for your Savior unless you also have him as Lord," Spurgeon said.[8] Pages of material could be adduced from Spurgeon's preaching to debunk no-lordship teaching.

Spurgeon stands with all the Puritans and Reformers on the question of whether practical sanctification is an essential evidence of justification. Preaching on Matthew 22:11–14, for example, Spurgeon said,

> Holiness is always present in those who are loyal guests of the great King, for "without holiness no man shall see the Lord." Too many professors pacify themselves with the idea that they possess imputed righteousness, while they are indifferent to the sanctifying work of the Spirit. They refuse to put on the garment of obedience, they reject the white linen which is the righteousness of the saints. They thus reveal their self-will, their enmity to God, and their non-submission to his Son. Such men may talk what they will about justification by faith, and salvation by grace, but they are rebels at heart, they have not on the wedding dress any more than the self-righteous, whom they so eagerly condemn. The fact is, if we wish for the blessings of grace, we must in our hearts submit to the rules of grace without picking and choosing.[9]

In another context, Spurgeon said,

> Christ Jesus did not come in order that you might continue in sin and escape the penalty of it; he did not come to prevent the disease being mortal, but to take the disease itself away. Many people think that when we preach salvation, we mean salvation from going to hell. We do not mean [only] *that,* but we mean a great deal more; we preach salvation *from sin;* we say that Christ is able to save a man; and we mean by that that he is able to save him from sin and to make him holy; to make him a new man. No person has any right to say, "I am saved," while he continues in sin as he did before. How can you be saved from sin while you are living in it? A man that is drowning cannot say he is saved from the water while he is sinking in it; a man that is frost-bitten cannot say, with any truth, that he is saved from the cold while he is stiffened in the wintry blast. No, man, Christ did not come to save thee *in* thy sins, but to save thee *from* thy sins; not to make the disease so that it should not kill thee,

---

[8]C. H. Spurgeon, *The Metropolitan Tabernacle Pulpit,* vol. 47 (reprint, Pasadena, Tex.: Pilgrim, 1986), 570.

[9]C. H. Spurgeon, *The Metropolitan Tabernacle Pulpit,* vol. 17 (London: Passmore & Alabaster, 1894), 99.

but to let it remain in itself mortal, and, nevertheless, to remove it from thee, and thee from it. Christ Jesus came then to heal us from the plague of sin, to touch us with his hand and say, "I will, be thou clean."[10]

Spurgeon attacked an incipient variety of no-lordship doctrine in an 1872 sermon:

There are some who seem willing to accept Christ as Saviour who will not receive him as Lord. They will not often state the case quite as plainly as that; but, as actions speak more plainly than words, that is what their conduct practically says. How sad it is that some talk about their faith in Christ, yet their faith is not proved by their works! Some even speak as if they understood what we mean by the covenant of grace; yet, alas! there is no good evidence of grace in their lives, but very clear proof of sin (not grace) abounding. I cannot conceive it possible for anyone truly to receive Christ as Saviour and yet not to receive him as Lord. One of the first instincts of a redeemed soul is to fall at the feet of the Saviour, and gratefully and adoringly to cry, "Blessed Master, bought with thy precious blood, I own that I am thine,—thine only, thine wholly, thine for ever. Lord, what wilt thou have me to do?" A man who is really saved by grace does not need to be told that he is under solemn obligations to serve Christ; the new life within him tells him *that*. Instead of regarding it as a burden, he gladly surrenders himself—body, soul, and spirit, to the Lord who has redeemed him, reckoning this to be his reasonable service. Speaking for myself, I can truthfully say that, the moment I knew that Christ was my Saviour, I was ready to say to him,—

> I am thine, and thine alone,
> This I gladly, fully own;
> And, in all my works and ways,
> Only now would seek thy praise.
>
> Help me to confess thy name,
> Bear with joy thy cross and shame,
> Only seek to follow thee,
> Though reproach my portion be.

It is not possible for us to accept Christ as our Saviour unless he also becomes our King, for a very large part of salvation consists in our being saved from sin's dominion over us, and the only way in

---

[10]C. H. Spurgeon, *The Metropolitan Tabernacle Pulpit,* vol. 11 (reprint, Pasadena, Tex.: Pilgrim, 1979), 138.

which we can be delivered from the mastery of Satan is by becoming subject to the mastery of Christ. . . . If it were possible for sin to be forgiven, and yet for the sinner to live just as he lived before, he would not really be saved.[11]

American Evangelicalism and No-lordship Theology

I stated in chapter 2 my conviction that the contemporary no-lordship movement is a chiefly American phenomenon. Yet I would also add that no-lordship theology is a radical *departure* from historic fundamentalist and evangelical belief in America. American Protestant belief has its roots, of course, in the English Puritan movement. The great evangelical awakenings of the eighteenth and nineteenth centuries, the Methodist movement, and the rise of revivalism at the beginning of this century all featured Christ's lordship at the heart of the gospel they proclaimed. Jonathan Edwards, perhaps the greatest theological mind America has ever produced, wrote,

> As to that question, Whether closing with Christ in his kingly office be of the essence of justifying faith? I would say: 1. That accepting Christ in his kingly office, is doubtless the proper condition of having an interest in Christ's kingly office, and so the condition of that salvation which he bestows in the execution of that office; as much as accepting the forgiveness of sins, is the proper condition of the forgiveness of sin. Christ, in his kingly office, bestows salvation; and therefore, accepting him in his kingly office, by a disposition to sell all and suffer all in duty to Christ, and giving proper respect and honor to him, is the condition of salvation. This is manifest by Heb v.9 "And being made perfect, he became the author of eternal salvation to all them that obey him."[12]

Of course the strong Reformed tradition of Princeton Seminary, which produced Charles Hodge, B. B. Warfield, and J. Gresham Machen, featured a clear lordship message. Hodge wrote,

> That good works are the certain effects of faith is included in the doctrine that we are sanctified by faith. For it is impossible that there

---

[11]C. H. Spurgeon, *The Metropolitan Tabernacle Pulpit,* vol. 56 (reprint, Pasadena, Tex.: Pilgrim, 1979), 617.

[12]Cited in John Gerstner, *The Rational Biblical Theology of Jonathan Edwards* (Orlando: Ligonier, 1991), 301.

should be inward holiness, love, spirituality, brotherly kindness, and zeal, without an external manifestation of these graces in the whole outward life. Faith, therefore, without works, is dead. We are saved by faith. But salvation includes deliverance from sin. If, therefore, our faith does not deliver us from sin, it does not save us. Antinomianism involves a contradiction in terms.[13]

Only one strand of American evangelicalism has embraced and propagated no-lordship theology, and that is the branch of dispensationalism I described in Appendix 2.

D. L. Moody on Repentance

D. L. Moody, evangelist and founder of Moody Bible Institute, featured a clear call to repentance in his preaching:

There is a good deal of trouble among people about what repentance really is. If you ask people what it is, they will tell you "It is feeling sorry." If you ask a man if he repents, he will tell you: "Oh, yes; I generally feel sorry for my sins." That is not repentance. It is something more than feeling sorry. Repentance is turning right about, and forsaking sin. I wanted to speak Sunday about that verse in Isaiah, which says: "Let the guilty forsake his way, and the unrighteous man his thoughts." That is what it is. If a man don't turn from his sin, he won't be accepted of God; and if righteousness don't produce a turning about—a turning from bad to good—it isn't true righteousness.[14]

Moody stated,

We do not walk in the same way as before we were converted. A man or a woman who professes Christianity and yet goes on in the same old way has not been born again. When we are born again, we are born in a new way; and Christ is that new way himself. We give up our old way, and take his. The old way leads to death, the new way to life everlasting. In the old way, Satan leads us; in the new way the Son of God leads us. We are led by Him, not into bondage and darkness, but into the way of peace and joy.[15]

---

[13]Charles Hodge, *Systematic Theology* (reprint, Grand Rapids, Mich.: Eerdmans, 1989), 3:110.

[14]D. L. Moody, "True Repentance," in *The Gospel Awakening* (Chicago: Fairbanks, Palmer, 1883), 417.

[15]"Signs of the New Birth," ibid., 658.

R. A. Torrey on Lordship

R. A. Torrey, first president of Moody Bible Institute, instructed students on leading people to Christ:

Show them Jesus as Lord.

It is not enough to know Jesus as a Saviour, we must know Him as Lord also. A good verse for this purpose is Acts 2:36:

"Therefore let all the house of Israel know assuredly, that *God hath made that same Jesus,* whom ye have crucified, *both Lord and Christ.*"

When the inquirer has read the verse, ask him what God hath made Jesus, and hold him to it until he replies, "Both Lord and Christ." Then say to him, "Are you willing to accept Him as your Divine Lord, the one to whom you will surrender your heart, your every thought, and word, and act?"

Another good verse for this purpose is Rom. 10:9:

"That if thou shalt confess with thy mouth *the Lord* Jesus, and shalt believe in thine heart that God hath raised him from the dead, thou shalt be saved."

When the inquirer has read the verse, ask him what we are to confess Jesus as. He should reply, "Lord." If he does not so reply, ask him other questions until he does answer in this way. Then ask him, "Do you really believe that Jesus is Lord, that He is Lord of all, that He is rightfully the absolute Lord and Master of your life and person?" Perhaps it will be well to use Acts 10:36 as throwing additional light upon this point:

"The word which God sent unto the children of Israel, preaching peace by Jesus Christ: (*he is Lord of all*)."[16]

James M. Gray on Salvation

James M. Gray, second president of Moody Bible Institute, wrote,

The design of the atonement is stated in the words: "*That we being dead to sins, should live unto righteousness,*" a two-fold design, as we see. The thought of God was not only punitive but remedial. He gave His Son not only to take away our guilt but to change our lives. . . .

---

[16]R. A. Torrey, *How to Work for Christ* (Old Tappan, N.J.: Revell, n.d.), 37–38.

The moment we receive Christ by faith, we do also receive the Holy Spirit to dwell within us, regenerating us, creating within us a clean heart and renewing within us a right spirit, so that we become "dead to sins" not only in the judicial or imputed sense . . . but in the actual and experimental sense as well. That is not to say that sin becomes eradicated from our hearts and no longer dwells even latently within us (1 John 1:8); but that its power over us is broken. We do really come to hate the sins we used to love and to love the holiness we used to hate.

. . . Christ died not merely that we should be dead to sins judicially and experimentally but that we might "*live unto righteousness.*" As our substitute and representative He both died *and rose again.* . . .

Now Paul tells us also in the sixth chapter of Romans already quoted that if we are united with Christ in the likeness of His death, we are also in the likeness of His resurrection. If we died with Him we also live with Him.

This is not merely that we *shall* live with Him by and by in a physical state of resurrection glory, but that we live with Him now in a spiritual state of resurrection glory. The death He died He died unto sin once, but the life He liveth, He liveth unto God. He liveth it unto God now. Even so we are to reckon ourselves not only to be dead indeed unto sin as we have already considered, but alive unto God in Christ Jesus (6:11), alive *now.* . . .

Nor is it *only* in an imputed sense that this is true; but, as in the other half of this declaration, in an experimental sense as well. As we have just seen, the Holy Spirit within the regenerated man, not only enables him to hate sin but to love holiness and follow after it. No longer yields he his "members (as) servants to uncleanness and to iniquity unto iniquity," but as "servants to righteousness unto holiness." He crucifies the flesh with its affections and lust. He not only puts off all these: "Anger, wrath, malice, railing, shameful speaking out of his mouth"; but he puts on, as the elect of God, "a heart of compassion, kindness, humility, meekness, long-suffering, and above all these, love, which is the bond of perfection."

It is thus that "*by His stripes we are healed.*" Perfectly healed. God having begun the good work in us perfects it until the day of Jesus Christ (Philippians 1:6). The man who receives Christ as his Saviour, and confesses Him as his Lord, need not fear as to whether he shall be "able to hold out."[17]

---

[17]James M. Gray, *Salvation from Start to Finish* (Chicago: Moody, n.d.), 39–44.

W. H. Griffith Thomas on Surrender

W. H. Griffith Thomas, co-founder of Dallas Theological Seminary, wrote,

> God says "Here I am" to man, and then man welcomes this and responds with "Here am I" to God.
>
> The words imply *Surrender*. When the believer says "Here am I" to God, he places himself at God's disposal. This whole-hearted response is the natural outcome of the reception of God's revelation to the soul. We can see this truth on every page of the New Testament. God comes to the soul, enters the heart and life, and then man yields himself entirely to God as belonging to Him. "Ye are not your own, ye are bought." This is the meaning of St. Paul's great word translated "yield" in Rom. vi. 13, 19, and "present" in ch. xii. 1. In the latter passage the Apostle bases his exhortation on the "mercies of God," on the revelation of God saying "Here I am" to man, and after urging his readers to "present" their bodies as a sacrifice to God he speaks of this surrender as their "logical service," the rational, logical, necessary outcome of their acceptance of "the mercies of God." The Gospel does not come to the soul simply for personal enjoyment, it comes to awaken in it a sense of its true life and marvelous possibilities. Consequently, when God says to the believer, "I am thine," the believer responds, "I am Thine" (Psalm cxix. 94), "I am the Lord's" (Isa. xliv. 5). This was one part of the purpose of our Lord's redemption work, "that He might be Lord" and now, "we are the Lord's" (Rom. xiv. 8 and 9). This whole-hearted response should be made from the first moment of acceptance in and of Christ. "Christ is all" to us from the outset; and we should be "all to Him." There should be no *hiatus,* no gap, no interval, between the acceptance of Christ as Saviour and the surrender to Him as Lord. His full title is "Jesus Christ our Lord"; and the full extent of its meaning (though of course not its full depth) is intended to be realised from our very first experience of His saving presence and power. . . .
>
> This initial act of surrender, however, is but the beginning of a life of surrender. The act must develop into an attitude. This has been recognised by God's true children in all ages as their "bounden duty and service."[18]

---

[18]W. H. Griffith Thomas, *The Christian Life and How to Live It* (Chicago: Moody, 1919), 46–49.

H. A. Ironside on Assurance

Dr. H. A. Ironside, pastor of Moody Memorial Church in Chicago, wrote,

> Perhaps some one may ask, "But does it make no difference to God what I am myself? May I live on in my sins and still be saved?" No, assuredly not! But this brings in another line of truth. The moment one believes the gospel, he is born again and receives a new life and nature—a nature that hates sin and loves holiness. If you have come to Jesus and trusted Him, do you not realize the truth of this? Do you not now hate and detest the wicked things that once gave you a certain degree of delight? Do you not find within yourself a new craving for goodness, a longing after holiness, and a thirst for righteousness? All this is the evidence of a new nature. And as you walk with God you will find that daily the power of the indwelling Holy Spirit will give you practical deliverance from the dominion of sin.[19]

Regarding 1 John 3:9, Ironside wrote,

> See how the two families, the unregenerated and the regenerated, are here depicted. Unsaved men practice sin. Whatever fine things there may be in their characters, as judged by the world's standards, they delight in having their own way. This is the essence of sin. "Sin is lawlessness." All careful scholars agree that this is a more correct translation than "Sin is the transgression of the law." We are told that "until the law sin was in the world," and although sin was not imputed as transgression because no written standard had yet been given, nevertheless sin manifested itself as self-will, or lawlessness, and was seen everywhere among fallen mankind. Lawlessness is the refusal of a person to submit his will to Another, even to God Himself, who has the right to claim his full obedience. In this the children of the devil show plainly the family to which they belong.
>
> But with the believer it is otherwise. Turning to Christ he is born from above, as we have seen, and thus possesses a new nature. This new nature abominates sin, and henceforth dominates his desires and his thinking. Sin becomes detestable. He loathes himself for the follies and iniquities of his past, and he yearns after holiness. Energized by the Holy Spirit, his life-trend is changed. He practices righteousness. Though ofttimes conscious of failure, the whole trend of his life is altered. The will of God is his joy and delight. And

---

[19]H. A. Ironside, *Full Assurance* (Chicago: Moody, 1937), 33.

as he learns more and more the preciousness of abiding in Christ, he grows in grace and in knowledge, and realizes that divine power is given him to walk in the path of obedience. His new nature finds joy in surrendering to Jesus as Lord, and so sin ceases to be character-istic of his life and character.[20]

A. W. Tozer on Following Christ

A. W. Tozer wrote much on the lordship issue. He began to see the dangers of a no-lordship gospel nearly half a century ago, and he sounded many warning blasts to the church. Here are a few excerpts:

Allowing the expression "Accept Christ" to stand as an honest effort to say in short what could not be so well said any other way, let us see what we mean or should mean when we use it.

To accept Christ is to form an attachment to the Person of our Lord Jesus altogether unique in human experience. The attachment is intellectual, volitional and emotional. The believer is intellectually convinced that Jesus is both Lord and Christ; he has set his will to follow Him at any cost and soon his heart is enjoying the exquisite sweetness of His fellowship.

This attachment is all-inclusive in that it joyfully accepts Christ for all that He is. There is no craven division of offices whereby we may acknowledge His Saviourhood today and withhold decision on His Lordship till tomorrow. The true believer owns Christ as his All in All without reservation. He also includes all of himself, leaving no part of his being unaffected by the revolutionary transaction.

Further, his attachment to Christ is all-exclusive. The Lord becomes to him not one of several rival interests, but the one exclu-sive attraction forever. He orbits around Christ as the earth around the sun, held in thrall by the magnetism of His love, drawing all his life and light and warmth from Him. In this happy state he is given other interests, it is true, but these are all determined by his relation to his Lord.

That we accept Christ in this all-inclusive, all-exclusive way is a divine imperative. Here faith makes its leap into God through the Person and work of Christ, but it never divides the work from the Person. It never tries to believe on the blood apart from Christ Himself, or the cross or the "finished work." It believes on the Lord Jesus Christ, the whole Christ without modification or reservation, and thus it receives and enjoys all that He did in His work of

---

[20]Ibid., 82–83.

redemption, all that He is now doing in heaven for His own and all that He does in and through them.

To accept Christ is to know the meaning of the words "as he is, so are we in this world" (I John 4:17). We accept His friends as our friends, His enemies as our enemies, His ways as our ways, His rejection as our rejection, His cross as our cross, His life as our life and His future as our future.

If this is what we mean when we advise the seeker to accept Christ we had better explain it to him. He may get into deep spiritual trouble unless we do.[21]

Tozer wrote, "The Christian is saved from his past sins. With these he simply has nothing more to do; they are among the things to be forgotten as the night is forgotten at the dawning of the day."[22]

This essay hits several themes that Tozer emphasized again and again:

We are under constant temptation these days to substitute another Christ for the Christ of the New Testament. The whole drift of modern religion is toward such a substitution.

To avoid this we must hold steadfastly to the concept of Christ as set forth so clearly and plainly in the Scriptures of truth. Though an angel from heaven should preach anything less than the Christ of the apostles let him be forthrightly and fearlessly rejected.

The mighty, revolutionary message of the Early Church was that a man named Jesus who had been crucified was now raised from the dead and exalted to the right hand of God. "Therefore let all the house of Israel know assuredly, that God hath made that same Jesus, whom ye have crucified, both Lord and Christ." . . .

Salvation comes not by "accepting the finished work" or "deciding for Christ." It comes by believing on the Lord Jesus Christ, the whole, living, victorious Lord who, as God and man, fought our fight and won it, accepted our debt as His own and paid it, took our sins and died under them and rose again to set us free. This is the true Christ, and nothing less will do.

But something less is among us, nevertheless, and we do well to identify it so that we may repudiate it. That something is a poetic fiction, a product of the romantic imagination and maudlin religious fancy. It is a Jesus, gentle, dreamy, shy, sweet, almost effeminate,

---

[21]A. W. Tozer, *That Incredible Christian* (Harrisburg, Pa.: Christian Publications, 1964), 18–19.

[22]Ibid., 44.

and marvelously adaptable to whatever society He may find Himself in. He is cooed over by women disappointed in love, patronized by pro tem celebrities and recommended by psychiatrists as a model of a well-integrated personality. He is used as a means to almost any carnal end, but He is never acknowledged as Lord. These quasi Christians follow a quasi Christ. They want His help but not His interference. They will flatter Him but never obey Him.[23]

Tozer called no-lordship teaching a "discredited doctrine" that divides Christ. He described the teaching he opposed:

It goes like this: Christ is both Saviour and Lord. A sinner may be saved by accepting Him as Saviour without yielding to Him as Lord. The practical outworking of this doctrine is that the evangelist presents and the seeker accepts a divided Christ. . . .

Now, it seems odd that none of these teachers ever noticed that the only true object of saving faith is none other than Christ Himself; not the "saviourhood" of Christ nor the "lordship" of Christ, but Christ Himself. God does not offer salvation to the one who will believe on one of the offices of Christ, nor is an office of Christ ever presented as an object of faith. Neither are we exhorted to believe on the atonement, nor on the cross, nor on the priesthood of the Saviour. All of these are embodied in the person of Christ, but they are never separated nor is one ever isolated from the rest. Much less are we permitted to accept one of Christ's offices and reject another. The notion that we are so permitted is a modern day heresy, I repeat, and like every heresy it has had evil consequences among Christians. No heresy is ever entertained with impunity. We pay in practical failure for our theoretical errors.

It is altogether doubtful whether any man can be saved who comes to Christ for His help but with no intention to obey Him. Christ's saviourhood is forever united to His lordship. Look at the Scriptures: "If thou shalt confess with thy mouth the Lord Jesus, and shalt believe in thine heart that God hath raised him from the dead, thou shalt be saved . . . for the same Lord over all is rich unto all that call upon him. For whosoever shall call upon the name of the Lord shall be saved" (Rom. 10:9–13). There the *Lord is* the object of faith for salvation. And when the Philippian jailer asked the way to be saved, Paul replied, "Believe on the Lord Jesus Christ, and thou shalt be saved" (Acts 16:31). He did not tell him

[23]A. W. Tozer, *Man: The Dwelling Place of God* (Camp Hill, Pa.: Christian Publications, 1966), 140–43.

to believe on the Saviour with the thought that he could later take up the matter of His lordship and settle it at his own convenience. To Paul there could be no division of offices. Christ must be Lord or He will not be Saviour.[24]

This penetrating analysis on faith shows how deeply Tozer had thought about the dangers of no-lordship doctrine:

> For a number of years my heart has been troubled over the doctrine of faith as it is received and taught among evangelical Christians everywhere. Great emphasis is laid upon faith in orthodox circles, and that is good; but still I am troubled. Specifically, my fear is that the modern conception of faith is not the Biblical one; that when the teachers of our day use the word they do not mean what Bible writers meant when they used it.
>
> The causes of my uneasiness are these:
>
> 1. The lack of spiritual fruit in the lives of so many who claim to have faith.
>
> 2. The rarity of a radical change in the conduct and general outlook of persons professing their new faith in Christ as their personal Saviour.
>
> 3. The failure of our teachers to define or even describe the thing to which the word *faith* is supposed to refer.
>
> 4. The heartbreaking failure of multitudes of seekers, be they ever so earnest, to make anything out of the doctrine or to receive any satisfying experience through it.
>
> 5. The real danger that a doctrine that is parroted so widely and received so uncritically by so many is false as understood by them.
>
> 6. I have seen faith put forward as a substitute for obedience, an escape from reality, a refuge from the necessity of hard thinking, a hiding place for weak character. I have known people to miscall by the name of faith high animal spirits, natural optimism, emotional thrills and nervous tics.
>
> 7. Plain horse sense ought to tell us that anything that makes no change in the man who professes it makes no difference to God either, and it is an easily observable fact that for countless numbers of persons the change from no-faith to faith makes no actual difference in the life. . . .

[24]A. W. Tozer, *The Root of the Righteous* (Harrisburg, Pa.: Christian Publications, 1955), 84–86.

Any professed faith in Christ as personal Saviour that does not bring the life under plenary obedience to Christ as lord is inadequate and must betray its victim at the last.

The man that believes will obey; failure to obey is convincing proof that there is not true faith present. To attempt the impossible God must give faith or there will be none, and He gives faith to the obedient heart, only. Where real repentance is, there is obedience; for repentance is not only sorrow for past failures and sins, it is a determination to begin now to do the will of God as He reveals it to us.[25]

Arthur Pink on No-lordship Evangelism

Arthur W. Pink was a largely self-taught classic Reformed theologian. He wrote and distributed short studies on theological and biblical topics through a monthly magazine, *Studies in the Scriptures*. His understanding of Scripture and ability to express himself in writing are legendary.

Pink often wrote with an acid pen, however, and he reserved some of his harshest criticism for those whom he saw corrupting the gospel message with easy-believism. It is fair to say that he held no-lordship doctrine in utter contempt. "The evangelism of the day is not only superficial to the last degree, but it is *radically defective*," Pink wrote.[26]

As early as the 1930s, decades before the lordship debate became a familiar issue, Pink clearly saw major problems with emerging no-lordship doctrine:

> Saving faith consists of the complete surrender of my whole being and life to the claims of God upon me: "But first gave their own selves to the Lord" (2 Cor. 8:5).
>
> It is the unreserved acceptance of Christ as my absolute Lord, bowing to His will and receiving His yoke. Possibly someone may object, Then why are Christians exhorted as they are in Romans 12:1? We answer, All such exhortations are simply a calling on them to *continue as they began:* "As ye have therefore received Christ Jesus the Lord, so walk ye in Him" (Col. 2:6). Yes, mark it well that Christ is "received" as *Lord.* Oh, how far, far below the New Testament standard is this modern way of begging sinners to receive Christ as their own personal "Saviour." If the reader will consult his

---

[25]Tozer, *Man: The Dwelling Place of God*, 30–33.

[26]Arthur Pink, *Studies on Saving Faith* (Swengel, Pa.: Reiner, n.d.), 5.

concordance, he will find that in *every passage* where the two titles are found together it is *always* "Lord and Saviour, and never vice versa: see Luke 1:46, 47; 2 Peter 1:11; 2:20; 3:18.[27]

He decried the disaster he saw happening as no-lordship evangelism grew more and more popular:

> The terrible thing is that so many preachers today, under the pretence of magnifying the grace of God, have represented Christ as the Minister of *sin;* as One who has, through His atoning sacrifice, procured an indulgence for men to continue gratifying their fleshly and worldly lusts. Provided a man professes to believe in the virgin birth and vicarious death of Christ and claims to be resting upon Him alone for salvation, he may pass for a real Christian almost anywhere today, even though his daily life may be no different from that of the moral worldling who makes no profession at all. The Devil is chloroforming thousands into hell by this very delusion. The Lord Jesus asks, "Why call ye Me, Lord, Lord, and *do not* the things which I say?" (Luke 6:46); and insists, "Not every one that saith unto Me, Lord, Lord, shall enter into the kingdom of heaven; but he that *doeth* the will of My Father which is in heaven" (Matt. 7:21).[28]

Pink gave this advice on how to deal with the purveyors of the doctrine he saw corrupting the church:

> It is the bounden duty of every Christian to have no dealings with the "evangelistic" monstrosity of the day: to *withhold* all moral and financial support of the same, to attend none of their meetings, to circulate none of their tracts. Those preachers who tell sinners they may be saved *without* forsaking their idols, *without* repenting, without-surrendering to the Lordship of Christ are as erroneous and dangerous as others who insist that salvation is by works and that Heaven must be earned by our own efforts.[29]

Startling words. But Pink felt the seriousness of the no-lordship error called for the strongest possible warning. One wonders what his reaction would have been if he had seen the radical no-lordship doctrine that has emerged in recent years.

---

[27]Arthur Pink, *Practical Christianity* (Grand Rapids, Mich.: Baker, 1974), 20.

[28]Ibid., 24–25.

Summary

No-lordship soteriology departs from the mainstream of evangelical orthodoxy. The fact remains that prior to this century and the rise of Chafer-Scofield dispensationalism, no prominent theologians or pastors ever embraced the tenets of no-lordship doctrine.[30]

The church as a whole needs to study this issue very carefully. None of us enjoys controversy, but the issues we are dealing with here are more important than mere matters of preference. It is the *gospel* that is at stake. We must get the message right. It is no mere academic question. These are the very issues many great men of God in the past have given their lives for.

We cannot continue to compromise and tolerate and sweep the error under the rug. That kind of response to the controversy has only contributed to the decline of the biblical gospel. It has decimated the church of our generation:

> Today's "Christianity" is in a state of disarray and decay, and the condition is deteriorating year by year. The truth of God's Word has been watered down and compromised to reach a common denominator that will appeal to and accommodate the largest number of participants. The result is a hybrid Christianity which is essentially man-centered, materialistic and worldly, and shamefully dishonouring to the Lord Jesus Christ. This shameful degeneracy is due in large part to the erroneous gospel that is presented by many today around the world.[31]

Let us search the Scriptures, ask the hard questions, and come to accord on the gospel.

---

[29]Pink, *Studies on Saving Faith,* 14.

[30]It might be possible, through selective quotations, to find comments from dependable theologians that appear to support some of the *ideas* advanced by various no-lordship teachers. But you will find no leading figures in the Reformation, Post-Reformation, or evangelical movements who ever endorsed the *system* of no-lordship soteriology Dr. Ryrie defends, much less the more extreme variety Professor Hodges espouses.

The true historical forerunners of no-lordship teaching include the Sandemanian antinomians (also known as "Glasites") in eighteenth-century Scotland. That movement was roundly denounced by the Puritans. D. Martyn Lloyd-Jones gives an overview of the Sandemanian sect and their doctrine in *The Puritans: Their Origins and Successors* (Edinburgh: Banner of Truth, 1987), 170–90.

[31]Jeffrey E. Wilson, "The Authentic Gospel" (Edinburgh: Banner of Truth, 1990), 1.

Glossary

antinomianism: the idea that behavior is unrelated to faith, or that Christians are not bound by any moral law. Antinomianism radically separates justification and sanctification, making practical holiness elective.

assensus: see *assent.*

assent (assensus): one of three elements of true faith; the settled confidence and affirmation that Christ's salvation is applicable to one's own soul (see *knowledge* and *trust*).

cheap grace: self-imparted grace that promises forgiveness without the need for repentance; pseudograce, which makes no change in the recipient's character.

common grace: divine grace bestowed to mankind in general. Common grace restrains sin, mitigates sin's destructive effects in human society, and imparts blessings of all kinds to all peoples. This grace is not redemptive (see *special grace*).

conversion: turning to God in repentance and faith.

decisionism: the idea that eternal salvation may be secured by the sinner's own movement toward Christ, a "decision for Christ" that is usually signified by some physical or verbal act—raising a hand, walking an aisle, reciting a prayer, signing a card, repeating a pledge, or something similar.

dispensation: the plan of God by which He adminsters His rule within a given era in His eternal program.

dispensationalism: a system of biblical interpretation that sees a distinction between God's program for Israel and His dealings with the church.

easy-believism: the view that saving faith is a solely human act. Those who adopt such a view must then scale back the definition of faith so that believing is something depraved sinners are capable of.

ecclesiology: the doctrine of the church.

efficacious grace: grace that is certain to produce the desired effect. God's grace is always efficacious.

eschatology: the doctrine of future things; prophecy.

faith: see *saving faith.*

fiducia: see *trust.*

flesh: the principle of human frailty—especially our sinful selfishness—which remains with us after salvation until we are ultimately glorified.

grace: the free and benevolent influence of a holy God operating sovereignly in the lives of undeserving sinners.

irresistible grace: grace that transforms the heart and thus makes the believer wholly willing to trust and obey. Saving grace is always irresistible.

justification: an act of God's grace whereby He declares that all the demands of the law are fulfilled on behalf of the believing sinner through the righteousness of Jesus Christ. Justification is the reversal of God's attitude toward the sinner. Whereas He formerly condemned, He now vindicates—not because of any good thing found in the sinner himself, but because of the imputed righteousness of Christ. Because of justification believers not only are perfectly free from any charge of guilt, but also have the full merit of Christ reckoned to their personal account. Justification and sanctification are both essential elements of salvation (see *sanctification*).

knowledge (notitia): one of three elements of true faith; a recognition and understanding of the truth that Christ saves (see *assent* and *trust*).

legalism: the teaching that people can earn favor with God by doing certain things. Some legalists teach that salvation must be earned by works. Others practice extreme ritualism or live by rigid codes of conduct. Even Christians can fall into legalism if they focus too much on externals and neglect to cultivate the right heart attitudes (cf. Rom. 2:29).

lordship salvation: the belief that the gospel call to faith presupposes that sinners must repent and yield to Christ's authority.

meritorious works: ritual or conduct that earns merit with God or is worthy of His rewards or honor. Scripture is clear that human works can *never* be meritorious (Isa. 64:6; Rom. 6:23; 8:8; Titus 3:5). No works of merit are necessary for salvation, but grace will produce works through faith as manifestations of God's saving work in every believer's life.

notitia: see *knowledge*.

ordo salutis: the order of salvation, a logical arrangement of various aspects of saving grace. A typical *ordo salutis* in Reformed theology would be: election, calling, regeneration, conversion, repentance, faith, justification, sanctification, perseverance, and glorification. Obviously, the part of the sequence from regeneration through sanctification is logical, not chronological. These events all happen in the same moment.

penance: an activity performed to try to atone for one's own sins.

premillennialism: the belief that Christ will come again, then inaugurate a thousand-year reign on earth.

Puritans: seventeenth-century English Reformers.

regeneration: the new birth—the work of the Holy Spirit that imparts new life to the sinner.

repentance: a change of heart involving turning from sin to embrace Jesus Christ. Repentance and *faith* are distinguishable elements that blend in one composite work by God's gracious moving in genuine *conversion.*

sanctification: the continuous operation of the Holy Spirit in believers, making us holy by conforming our character, affections, and behavior to the image of Christ.

saving faith: The soul's appropriation of and surrender to the Lord Jesus Christ as the solitary hope for eternal life and deliverance from sin. This faith is a work of God in the heart of the believing sinner.

saving grace: see *special grace.*

special grace: the irresistible work of God that frees men and women from the penalty and power of sin, renewing the inner person and sanctifying the sinner through the operation of the Holy Spirit. Also called *saving grace* and *irresistible grace.*

soteriology: doctrine of salvation.

spurious faith: counterfeit or defective faith. Radical no-lordship teaching denies the possibility of spurious faith in Christ as Savior. That view asserts that if the *object* of faith is trustworthy, the character of the faith itself is not to be challenged.

total depravity: corruption by sin in every aspect of being. Unredeem-ed sinners are totally depraved; that is, they are spiritually dead, unable to respond to or please God, and in total need of God's gracious inclining.

trust (fiducia): one of three elements of true faith; a personal commitment to and appropriation of Christ as the only hope for eternal salvation (see *assent* and *knowledge*).

ultradispensationalism: an extreme brand of dispensationalism that places the beginning of the church at varying points later than Acts 2. Many ultradispensationalists reject water baptism and the Lord's Supper as ordinances intended for another age, and they believe the only Scripture directly applicable for this age is contained in the Pauline epistles.

Scripture Index

Subject Index